Our self-centred culture sorely nee
The Lord alone is worthy of prais
Therefore He cannot be satisfied with anything less than the exclusive devotion of His people. On the human side, jealousy is most godly when it has only the glory of God as its goal. Powerful examples of this are seen in both the Old and New Testaments. Here is biblical exegesis at its best. While realistic in application to the world, Dr. Thoennes lifts the reader heavenward, and leaves one with a deeper sense of the greatness of God.

Robert E. Coleman
Distinguished Professor of Evangelism and Discipleship,
Gordon-Conwell Theology Seminary, Boston, Massachusetts

This is an important book on a neglected subject! Erik Thoennes shows that God is pleased with those today who, like Phineas, David, Paul, and Jesus himself, are jealous for the honor of our great God in an age that increasingly disregards him and his commands. Carefully researched and clearly written, this book shows that there is a good kind of godly jealousy which will give backbone and courage to our Christian lives.

Wayne Grudem
Research Professor of Bible and Theology
Phoenix Seminary, Phoenix, Arizona

Because the virtues are mutually reinforcing and require the presence of other virtues to be developed fully, a life of character will remain elusive if a particular virtue is disregarded. Today, jealousy has a public relations problem: It is widely misunderstood and regarded as a vice. In this scholarly yet accessible book, professor Thoennes fills a huge void regarding godly jealousy. With skill and admirable familiarity with the relevant literature, he restores godly jealousy to its proper place in a life well lived. Those concerned about character development cannot afford to neglect this book.

J. P. Moreland,
Distinguished Professor of Philosophy,
Talbot School of Theology, Biola University, La Mirada, California

Godly Jealousy
A Theology of Intolerant Love

K. Erik Thoennes

ΠENTOR

To my faithful wife, Donna.

'This is my beloved and this is my friend'
(Song of Songs 5:16).

Scripture quotations (unless otherwise noted) are taken from the New American
Standard Bible®, Copyright © 1960, 1962, 1963, 1968, 1971, 1972, 1973, 1975, 1977,
1995 by The Lockman Foundation used by permission. (www.lockman.org)

French and German translations are the author's own.

Copyright © Erik Thoennes 2005

10 9 8 7 6 5 4 3 2 1

ISBN 1-84550-027-X
ISBN 978-1-84550-027-6

Published in 2005
Reprinted 2008
in the
Mentor Imprint
by
Christian Focus Publications Ltd.,
Geanies House, Fearn, Ross-shire,
IV20 1TW, Scotland, UK

www.christianfocus.com

Cover design by Alister MacInnes

Printed and bound by
CPD Wales, Ebbw Vale

Contents

Acknowledgments

I would like to thank the following: Wayne Grudem and the late Harold O. J. Brown, and my friend and co-laborer David Talley. They helped me greatly with this study, in both their scholarly advice, and their living examples of godly men who are jealous for God's honor; My first theology professor, Timothy Phillips, whose faith became sight as this book was nearing completion taught me that the first *and final* question of theology should be, "am I being obedient to Jesus Christ?"; Dennis Dirks, Mike Wilkins, J. P. Moreland and the rest of my colleagues at Talbot School of Theology for encouraging and enabling me to finish and publish this book; My students at Biola University, the saints at Grace Evangelical Free Church in La Mirada, and our Grace Group whose sincere hunger to know and glorify Christ make them a joy to teach and shepherd; Ed Uszynski for his friendship and courage; Bob and Audrey Thompson for their generous support and encouragement; Joe and Fera Gorra for their meticulous editing; The good people at Christian Focus for their sincere desire to honor Christ and edify the church with the books they publish; My family who prays for me, especially my devoted loving wife and ministry partner, Donna. Her love, wisdom, patience, joy, encouragement, companionship, intelligence, sense of humor, and proofreading, have been invaluable; My deepest gratitude goes to the one true God who relentlessly loves us with a jealous love.

Chapter 1

Introduction

That God is a jealous God is a clear teaching of the Bible. Gerhard von Rad considers God's jealousy to be one of the most foundational divine attributes. He understands it as 'an emotion springing from the very depths of [God's] personality.'[1] Walter Eichrodt believes divine jealousy to be the 'basic element of the whole Old Testament idea of God.'[2] Jealousy is the reason God gives for the second commandment:

> You shall have no other gods before Me. You shall not make for yourself an idol, or any likeness of what is in heaven above or on the earth beneath or in the water under the earth. You shall not worship them or serve them; *for I, the* LORD *your God, am a jealous God*, visiting the iniquity of the fathers on the children, on the third and the fourth generations of those who hate Me. (Exod. 20:3-5)

When God renews the covenant with Moses in Exodus 34:10-28, he tells him that he is a jealous God. In the same verse, he goes to the extent of affirming that 'Jealous' is an appropriate personal name for himself: 'for you shall not worship any other god, for the LORD, whose name is Jealous, is a jealous God.' Repeatedly throughout the Bible God reminds his people that he is a jealous God.[3] His jealousy is for his own honor, and for the faithfulness

---

[1]Gerhard von Rad, *Old Testament Theology*, trans. D. G. M. Stalker (Edinburgh: Oliver and Boyd, 1962), 1:207.

[2]Walter Eichrodt, *Theology of the Old Testament* (Philadelphia: Westminster, 1961), 1:44.

[3]E.g., Exodus 20:5; 34:14; Numbers 25:11; Deuteronomy 4:24; 5:9; 6:15; 29:20; 31:16; 32:16, 21; Joshua 24:19; 1 Kings 14:22; 2 Kings 19:31; Psalms 78:58; 79:5; Isaiah 9:7; 26:11; 37:32; 42:13; 59:17; 63:15; Ezekiel 5:13; 8:3-5; 16:38, 42; 23:25; 36:5-6; 39:25; Joel 2:18; Nahum 1:2; Zephaniah 1:18; 3:8; Zechariah 1:14-15; 8:2; John 2:17; 1 Corinthians 10:22; 11:2; James 4:5.

of those with whom he has established a covenant relationship. Any violation of the exclusive favor in this relationship is met with a strong emotional response of jealousy, which results in wrathful and restorative action.

In the Bible we also see that humans demonstrate godly jealousy in relationship to other persons and on behalf of God.[4] Although human jealousy is seldom uncontaminated with sin, can be unwarranted,[5] and taken to ungodly extremes,[6] there is, nevertheless, an important place in the Bible for human jealousy that is righteous and godly.

The Definition of Godly Jealousy

This book will focus on occurrences where the concept of jealousy is present in the Bible even if the word is not. However, while this study of godly jealousy in the Bible is not limited to the occurrence of the Greek and Hebrew words that may be translated 'jealousy,' these words are nevertheless vital to a proper understanding of the Biblical understanding of this concept.

Most of the biblical reference sources provide good general definitions of jealousy and acknowledge the possibility of a positive sense for it.[7] The Hebrew and Greek words קִנְאָה (*qinah*) and ζῆλος (*zēlos*), which may be translated 'jealousy,' have a similar, and broad range of meanings. In addition to

---

[4]E.g., Numbers 5:11-31; 11:29; 25:11, 13; Deuteronomy 32:21; 1 Kings 19:10, 14; 2 Kings 10:16; Psalms 69:9; 119:139; Proverbs 6:34; 23:17; Song of Songs 8:6; John 2:17; 2 Corinthians 11:2.

[5]The rituals for determining the justification of the jealousy of a husband detailed in Numbers 5 assume that there were times that the husband's jealousy was unjustified. Joshua's jealousy on behalf of Moses was also unwarranted in Numbers 11:29.

[6]As it was with Jehu in 2 Kings 10:16 who seems to have had an appropriate godly jealousy that was taken too far in the massacre at Jezreel, as Hosea 1:4 indicates.

[7]One notable exception is the *Anchor Bible Dictionary*, which has no entry for jealousy. It does have an extensive entry for 'Zealots,' in which it deals with the concept of zeal. It defines zeal as 'behavior motivated by the desire to protect one's self, group, space, or time against violations.' David Rhoads, 'Zealots,' in *The Anchor Bible Dictionary*, ed., David Noel Freedman (Garden City, N.J.: Doubleday, 1992) 6:1044.

'jealousy,' other possible translations are 'zeal,' 'envy,' 'ardor' or 'emulation.'[8] The focus of this study will not examine the occurrences in Scripture where the meanings of קִנְאָה (*qinah*) and ζῆλος (*zēlos*) are envy, zeal, or emulation. Our focus will be upon the instances in the Bible where, as indicated by the context, a positive and relational 'jealousy' is the intended meaning.

קנא (*qna*) has an etymological connection with the Akkadian *uqnû*, meaning 'to become red or alternatively black.'[9] *BDB* provides 'ardor,' 'zeal' and 'jealousy' as possible translations of the noun form of קנא (*qna*) and connects it with the 'colour produced in [the] face by deep emotion.'[10] The possible definitions *BDB* provides for the noun forms are: (1) Ardour of jealousy of husband; (2) Ardour of zeal: a. of men for God, b. of God for his people especially in battle; (3) Ardour of anger: a. of men against adversaries, b. of God against men. For the verb forms the definitions it provides are: (1) Be jealous. (2) Be envious. (3) Be zealous for: a. of man, for God, b. of God. (4) Excite to jealous anger. *BDB* also defines the adjective form as 'jealous,' and points out that it is used only of God, and in the context of his 'demanding exclusive service.'[11] Hendrik G. L. Peels defines קנא as an 'intense energetic state of mind towards action which is caused by an infringement of someone's rights or injury to the subject's honor.'[12] He also adds 'furious' as a possible translation of the verb form. When used of humans in a positive sense, he notes that קנא (*qna*) is used 'to express

---

[8]Please see the charts in appendix 1 and 2 for all of the occurrences of the קנא (*qna*)and ζῆλ(*zēl*-) roots in the Bible, along with the subject, object, cause, positive or negative use, and the translation I believe fits best.

[9]Ludwig Koehler, Walter Baumgartner, and Johann J. Stamm, *The Hebrew and Aramaic Lexicon of the Old Testament*, ed. and trans. M. E. J. Richardson (New York: E. J. Brill, 1996), 3:109-10; cf. Hendrik G. L. Peels, 'קנא(*qna*),' in *NIDOTTE*, ed. Willem A. VanGemeren (Grand Rapids: Zondervan, 1996), 3:937.

[10]Francis Brown, et al., *The New Brown-Driver-Briggs-Genesis Hebrew-English Lexicon* (Peabody, Mass.: Hendrickson, 1979), 888.

[11]Ibid.

[12]Peels, *NIDOTTE*, 3:938.

religious fervor, impassioned devotion to God.'[13] As examples
of this religious fervor he gives Phinehas (Num. 25:11),
David's words in Psalm 69:9, Elijah (1 Kings 19:10), and Paul
(2 Cor 11:2). When used of God, Peels observes קָנָא (*qna*) is
often the response to Israel's idolatry and is God's 'fiery, angry
reaction to the infringement of his rights *vis-à-vis* Israel and the
violation of the *berît*.'[14]

Leonard Coppes defines קָנָא (*qna*) as 'a very strong emotion
whereby some quality or possession of the object is desired by
the subject.'[15] While he acknowledges that 'envy' or 'zeal' are
legitimate translations, he says that the 'central meaning of our
word, however, relates to "jealousy" especially in the marriage
relationship.'[16] As we shall see as our study develops, for God,
his jealous response is based in his love, for his people, love
that he expects to be reciprocated by them. This love God
expects from his people is not only an emotional response, but
also necessarily results in obedient behavior. When a person
experiences godly jealousy, he has a 'passionate, consuming
"zeal" focused on God that results in the doing of his will and
the maintaining of his honor in the face of the ungodly acts of
men and nations.'[17]

The Theological Lexicon of the Old Testament adds 'fervor'
to the possible translations of קִנְאָה־ (*qinah*). It recognizes that
meaning when there is an interpersonal context for the word
family; 'it indicates the attitude, often accompanied by a
strong emotional component, of one partner toward the other
regular partner.'[18] It also recognizes the strong link between

---

[13]Ibid.

[14]Ibid.

[15]Leonard J. Coppes, 'קָנָא,' (*qna*) in *TWOT*, ed. Harris, R. L., Gleason L. Archer,
and Bruce K. Waltke (Chicago: Moody, 1980), 2:802.

[16]Ibid.

[17]Ibid., 803. Coppes gives Phinehas, Elijah, and the Messiah (Ps. 69:9) as examples
of this kind of jealousy.

[18]G. Sauer, 'קִנְאָה,'(*qinah*) in *Theological Lexicon of the Old Testament*, trans. Mark
E. Biddle, ed. Ernst Jenni and Claus Westermann (Peabody, Mass.: Hendrickson,
1997), 3:1146.

God's jealousy and his holiness. Sauer agrees with Eichrodt when he says that '[t]he concept of Yahweh's jealousy that corresponds to his transcendence, majesty, and holiness is "the basic element in the whole Old Testament idea of God."'[19]

In the New Testament, the definitions and possible translations of ζῆλος (*zēlos*) are very close to those of קנא (*qna*). When used positively, Hans-Christoph Hahn defines ζῆλος (*zēlos*) generally as 'an emotional going out to a person, idea or cause.'[20] *BDAG* and *TDNT* leave little place for a positive translation rendered 'jealousy,' and limit the possible positive translations to 'zeal' or 'ardor.'[21] *BDAG* gives the following definitions for the noun form: (1) Intense positive interest in something, zeal, ardor, marked by a sense of dedication; (2) Intense negative feelings over another's achievements or success, jealous, envy. For the verb form *BDAG* gives the following definitions: (1) Be positively and intensely interested in something, strive, desire, exert oneself earnestly, be dedicated; (2) To have intense negative feelings over another's achievements or success, be filled with jealous, envy.[22] Liddell and Scott gives 'jealousy,' 'zeal,' 'envy,' 'fervour,' 'indignation,' and 'emulation' as possible translations of ζῆλος (*zēlos*).[23]

Boyd Luter does recognize a distinction between the positive use of 'jealousy' and the more general 'zeal.' When used in a positive sense he says, 'jealousy is the relational counterpart to zeal, primarily a focusing of emotion toward a person in the

---

[19]Ibid.

[20]Hans-Christoph Hahn, 'ζῆλος' (*zēlos*) *NIDNTT*, ed. Colin Brown (Grand Rapids: Zondervan, 1978), 3:1166.

[21]Walter Bauer, *A Greek English Lexicon of the New Testament and Other Early Christian Literature*, 3rd edition, revised and edited by Fredrick W. Danker (Chicago: University of Chicago, 2000), 427; Albrecht Stumpff, 'ζῆλος' (*zēlos*) trans. G. W. Bromiley, in *TDNT*, ed. Gerhardt Kittel and G. Friedrich (Grand Rapids: Eerdmans, 1965), 2:279-290.

[22]Bauer, *BDAG*, 427.

[23]Henry G. Liddell and Robert Scott, *A Greek-English Lexicon*, revised and augmented by Henry A. Jones (Oxford: Clarendon, 1968), 755.

desire for a closer or renewed bond.'[24] Other sources I examined
did not add anything more to the basic definitions given for
קִנְאָה(*qinah*) and ζῆλος (*zēlos*) than we have seen thus far.[25]

As the aforementioned lexical studies indicate, and as
my analysis of the ninety occurrences of these words in the
Bible shows, קִנְאָה (*qinah*) and ζῆλος (*zēlos*) both represent
exclusive single-mindedness of emotion, which may be morally
blameworthy or praiseworthy, depending on the object and
motive of the jealousy.[26] The objects of God's holy jealousy
are the honor of his name and his people who are bound to him
through covenant. The jealousy of God is vital to the essence of
his moral character, a major cause for worship and confidence
on the part of his people, and a ground for fear on the part of
his enemies.

For the purposes of this study, jealousy, in distinction to
envy and zeal, will be understood always to carry with it a
relational element in which the one who is jealous desires
exclusive favor in the relationship.[27] Zeal is the more general
emotion of which jealousy is a sub-category. Jealousy is always
a zealous emotion, but zeal is not always a jealous emotion. At
its core jealousy is an emotion based on a perceived infidelity
to covenant exclusivity. This desire to remain exclusively

---

[24]Boyd A. Luter, 'Jealousy, Zeal,' in *Dictionary of Paul and His Letters*, ed. Ralph
P. Martin, Gerald F. Hawthorne, Daniel G. Reid (Downers Grove, Ill.: InterVarsity,
1993), 461.

[25]Other sources I consulted were: E. M. Good, 'Jealousy,' *IDB* (N.Y.: Abingdon,
1962), 2; Bruce A. Miline, 'Jealousy,' in *New Bible Dictionary*, ed. J. D. Douglas,
(Wheaton, Ill.: Tyndale, 1962), 553; Norman H. Snaith, 'Jealous, Zealous,' in *A
Theological Wordbook of the Bible*, ed. Alan Richardson (London: SCM, 1957),
115-16. N. J. Opperwall, 'Jealous,' in *International Standard Bible Encyclopedia*,
ed. Geoffery W. Bromiley, et al (Grand Rapids: Eerdmans, 1982), 971.

[26]In my study of the 90 occurrences of the קנא (*qna*) and ζῆλ (*zēl-*) roots that
could be translated with the 'jealous' words, 64 are used positively and 43 are used
to describe God himself.

[27]This relational distinction is explained in Daniel M. Farrell, 'Jealousy,' *The
Philosophical Review* 89, no. 4 (1980): 527-59 and D. H. Semdahl, 'God and the
Concept of Jealousy' (Th.M. thesis, Dallas Theological Seminary, 1983). See also
Daniel M. Farrell, 'Jealousy and Desire,' *Love Analyzed* (ed. Roger E. Lamb),
Boulder: Co., Western Press, 1997.

favored in covenant relationship grows out of recognition of the righteousness of this fidelity. It is also based in the desire for the pleasure this fidelity produces.

Jealousy expresses the unique character of the covenant relationship between Yahweh and his people. The word 'jealousy' translates קנא (*qna*) and ζῆλος (*zēlos*) most accurately, when it is intended to describe the emotional response to infidelity that a personal being experiences. God's transcendent qualities do not diminish his personal immanence. Indeed, 'God is not only the master who commands, he is the Father who loves and passes this love into the reality of the life of human history.'[28]

To refrain from using 'jealousy' as a translation and opt for the less particular 'zeal' means that the relational sense of the concept is lost, and God's genuine intimacy with, and love for, his people is diminished. 'Zeal' is a far too broad word for many of the contexts with which we will be dealing. In these inter-personal contexts, jealousy is the preferable translation 'on the condition that from it we eliminate all pejorative characteristics of narrowness and pettiness and to situate jealousy in a larger context than that of conjugal symbolism.'[29]

Definitions of Jealousy and Related Words
In this study, the following definitions for jealousy and related words will be employed:

♦ *Jealousy*: The ardent desire to maintain exclusive devotion within a relationship in the face of a challenge to that exclusive devotion. Necessary requirements for jealousy to be present are:

---

[28]Bernard Renaud, *Je Suis un Dieu Jaloux* (I am a Jealous God), (Paris: Les Editions du Cerf, 1963), 70-71. 'Dieu n'est pas seulement le Maître qui commande, il est le Père qui aime et qui fait passer cet amour dans la réalité de la vie et de l'histoire humaine.'

[29]Ibid., 153. 'à condition d'en éliminer tout caractère péjoratif d'étroitesse et de mesquinerie, et de le situer dans un cadre plus large que celui du symbolisme conjugal.'

(1) A Lover
(2) A Beloved
(3) A Rival
(4) Infidelity Expressed In Some Way by the Beloved[30]
(5) An Emotional Response to that Infidelity

The covenant, and metaphors, of sexual relations, father-son relationships, and marriage relationships[31] are common in the biblical expressions of jealousy. The Bible understands jealousy as a very powerful emotion. 'Wrath is fierce and anger is a flood, but who can stand before jealousy?' (Prov 27:4).

♦ *Zeal*: An ardent general desire to see a particular result come about. This emotion differs from jealousy in that it is a much less specific desire. Zeal is the most general of the translations, and means the eager ardent desire for something.[32] This emotion is clearly evident in Nehemiah 3:20. 'Baruch the son of Zabbai *zealously* repaired another section, from the angle to the doorway of the house of Eliashib the high priest.'

♦ *Envy*: The ardent desire to gain possession of something that is not currently possessed. This emotion differs from jealousy in that it is never godly, is not necessarily a relational emotion (one can be envious of inanimate objects), and the object desired is not the possession of the one experiencing the emotion. While jealousy desires the protection of something

---

[30]For the sake of clarity in this book, for godly jealousy to be present, there must be due cause. This means that even if the beloved is enticed to infidelity, godly jealousy will not be present unless the beloved is in some way unfaithful. A range of other godly emotions may be felt in response to the attempt of a rival to seduce a beloved (indignation, anger, a sense of betrayal, etc.), but godly jealousy is always in response to the expressed or intended infidelity of the beloved.

[31]קנא (*qna*) and ζῆλ (*zēl-*) are used in relation to the marriage metaphor in the Bible at least seventeen times: Genesis 30:1; Numbers 5:14-30 (10 times); Proverbs 6:34; Song of Songs 8:6; Ezekiel 16:38, 42; 23:25; 2 Corinthians 11:2. Although the words occur in relation to marriage in only in these passages, as we shall see, jealousy is expressed in many more passages in relation to the marriage metaphor even when the words for jealousy are not used.

[32]Noah Webster, *Webster's Tenth New International Dictionary of the English Language* (Chicago: Encyclopedia Britannica, Inc., 1993), 760.

possessed, envy is the resentful desire to possess something not currently possessed. Envy never carries a positive connotation.[33]

♦ *Malicious envy*: The ardent desire to gain possession of something not currently possessed, *and to deny it of the current possessor*. This is the especially evil form of envy.[34]

♦ *Desire to emulate*: A positive desire to gain possession of a trait or ability of another. Emulation is to aspire to be like someone in a particular characteristic while not wanting to deny him of that characteristic.

♦ *Covetousness*: A selfish inordinate desire to gain wealth or possessions.

♦ *Resentment*: A feeling of indignant displeasure or persistent ill will at something regarded as a wrong, insult, or injury (Webster). Resentment often accompanies these other emotions of possession.

---

[33]This usage is found in passages such as Genesis 26:14, where the Philistines were envious of Isaac's possessions and Psalm 73:3, 'For I was envious of the arrogant, when I saw the prosperity of the wicked.'

[34]This category of envy comes from Peter Salovey's very helpful, *The Psychology of Jealousy and Envy* (New York: Guilford, 1991). Although based upon naturalistic presuppositions, this is the definitive book on jealousy from a psychological perspective, and very helpful for thinking through the concept and experience of human jealousy. The field of psychology has studied this emotion, and emotions in general, more than any other. Philosophy is a distant second with works like Daniel Farrell's, 'Jealousy,' *The Philosophical Review* 89, no. 4 (Oct. 1980): 527-59 and Immanuel Kant's, 'Jealousy, Envy, and Spite,' trans. Louis Enfield, in *Virtue and Vice in Everyday Life*, ed. Christina Sommers and Fred Sommers (New York: Harcourt Brace Janovich College Publishers, 1993), 384-92. Aaron Ben-Ze'ev, 'Are Envy, Anger, and Resentment Moral Brothers?' *Philosophical Explorations* 5:2 (May 2002), 148-54. Aaron Ben-Ze'ev, 'Envy and Jealousy,' *Canadian Journal of Philosophy* (December 1990), 487-516. Kristjan Kristjansson, *Justifying Emotions, Pride and Jealousy* (NY: Routledge, 2002). Kristjan Kristjansson, 'Why Persons Need Jealousy,' *Personalist Forum*, 12.2 (Fall 1996), 163-81. Michael Wren, 'Jealousy,' *Nous* 23.5 (December 1989), 635-52. Theologians and biblical scholars have woefully neglected jealousy and the issue of emotions in general. One notable exception is Dan Allender and Tremper Longman's, *The Cry of the Soul: How Our Emotions Reveal Our Deepest Questions About God* (Colorado Springs, Colo.: NavPress 1994), 132, a book co-authored by a psychologist and an Old Testament scholar.

♦ *Honor*: Respect, esteem, or devotion shown one as his due or claimed by one as a right. This concept is related to jealousy, because often honor is the key relational element that is denied when jealousy is aroused.

♦ *Indignation* (righteous): Anger aroused by something unjust, unworthy, or mean.

♦ *Vengeance* (revenge): Punishment inflicted in retaliation for an injury or offense.

♦ *Devotion*: The fact or state of being ardently dedicated and loyal (as to an idea or person).

♦ *Ambition*: An ardent desire for rank, fame, or power.

It is important to point out here that emotions are never experienced to the exclusion of, or in isolation from, other emotions. One might add, as philosopher Richard Swinburne points out, 'Emotional states differ from each other according to the different thoughts, beliefs and desires which enter into them.'[35] I might add, then, that having proper belief-desire sets will make for mature decision-making. Furthermore, Jennifer Robinson has argued that it is characteristic of the role of desire in emotion that the desire causes the thought (viz. judgment).[36]

Jealousy is often experienced as a blended emotion, along with zeal, anger, indignation, or even grief. It is even possible to have godly and ungodly emotions at the same time. It is no easy task figuring out what emotions are at work in someone, even in oneself. This may be why the study of emotions tends to be neglected. However, the Bible puts significant emphasis on the importance of the internal emotions that motivate behavior. For this reason, and because emotions are such a vital part of the human experience this study on jealousy is greatly needed and has vital implications for the church.

---

[35]Richard Swinburne, *The Evolution of the Soul*, revised edition (Oxford, 1997), 140.

[36]Jennifer Robinson, 'Emotion, Judgment, and Desire,' *Journal of Philosophy* (1983), 80

Contemporary Views of Jealousy

In spite of the considerable emphasis on the jealousy of God, and godly human jealousy in the Bible, the common understanding of jealousy in the secular *and* Christian realms is mostly negative. A survey of the relevant literature shows relatively little written on this subject.[37] When it is dealt with in secular literature, jealousy is often seen as the main cause of wife abuse and is generally considered a destructive primitive emotion for God or mankind to exhibit.[38] Because jealousy is primarily seen as a result of personal and relational insecurity[39] it is assumed that a God who is jealous must therefore be insecure. 'Thus the jealousy of God correlates with the insecurity of his Chosen People.'[40] A good example of the disdain for divine jealousy can be seen in Gerald Ringer's article on contemporary spirituality, 'Report from a Far Meridian: Yahweh, God of the Fireball,' where he blames the idea of divine jealousy for much of the destruction in history including the dropping of the atom bomb on Japan.[41]

In a balance of terror maintained by nuclear arsenals, the jealousy of God and the insecurity of people together induce structural

---

[37]Bernard Renaud's, *Je Suis un Dieu Jaloux* (I am a Jealous God), was the only monograph I was able to find that is devoted to jealousy from a biblical perspective. There are two Th.M. theses on the subject, which both leave considerable work to be done. Cf. Arnold G. Fruchtenbaum, 'A Study of the Root קנא' (*qna*) (Th.M. thesis, Dallas Theological Seminary, 1971); D. H. Semdahl, 'God and the Concept of Jealousy' (Th.M. thesis, Dallas Theological Seminary, 1983).

[38]Examples of secular literature that have this strongly negative understanding of jealousy can be found in the following: James B. Ashbrook, *The Humanizing Brain: Where Science and Religion Meet* (Cleveland, Ohio: Pilgrim Press, 1997); Charles Darwin, *The Expression of the Emotions in Man and Animals* (Chicago: University of Chicago Press, 1965); Carolyn Gard, 'Taming Jealousy: 'The Green-Eyed Monster,'' *Current Health* 25, no. 7 (1999): 26-28; Salovey, *The Psychology of Jealousy and Envy*; Ira L. Reiss, 'A Sociological Journey Into Sexuality,' *Journal of Marriage and Family* 48, no. 2 (1986): 233-42; Gerald Ringer, 'Report from a Far Meridian: Yahweh, God of the Fireball,' in *Fireball and the Lotus: Emerging Spirituality from Ancient Roots*, ed. Ron Miller and Jim Kenney (Santa Fe, N.M.: Bear & Co., 1987), 85; Swami Anand Veereshwar, 'Jealousy and the Abyss (Ego Defenses Against Nothingness),' *Journal of Humanistic Psychology* 23, no. 2 (1983): 70-84.

[39]Ringer, *Yahweh, God of the Fireball*, 85.

[40]Ibid.

[41]Ibid.

instability. Yahweh, whether under the banner of Adam Smith or Karl Marx, remains the jealous God of the fireball of righteous wrath.[42]

Ringer believes that the repression of 'the matrist sensitivity to mercy'[43] and the idea of the jealousy of God are responsible for the nuclear destruction he believed loomed on the horizon. For Ringer, and most people in our culture today, the idea of a wrathful jealous God is an 'unutterable horror.'[44]

While there are notable exceptions,[45] many in the field of psychology view the idea of God's jealousy as a great evil that is the result of the 'territorial imperative of the primal mind,'[46] which produces the 'my turf'[47] mentality of territorial religion. It is also seen as the reason for hierarchical, watchful, persistent, unchanging ideas of God.[48] Jealousy is often explained as the product of the evolutionary process. Among men, jealousy is viewed as an emotion that is intended to 'defend paternity confidence.'[49] This jealousy often results in violence done in order to achieve sexual exclusivity and control over women, thereby satisfying their motive—their inclination (stemming from evolution) for assurance that they are passing on their own gene pool and not wasting their resources on raising the children

---

[42]Ibid., 86.

[43]Ibid., 85.

[44]Ibid., 86.

[45]One of these exceptions can be seen in the following statement of psychologist Bram P. Buunk in his chapter, 'Jealousy in Close Relationships: An Exchange Theoretical Perspective,' in *The Psychology of Jealousy and Envy*, ed. Peter Solovey, 172, who recognizes a positive sense of jealousy:

It has been shown that some forms of jealousy may arise from the desire to protect a valued and satisfying relationship whereas other types of jealousy seem to be indicative of insecurity, too much dependence and lack of trust.... Interdependence theory makes it quite clear that to attempt to eradicate all forms of jealousy completely would mean to give up all forms of interdependence. And that would mean giving up what can be considered the core of intimate relationships.

[46]Ashbrook, *Humanizing Brain*, 63.

[47]Ibid.

[48]Ibid.

[49]Ralph B. Hupka, 'The Motive for the Arousal of Romantic Jealousy: Its Cultural Origin,' in *The Psychology of Jealousy and Envy*, ed. Peter Solovey, 257.

of interlopers.[50] It is even believed that the idea of a jealous God is the result of vestiges of our reptilian brains.[51]

The perception of jealousy in the church does not fare much better than outside of it. Emotions in general and jealousy as a positive emotion suffer from neglect and ignorance in the church. Like those outside the church, few Christians realize that a godly jealousy exists, and seldom is any distinction made between jealousy, which can be godly, and envy, which never is. Part of the problem is that for most English speakers envy (which is the desire to gain possession of something that does not belong to you) and jealousy (which is the desire to maintain possession of something that does belong to you) are used synonymously.

When human jealousy is spoken of in Christian literature, it is more often than not used as Catherine Clark Kroeger does when she describes an 'insanely jealous' husband who abuses his wife.[52] Few Christian authors leave much room for a positive understanding of jealousy. Most see the emotion as do secular psychologists who view jealousy as little more than 'the motive in homicide and wife beating.'[53]

While it is likely that the jealousy of God has never been easy for students of the Bible to feel comfortable with or understand, this is especially true in contemporary western culture, with its increasing disrespect for exclusive relationship in general, as well as a de-emphasis on God's transcendent holiness. The negative connotations that commonly accompany the concept of jealousy have left little place for a positive idea of it, even among Bible scholars. H. C. Hahn and Albrecht Stumpff believe the term 'jealousy,' when used of God, is a 'misleading and unfortunate' rendering of the קנא (*qna*) and ζῆλ (*zēl-*) word

---

[50]Ibid.

[51]Ashbrook, *Humanizing Brain*, 63.

[52]Catherine Clark Kroeger, Prologue in *Women, Abuse and the Bible: How Scripture Can Be Used to Hurt or Heal*, ed. Catherine Clark Kroeger and James R. Beck (Grand Rapids: Baker, 1996), 9-12.

[53]Hupka, 'Romantic Jealousy,' 257.

groups.[54] Because of the negative connotation that jealousy carries, there seems to be an increasing tendency to opt for the more general and vague 'zeal.' This is true even when context indicates that the emotion exhibited is the result of the violation of an exclusive relationship.

The emotions of God in general present a difficulty in light of traditional views of God's immutability.[55] God's immutability can be emphasized to the point where his emotions are not sufficiently acknowledged.[56] Or God's emotions can be emphasized to the point where the result is a god who is impotent and capricious. Orthodox priest Theodore Pulcini represents an increasingly common view when he quotes John Cassian[57] who says of anger, 'one dare not attribute this most pernicious disease of the soul to God.'[58] Pulcini allows for none of the 'taint of human passions' to be attributed to God and believes that to apply these and other 'gross anthropomorphisms' to the immutable nature of God is nothing short of blasphemy.[59] At times, negatively perceived emotions of God have been underappreciated and dismissed as merely incomprehensible anthropopathisms.[60] One wonders why this is not the approach

---

[54]Hahn, 'ζῆλος,' (*zēlos*) *TNIDNTT*, ed. Colin Brown, 3:1166-69; Stumpff, 'ζῆλος,' (*zēlos*) in *TDNT*, ed. Gerhardt Kittel and G. Friedrich, 2:279-90.

[55]For a helpful treatment on this difficulty see, Joseph M. Hallman, 'The Emotions of God in the Theology of St. Augustine,' *Recherches de Theologie Ancienne et Medievale* 51, no. 4 (Jan-Dec 1984): 5-19.

[56]Ibid.

[57]Cassian was an ascetic monk who died in AD 435. He was ordained a deacon by Chrysostom in Constantinople and is commemorated by the Eastern Church on February 29.

[58]Theodore Pulcini, 'Cultivating "Christian Anger": A Warning from the Fifth Century,' *Touchstone* 11, no. 1 (Jan-Feb 1998): 8-10.

[59]Ibid., 9.

[60]For instance John Chrysostom says, 'God is jealous, for He loves, God is wroth, not as yielding to passion, but for the purpose of chastising, and punishing.... For God also is said to be jealous, not that any should suppose passion, (for the Godhead is impassible,) but that all may know that He doeth all things from no other regard than their sakes over whom He is jealous.' John Chrysostom, *Nicene and Post Nicene Fathers, Series I, Vol. XIII, Homilies on First Corinthians*, available from the internet on *http://www.ceel.org/s/schaff/npnflld/cuchc/npnf112.pdf*. And even John Calvin shows a failure to fully appreciate God's genuine emotions when he says, 'Whenever we hear that God is angered, we ought not to imagine any emotion in him, but rather to

taken to God's positive emotions as well. Other theologians who want to have a place for genuine emotions in God at times only want to preserve ones that are popular with societal opinion. This diminishing of God's transcendent qualities easily heads down the road of process theism.[61]

Augustine recognized the frailty of human words when he said, 'nothing is able to be said that is worthy of God.'[62] Indeed, every time an infinite God reveals himself to finite creatures, he necessarily uses limiting analogical language.[63] When we use terms like 'jealousy' to describe God we are using limiting anthropopathisms, which run the risk of misunderstanding and misinterpretation. However, God has chosen to reveal himself in frail human language, and this language should be respected and understood to the best of our ability. The jealousy of God affirms his personhood and relational nature that must be acknowledged along with his immutability. The revelation of God's emotions must be taken seriously and appreciated along with his immutability. We speak truly of God when we speak about him as he has spoken about himself. And he has told us that he is a jealous God.

Human understanding of jealousy is often primarily based on our experience of it in our own lives, which is often unwarranted or sinfully expressed, and destructive. Because of this, it can be extremely difficult for many to understand how this could be a

---

consider that this expression has been taken from our own human experience; because God, whenever he is exercising judgment, exhibits *the appearance* of one kindled and angered (italics mine).' Calvin, *Institutes*, 1:227. See also, The Westminster Confession, Ch 2, which says that God is without passions.

[61]Examples of this approach can be found in: Clark H. Pinnock, *Most Moved Mover: a Theology of God's Openness* (Grand Rapids: Baker 2001); Gregory Boyd, *God of the Possible* (Grand Rapids, Baker, 2000) John Sanders, *The God Who Risks: A Theology of Providence* (Downers Grove, Ill.: InterVarsity, 1998) and Clark Pinnock et al., *The Open View of God: A Biblical Challenge to the Traditional View of God* (Downers Grove, Ill.: InterVarsity, 1994).

[62]Hallman, 'Emotions of God,' 14.

[63]For an excellent discussion of this idea, see Michael S. Horton, 'Hellenestic or Hebrew: Open Theism and Reformed Theological Method,' *Journal of the Evangelical Theological Society*, Vol. 45, No. 2 (June, 2002), 317-41.

godly emotion. Some would suggest that the concept of jealousy as a godly emotion has lost its ability to be intelligible to the modern mind. However, for those who base their understanding of God, humans and relationships on God's revelation, the teaching of the Bible must continue to be understood, affirmed and taught, regardless of contemporary sensibilities.

> But can we, when it concerns the question of our picture of God, ignore the source of our belief, the Holy Scriptures? Do not we give up too quickly, in the dangerous waters of religious projection, when we let our picture of God be determined by our experiences and buckle under the pressure of our own life relationships?[64]

God's Jealousy for His Own Glory

While godly human jealousy will be the main focus of this work, it is obvious that an accurate understanding of God's jealousy must first be understood before godly human jealousy can be. Therefore, the nature of the jealousy of God will be established in chapters 2, 3 and 4 before human jealousy is investigated. God's jealousy for his own glory is his inherent jealousy that desires that his glory be acknowledged and proclaimed.

God's jealousy is more than a passing mood; it springs from his innate character and is the foundation of all godly jealousy. It is one of the enduring characteristics that make up his communicable attributes.[65] It is with jealousy that God always responds to the abrogation of his exclusive right to be acknowledged as the only true God. God 'will admit no

---

[64] Christoph Dohmen, "Eifersuchtiger ist Sein Name' (Ex 34, 14): Ursprung und Bedeutung der Alttestamentlichen Rede von Gottes Eifersucht,' *Theologische Zeitschrift* 46, no. 4 (1990): 290. Aber können wir, wenn es um die Frage unseres Gottesbildes geht, die Urkunde unseres Glaubens, die Heilige Schrift, beiseite lassen? Geraten wir nicht allzuschnell in das gefährliche Fahrwasser religiöser Projektionen, wenn wir unter dem Druck eigener Lebensverhältnisse unser Gottesbild unmittelbar und ausschliesslich von unseren Erfahrungen und Bedürfnissen her bestimmen lassen?

[65] God's communicable attributes are those attributes that humans share with him in greater degree than his incommunicable attributes which we share in much lesser degree, if at all.

derogation from his majesty.'[66] God demands that his people recognize his exclusive claims on them (Deut. 6:13-15). When God is jealous, it means that he 'continually seeks to protect his own honor.'[67] It is not only the emotion that leads to divine wrath, it is also the cause of God's loving pursuit of his rebellious people when they go astray.

The key passages in this in this category are: Exodus 10:1-2; Isaiah 48:9-11; Ezekiel 20:42-44; 36:21-23; 39:25-27; Matthew 4:10; Mark 8:38; John 12:28-29; 17:1-5; Acts 12:21-23; 2 Corinthians 4:7, 15; and Hebrews 1:4-14.

♦ Exodus 10:2: I performed My signs among them, *that you may know that I am the LORD.*

♦ Isaiah 48:9-11: *For the sake of My name* I delay My wrath, and *for My praise I restrain it* for you, in order not to cut you off. Behold, I have refined you, but not as silver; I have tested you in the furnace of affliction. *For My own sake, for My own sake, I will act; for how can My name be profaned? And My glory I will not give to another.*

♦ Ezekiel 20:44: '*Then you will know that I am the LORD when I have dealt with you for My name's sake*, not according to your evil ways or according to your corrupt deeds, O house of Israel,' declares the Lord GOD.

♦ Ezekiel 36:21-23: But *I had concern for My holy name*, which the house of Israel had profaned among the nations where they went. Therefore say to the house of Israel, 'Thus says the Lord GOD, It is not for your sake, O house of Israel, that *I am about to act, but for My holy name*, which you have profaned among the nations where you went. I will vindicate the holiness of *My great name* which has been profaned among the nations, which you have profaned in their midst. Then the nations will know that I am the LORD,' declares the Lord GOD, '*when I prove Myself holy among you in their sight.*'

---

[66]Eichrodt, *Theology of the Old Testament*, 1:210.

[67]Wayne A. Grudem, *Systematic Theology: An Introduction to Biblical Doctrine* (Grand Rapids: Zondervan, 1994), 205.

♦ Ezekiel 39:25: Therefore thus says the Lord GOD, 'Now I will restore the fortunes of Jacob and have mercy on the whole house of Israel; and *I will be jealous for My holy name.*'

♦ Matthew 4:10: Then Jesus said to him, 'Go, Satan! For it is written, "YOU SHALL WORSHIP THE LORD YOUR GOD, AND SERVE HIM ONLY." '

♦ Acts 12:23: And immediately an angel of the Lord struck him *because he did not give God the glory*, and he was eaten by worms and died.

♦ 2 Corinthians 4:7: But we have this treasure in earthen vessels, so *that the surpassing greatness of the power will be of God and not from ourselves.*

This kind of self-directed jealousy for one's own glory is unique to God, for no created thing is in a position to rightly assume this right. Only God deserves absolute honor, worship, and glory and he reacts with jealousy and anger when those he has created do not ascribe it to him or when they desire it for themselves.[68] This kind of divine jealousy will be examined in chapter 2.

God's Jealousy for the Faithfulness of His People
The primary means by which God is glorified is through the faithfulness of his people with whom he has established a covenant relationship. When his people are unfaithful he naturally reacts with jealousy. The category dealt with in chapters 3 and 4 will be passages of Scripture where the emphasis of God's jealousy is most clearly on the faithfulness of his people. The key passages on this category are Exodus 20:1-6; 34:14; Deuteronomy 4:23-24; Ezekiel 16; 1 Corinthians 10:22; and James 4:5.

♦ Exodus 20:5: You shall not worship them or serve them; for *I, the LORD your God, am a jealous God.*

♦ Exodus 34:14: for you shall not worship any other god, for *the LORD, whose name is Jealous, is a jealous God.*

---

[68]Ibid., 1005.

♦ Deuteronomy 4:24: For the LORD your God is a consuming fire, *a jealous God.*

♦ Ezekiel 16:38, 42: Thus I will judge you like women who commit adultery or shed blood are judged; and *I will bring on you the blood of wrath and jealousy....* So I will calm My fury against you and *My jealousy will depart from you,* and I will be pacified and angry no more.

♦ 1 Corinthians 10:22: Or do we *provoke the Lord to jealousy?* We are not stronger than He, are we?

♦ James 4:5: Or do you think that the Scripture speaks to no purpose: *'He jealously desires the Spirit* which He has made to dwell in us'?

Here we see God's jealousy expressed toward his people who exclusively belong to him. Yahweh has the right of possession simply because he is God, and he specifically demands this exclusive favor from those with whom he has established his covenant relationship. His people are in a marriage relationship with him and any violation of it is cause for a jealous reaction. Jealousy is the foundational emotion underlying God's wrathful response to infidelity. God's jealousy when caused by the unfaithfulness of his people will be examined in chapters 3 and 4.[69]

---

[69]In addition to God's jealousy for his own glory and his jealousy for the faithfulness of his people, it is possible to consider a third kind of divine jealousy as well; namely, God's jealousy on behalf of his people. This is when God is intensely concerned with, and takes action for, the well being of his people. I have not included this category in this study because these passages did not clearly fit the definition of jealousy as it is being used in this dissertation. Jealousy is 'an ardent desire to maintain exclusive devotion within a relationship in the face of a challenge to that devotion. The passage where God seeks the well being of his people more clearly fits the more general definition of 'zeal.' The following forty-three passages fit this description (italicised passages contain the anq (*qna*) root). Genesis 12:2-3,17; 20:3; 22:12; 29:31; Exodus 9:17; Leviticus 20:10; Numbers 12:1-12; 14:13-19; 16:28-30; Deuteronomy 1:29-31; 21:15-17; 22:13-30; 32:40-43; 2 Kings 2:23-24; 19:31; 1 Chronicles 5:1; Psalm 105:12-15; Isaiah 9:7; *26:11*; 37:23, *32*; 43:3-4; 47:6-9; 51:22-23; *59:17-18*; *63:15*; Jeremiah 50:33-34; Ezekiel 35:10-11; *36:5-6*, 18; *38:18-19*; *Joel 2:18-19*; Nahum 1:2; 3:3-5; Zephaniah 2:10-11; *Zechariah 1:14-15*; *8:1-2*; 10:2; 13:2; Malachi 2:13-16; Revelation 18:19-20, 19:2.

Godly Human Jealousy

There are many instances in Scripture where humans express godly jealousy. These instances occur throughout every major phase of salvation history.[70] There are primarily three kinds of godly human jealousy: jealousy on behalf of God's honor, jealousy for the faithfulness of another person,[71] and jealousy on behalf of another person.[72] All three of these represent legitimate expressions of this righteous emotion. However, because it is most obviously representative of God's self-glorifying goal in salvation history, jealousy that is on behalf of God's honor is the purest and clearest type of godly jealousy. This type of jealousy will be the main focus of this study.

Human Jealousy on Behalf of God's Honor

Godly human jealousy that has God's honor as its object represents the highest form of human jealousy. This emotion earnestly desires that God be recognized for who he is, and that he be responded to accordingly. It is to take God's side, and represent his case before man. Many of the great leaders of God's people have exhibited this emotion. A godly perspective causes one to act on God's behalf to bring about covenant fidelity and obedience in the lives of his people. This emotion is a primary basis for the courage, boldness, and integrity with which great leaders of God's people lived their lives.

There are hundreds of examples in the Bible where men and women express this kind of jealousy. When Moses smashed the tablets and ground the golden calf to powder and made the Israelites drink it, he was most likely motivated by jealousy for God's exclusive right to be worshipped. Whenever religious

---

[70]Please see appendix 3 for an illustration showing some of the key examples of godly human jealousy as they occur in major events of salvation history.

[71]Genesis 49:3; Numbers 5:12-31; Proverbs 6:24-35; 7:1-27; Song of Songs 2:16; 6:3; 8:6; 2 Corinthians 11:1-4; 12:14.

[72]Genesis 34:7, 31; 49:5-7; 39:9-10; 48:17-18; Numbers 11:28-29; 1 Samuel 31:11-13; 2 Samuel 1:14-15; 1 Kings 1:17-18; 1 Chronicles 10:11-12; Job 31:9-12; Proverbs 2:16-17, 5:15-20; Malachi 2:13-16; Matthew 14:3-5, 19:4-9; Mark 6:18, 7:9-13, 10:11-12; Luke 3:19-20; John 3:29-30; Romans 7:1-4; 1 Corinthians 7:1-4.

reform and revival was brought about in Israel, behind it always stood a jealous leader. Whether it was Hezekiah smashing the sacred pillars and cutting down Asherah poles (2 Kings 18:3-4; 19:15-19), Jehoiada tearing down the house and altars of Baal (2 Kings 11:17-18), or Josiah removing the high places (2 Kings 23:19), jealousy on behalf of God, and his exclusive right to worship and covenant fidelity, is the motivating emotion behind these actions.

The limitations of this study do not allow for treatment of all of the passages that fit into this category of godly jealousy, so we will focus on the passages where jealousy on behalf of God's honor is most clearly expressed. Among the hundreds of examples and individuals we could focus on, five of them stand out as the strongest examples of godly jealousy: Phinehas, David, Elijah, Jesus, and Paul. The key passages that epitomize this attribute for each of them are Numbers 25 (Phinehas), Psalm 69:9 (David), 1 Kings 19:10-14 (Elijah), John 2:13-17 (Jesus), and 2 Corinthians 11:1-4 (Paul). Each of these passages use either קנא (*qna*) or ζῆλος (*zelos*) to describe these men, and they all show their intense desire for the preservation of God's honor in the face of a challenge to that honor.

The most obvious example of human jealousy on God's behalf is found in Numbers 25:11 where God says, 'Phinehas the son of Eleazar, the son of Aaron the priest, has turned away My wrath from the sons of Israel in that he was jealous with My jealousy among them, so that I did not destroy the sons of Israel in My jealousy.' The people had fallen into sexual immorality with Moabite women, which led to worshipping Baal. As a result, God's jealous anger went out against Israel in the form of a plague. In the midst of the tears of repentance, an Israelite takes a Midianite woman into his home in sight of the Tent of Meeting. With the jealousy and anger of God, Phinehas carries out justice by killing the guilty parties. Here Phinehas represents God before the people in his reaction to the gross public affront to God's covenant requirements that had just occurred. His action stops the plague, and God rewards

him with an everlasting right to the priesthood. This righteous
action causes Phinehas to stand as a type of Christ in that he
took action to atone for the sin of God's people and thereby
received a perpetual priesthood.

David stands as another leader of God's people who was
jealous for God's honor. This is what must have stood behind
his bravery and indignation as a young man, as he stood before
the giant from Gath and said, 'Your servant has killed both the
lion and the bear; and this uncircumcised Philistine will be like
one of them, since he has defied the armies of the living God'
(1 Sam. 17:36). It is David's jealous love for God and devotion
to preserving his honor that made him the passionate, fearless
leader he became. As he says in Psalm 69:10: 'For קִנְאַת (*qinah*)
for Your house has consumed me, and the reproaches of those
who reproach You have fallen on me.'

We see this same attitude expressed by Elijah as he flees from
Jezebel after killing the prophets of Baal on Mount Carmel. In
his despondence he reveals the emotion that was behind his
bravery and zeal in confronting the prophets. He cries to God,

I have been very jealous (קַנֹּא קִנֵּאתִי) (*qana qanah*) for the LORD, the God
of hosts; for the sons of Israel have forsaken your covenant, torn down
your altars and killed Your prophets with the sword. And I alone am
left; and they seek my life, to take it away.' (I Kings 19:14)

God then assures Elijah that he is not alone in his jealousy for
God's honor. He tells him to go and anoint Hazael, Jehu and
Elisha as his successors who will carry on his jealousy for the
honor of God and the fidelity of his people. God than lets Elijah
know that he has reserved 7000 in Israel who have stood with
him and not succumbed to playing the harlot for Baal.

The jealous attitude of these great leaders of God's people
also motivates the wrath of the God-man as he over-turned
tables in the temple and drove out the moneychangers with a
whip. His disciples recognized this attitude as the same one that
drove David. For it is his words from Psalm 69 they recall after
Jesus cleanses the temple, 'His disciples remembered that it was

written, "jealousy (ζῆλος, *zēlos*) for your house will consume me." ' The apostle Paul also shows his godly jealousy at the core of his ministry when he demands faithfulness to God in the lives of the believers in Corinth when he says: 'For I am jealous for you with a godly jealousy; for I betrothed you to one husband, that to Christ I might present you as a pure virgin' (2 Cor. 11:2).

For our discussion of godly human jealousy, we will focus on the five key passages for each jealous leader we have mentioned. These passages will be considered within biographical sketches that highlight the godly jealousy of these five persons. In chapter 5 we will consider the Old Testament examples of Phinehas, David, and Elijah. In chapter 6 we will examine the lives of Jesus and Paul.

The Goals and Methodology of the Study
Dynamic, progressive, visionary, strong, articulate, sensitive, energetic, are common adjectives used to describe the kind of leader churches are looking for today. However, if one were to peruse the want ads looking for church leaders, it is highly unlikely that 'jealous' would be among the desired character traits. What place does this often misunderstood and maligned emotion have among the important qualities of a leader of God's people? How do godly and sinful jealousies differ? What are proper objects of godly jealousy? The intent of this study is to answer these questions and thereby gain an accurate understanding of the role of godly jealousy in the life of the Christian. We will be asking the broad question, 'What does the Bible as a whole tell us about godly human jealousy, and what does this mean in the life and ministry of believers today?'

The greatest challenge to this study is the contemporary ignorance and disdain for all jealousy both in society and the church. The vital importance this emotion has for our understanding of God, man, love, and covenant relationships demands that we have a solid grasp of its meaning in the Bible.

The direction of the goal of the handling of the theme 'jealousy of God' is to be determined from the contemporary disinterest or even ignoring of this, in which it is attempted to show how the use of the 'jealousy of God' is to be understood. That means: where it has its worth and how it, in the context of Old Testament beliefs, is further developed and formulated, and that it in the center of Old Testament theology in the most narrow sense of the word belongs to God and therefore also is in the forefront of the Christian under-standing of the unity of the holy Scriptures as script in two parts has its place and cannot be suppressed without a loss of meaning.[73]

The doctrine of God is deeply influenced by an ignorance of or appreciation for the biblical teaching on God's jealousy. God's emotions in general and his jealousy in particular have significant implications for understanding his character. While God's jealousy is foundational for his wrath and indignation, it also motivates his relentless pursuit of his loved ones when they go astray. It does not allow him to remain ambivalent when his betrothed wanders from his side. 'It is our confidence that the divine Lover will win His bride.'[74]

In this study of godly human jealousy, I have no desire to draw theological meaning, even if it represents truth found elsewhere in Scripture, from a text where that meaning is not truly found. To that end, great effort will be made to consider each major passage with sensitivity to its historical and literary contexts.[75] While great effort will be made to understand each

---

[73]Dohmen, 'Eifersuchtiger ist Sein Name,' 290. Die sich daraus ergebene Zielrichtung der Behandlung des Themas 'Eifersucht Gottes'ist bestimmt von der Auseinandersetzung mit dem häufig anzutreffenden – zwar verständlichen – Desinteresse oder gar Verschweigen dieser Thematik, indem zu zeigen versucht wird, wie die Rede von der 'Eifersucht Gottes' zu verstehen ist, d.h. wo sie ihre Wurzeln hat und wie sie im Kontext alttestamentlicher Glaubengeschichte weiterentwickelt undformuliert worden ist, und dass sie ins Zentrum alttestamentlicher Theologie im engeren Sinn des Wortes als Rede von Gott gehört und deshalb auch und gerade im christlichen Verständnis der Einheit der Heiligen Schrift als einer Schrift aus zwei Teilen ihren Platz hat und nicht ohne Verlust unterdrückt werden kann.

[74]Allender, and Longman, *The Cry of the Soul*, 132.

[75]I will also strive to pay sufficient attention to the literary elements as described in Peter Cottrell's excellent article on the subject in 'Linguistics, Meaning Semantics,

relevant passage in its appropriate context, the unified coherent message of the Bible will be the goal.

While significant text-critical issues will be dealt with when they have bearing on the theological meaning of a passage, the text in its final canonical form will be the subject of the study.[76] This study is grounded in my understanding of the Bible to be the coherent, clear, inerrant, authoritative, inspired word of God. Because I believe that the Bible ultimately has one divine author, I also believe that it has one unified theological perspective. Because of these assumptions, I believe that when systematic theology is grounded in rigorous exegesis and sound biblical theology, it will elucidate God's definitive truth on a theological issue.

This study will search the whole Bible to learn about godly human jealousy. It will seek to show that God, and godly persons, are intensely jealous for God's glory and the faithfulness of his people.

---

and Discourse Analysis,' in *NIDOTTE*, ed. Willem A. VanGemeren, et al., (Grand Rapids: Zondervan, 1996), 1:134-60.

[76]For the student of the Bible who reads it to know God, and what he requires of those who wish to live in obedience to him, the questions of the historical critical method regarding the historicity, composition, and transmission of the biblical text can hold varying degrees of importance. Some may see the questions of the historical critical method as irrelevant to faith and practice. However, those who recognize that the Christian faith is inextricably tied to historical events will be concerned that the Biblical witness is historically accurate and compositionally reliable. One's understanding of the nature of inspiration will also determine the amount of importance one places on the methods of source, form, tradition and redaction criticism. If we grant that God used human processes in transmitting the text of the Bible, an interest in the sources and means he used can be appropriate.

When this interest is based in a belief in the inspiration and authority of the Bible, the quest must be dictated and controlled by the verifiable data that the text provides, not theories about the data. As the critical problems of the passages considered are examined in this book, the methodology of Timothy Ashley will be used, Timothy R. Ashley, *The Book of Numbers*, ed. R. K. Harrison, NICOT (Grand Rapids: Eerdmans, 1993), 7.

I will attempt to find a literary solution from within the text itself, rather than simply positing a combination of sources by an editor who had little appreciation for logic, cogency, and literary style. God was at work through all the stages. Inspiration should not be limited to any one stage of the transmission and composition of the text.

Chapter 2

God's Jealousy for His Own Glory

As discussed in the previous chapter, there is little place today for any positive idea of jealousy, whether it be human or divine. The thought of God possessing this troublesome emotion is hard for the contemporary mind to understand. Because jealousy invokes ideas of a fearful, capricious, and insecure husband who is needlessly suspicious of petty human rivalry, and then abuses his wife as a result, it is difficult for many to imagine this idea attributed to God. As the recognition of God-ordained relational exclusivity wanes, so does an appreciation for jealousy that demands exclusive fidelity. Adding to this neglect are the marketing strategies of the church growth movement, and a therapeutic self-help focus of the church, which leave little interest in a theocentric emphasis for the Christian life.

The purpose of this and the next two chapters is to examine God's jealousy in the Bible so that we have a foundation from which to understand and assess the human jealousy to be studied in chapters 5 and 6. The main opponents of this chapter are ignorance of, and an aversion to, the idea of divine jealousy. This ignorance and aversion result in an anthropocentric perspective and approach to corporate worship, Bible study, preaching, counseling, theology and mission. When jealousy for God's glory is neglected, the creature rather than the creator takes center stage. Recovery of the pervasive theme in Scripture of God's jealousy for his own glory will insure that God's people live to fulfill their highest purpose – to bring glory to God.

One of the most important potential contributions of this study could be to help recover a central attribute of God that has either been relegated to a meaningless anthropopathism, or dismissed as an antiquated, pagan idea. Those most concerned to preserve God's transcendence and holiness often assume that only an entirely impassable God can be transcendent and holy. In this perspective, God's emotions are often acknowledged, but then quickly ignored as almost embarrassing and frail anthropomorphic language. On the other end of the spectrum, those wanting to preserve a robust understanding of divine emotions tend to only want to preserve those emotions that appeal to the anthropocentric sensibilities of contemporary culture. God's love, patience, and grace are appreciated, but not his hatred, wrath, and jealousy. They embrace 'a wideness in God's mercy,' but not the severity of his jealousy.[1] In both approaches God's jealousy is effectually ignored.

In this and the next two chapters we will see that not only is jealousy an emotion that God experiences; it is a fundamental character trait. It will be shown that in the Bible, when understood properly, jealousy is not a minor incidental aspect of God's work in human history; rather, it is a deep and pervasive quality of his that is foundational to everything he does in human history.

There are two major kinds of divine jealousy. Which kind of jealousy we are dealing with is based upon the emphasis or focus of that jealousy. God is jealous (1) for his own glory, and (2) for the faithfulness of his people. The latter is related to, and based on, the former. God is ultimately jealous for the faithfulness of his people because he is jealous for his own glory.

Because the theology of the Bible unfolds within human history, God's character is usually revealed in the context of his relationship with humanity. So, as would be expected within this salvation history scheme, the majority of divine jealousy passages have God's people as the focus. Although God's self-directed jealousy is foundational for all other types of godly jealousy, passages where God's own honor is emphasized are not as common or consistently found through all parts of

---

[1]For this end of the spectrum among evangelicals, see Pinnock, *Most Moved Mover*; Boyd, *God of the Possible*; John Sanders, *The God Who Risks: A Theology of Providence* and Clark Pinnock et al., *The Open View of God: A Biblical Challenge to the Traditional View of God* (Downers Grove, Ill.: InterVarsity, 1994).

Scripture. This causes gaps in the progressive development of this kind of jealousy through the Old Testament canon. This does not make God's jealousy for his own glory any less significant or foundational, it merely points to the historical nature of God's revelation of himself. In this chapter, which deals with God's jealousy for his own glory, I have drawn from passages in which the emphasis is on God seeking honor for himself. When considered with the next two chapters, which examine passages in which God seeks honor or faithfulness from his people, a more consistent historical progression of this theme becomes evident.

God's jealous demand that he be supremely valued is a theme woven throughout salvation history. From the creation of the world, which declares his glory,[2] and of man and woman who bear his image,[3] to the final judgment,[4] and the eternal heavenly praise he will receive,[5] God's self-exalting goal can be clearly seen.[6] This type of godly jealousy is unique to God and is expressed in several ways. כבד (*kabod*) is followed closely in meaning by its LXX (Septuagint) and New Testament counterpart δόξα (*doxa*) and is related to the root idea of heaviness or weight. In relation to God, כבד (*kabod*) means, 'the revelation of God's being, nature and presence to mankind, sometimes with physical phenomena.'[7] When man accurately recognizes and appropriately responds to this revealed character of God in worship, obedience, and service, he gives glory to God. כבד (*kabod*) and δόξα (*doxa*) are often rendered 'honor,' and the cognate verbs mean to ascribe respect, homage, reverence.[8] When God demands that he be recognized as the one and only

---

[2]Psalm 19:1-2.

[3]Isaiah 43:7.

[4]Revelation 15:3-4.

[5]Revelation 4:6-11.

[6]This goal in no way detracts from his covenant love, which is also a central motive in his relationship with his people.

[7]R. E. Nixon, 'Glory,' *NBD*, 423.

[8]This definition is supported by John C. Collins in his article on כבד (*kabod*) in *NIDOTTE*, 2:577-587 and Sverre Aalen in his article on δόξα (*doxa)* in *NIDNTT*, 2:44-48.

true God, and worshiped and obeyed as such, he is jealously demanding the glory due him.

God's desire for glory drives his constant revelation of himself in the lives of his people. He wants to be known, and recognized for who he is, so that he will receive his deserved glory. God wants humanity *to know that he is the Lord*, and this motive is frequently given as the cause of his actions.[9] God expresses this desire in many places and ways.

♦ Exodus 8:10:   that you may know that there is no one like Yahweh our God.

♦ Exodus 9:14:   that you may know that there is no one like me in all the earth.

♦ Exodus 9:29:   that you may know that the earth is Yahweh's.

♦ Exodus 16:6:   that you may know that Yahweh has brought you out of Egypt.

♦ Deuteronomy 4:35: that you may know that Yahweh, he is God, there is no other besides him.

♦ 1 Samuel 17:46:   That all the earth may know that there is a God in Israel.

♦ Psalm 83:18:   that they may know that you alone, whose name is Yahweh, are the Most High over all the earth.

♦ Isaiah 49:26:   all flesh will know that I, Yahweh, am your Savior and your Redeemer.

♦ Isaiah 43:10:   that you may know and believe me and understand that I am he.

♦ Isaiah 45:3:   that you may know that it is I, Yahweh,

---

[9]Exodus 6:7; 7:5, 17; 10:2; 14:4, 18; 16:12; 29:46; 31:13; Deuteronomy 29:6; 1 Kings 20:13; 20:28; Isaiah 49:23; Ezekiel 6:7, 10, 13, 14; 7:4, 27; 11:10, 12; 12:15, 16, 20; 13:9, 14, 21, 23; 14:8; 15:7; 16:62; 17:24; 20:12, 20, 26, 38, 42, 44; 22:16; 23:49; 24:24, 27; 25:5, 7, 11, 17; 26:6; 28:22, 23, 24, 26; 29:6, 9, 16, 21; 30:8, 19, 25, 26; 32:15; 33:29; 34:27; 35:4, 9, 15; 36:11, 23, 38; 37:6, 13, 28; 38:23; 39:6, 7, 22, 28; Joel 3:17.

the God of Israel, who calls you by your name.

- ♦ Ezekiel 5:13: they will know that I, Yahweh, have spoken.
- ♦ Ezekiel 21:5: all flesh will know that I, Yahweh, have drawn my sword.
- ♦ Ezekiel 25:14: They shall know my vengeance.
- ♦ Ezekiel 34:30: know that I, Yahweh, their God, am with them.
- ♦ Ezekiel 38:16: that the nations may know me.
- ♦ Hosea 2:20: then you will know the Lord.
- ♦ Joel 2:27: know that I am in the midst of Israel.
- ♦ Micah 6:5: that you might know the righteous acts of Yahweh.[10]

True knowledge of God produces a healthy, holy fear of him. There is a cause and effect relationship between the cause of God's mighty acts and judgment and the effect of his people knowing who he is and fearing him. God receives glory when his people fear him and he acts so that they will.

> For the LORD your God dried up the waters of the Jordan before you until you had crossed, just as the LORD your God had done to the Red Sea, which He dried up before us until we had crossed; that all the peoples of the earth may know that the hand of the LORD is mighty, *so that you may fear the LORD your God forever.* (Josh. 4:23-24)

Holy fear of the Lord is the appropriate response to his revelation of himself and results in reverence for his authority, rejection of evil, and obedience to his commandments.[11] 'So you shall

---

[10]This list is from an unpublished paper presented at the November 15, 2000 annual meeting of the Evangelical Theological Society in Nashville, Tenn. by David Talley, 'Three Themes about Yahweh in the Old Testament—His Person, His Presence, and His Glory: A Foundation for Spiritual Formation.'

[11]J. D. Douglas, *Fear*, NBD, 372.

not wrong one another, but *you shall fear your God*; for I am
the LORD your God.' (Lev. 25:27)

Another central way God expresses his desire to maintain his
proper relational honor is through his desire to act for the sake
of his name. He often reveals the foundational motivation for
his acts by declaring them done 'for the sake of my name' (שְׁמִי
לְמַעַן, *lĕma'an šĕmi*).[12] God's glory and his name are closely
linked. Indeed, in the Old Testament, God's glory and his name
can be considered 'two ways of expressing the same thing.'[13] The
name of God is a major theme of biblical theology because the
name of God is a window into his character.[14] His name reveals
who he is and how he acts, and refers to 'the total complex of
God's identity and reputation.'[15] This is why David would say
in Psalm 9:10, 'Those who know your name will trust in you.'
God's name, his character, and his reputation are closely linked.[16]
This deep desire to be known through his name can be see in his
frequent declaration, אֲנִי יְהוָה ('*ăni yĕhwāh,* 'I am Yahweh').[17]
God's concern for his glory is expressed in his concern that his
name and reputation be rightly known among mankind.

There are major responses that God expects when his glory
is displayed. God's jealous desire for glory demands at least

---

[12]Cf. Psalms 79:9; 106:8; 143:11; Isaiah 48:9, 11; Ezekiel 20:9,14, 22; 36:22;
Daniel 9:19; 3 John 7.

[13]J. A. Motyer, *Name NBD*, 812.

[14]Names in general carry great significance in the Bible. Consider God's changing
of Abram's name, 'exalted father,' to Abraham, 'father of many' in Genesis 17:5, and
Jacob 'the deceiver' to Israel, 'he struggles with God' in Genesis 32:28. Jesus name
points us to his earthly purpose of saving his people from their sins (Matt. 1:21).

[15]John N. Oswalt, *The Book of Isaiah: 1-39*, NICOT, ed., R. K. Harrison and Robert
L. Hubbard, (Grand Rapids: Eerdmans, 1988), 270.

[16]Allen P. Ross, 'שֵׁם,' *NIDOTTE*, 4:148.

[17]Cf. Genesis 15:7; 28:13; Exodus 6:2, 6, 7, 8, 29; 7:5, 17; 8:22; 10:2; 12:12;
14:4, 18; 15:26; 16:12; 20:2; 29:46; 31:13; Leviticus 11:44, 45; 18:2, 4, 5, 6, 21,
30; 19:2, 3, 4, 10, 12, 14, 16, 18, 25, 28, 30, 31, 32, 34, 36, 37; 20:7, 8, 24; 21:12,
15, 23; 22:2, 3, 8, 9, 16, 30, 31, 32, 33; 23:22, 43; 24:22; 25:17, 38, 55; 26:1, 2, 13,
44, 45; Numbers 3:13, 41, 45; 10:10; 15:41; Deuteronomy 5:6; 29:6; Judges 6:10;
1 Kings 20:13, 28; Psalm 81:10; Isaiah 41:13; 42:6, 8; 43:3, 11, 15; 44:24; 45:5,
6, 7, 18; 48:17; 49:23; 51:15; Jeremiah 9:24; 24:7; 32:27; Ezekiel 6:7, 10, 13, 14;
7:4, 9, 27; 11:10, 12; 12:15, 16, 20, 25; 13:9, 14, 21, 23; 14:8; 15:7; 16:62; 17:24;
20:5, 7, 12, 19, 20, 26, 38, 42, 44; 22:16; 23:49; 24:24, 27; 25:5, 7, 11, 17; 26:6;

the following manifestations: (1) worship, (2) obedience, (3) knowledge that he is the Lord, (4) fear of the Lord, and (5) reverence for his name. These key biblical concepts are normative responses when God's glory is recognized and result in honoring him. When any of these ideas is used in this study it will be assumed that the glory of God is understood as the ultimate purpose in these ways of relating to God.

While there are many passages that demonstrate God's jealousy for his glory,[18] five of these passages most clearly express or typify key aspects of this concept and are looked at more closely in this chapter. They are Exodus 10:1-2; Isaiah 48:9-11; Ezekiel 20:42-44; 36:21-23; 39:25-27.[19]

The Old Testament

We will now examine the key examples of God's jealousy for his own glory in the Old Testament. The first of these is found in the Exodus narrative.

The Exodus[20]

The Exodus was the liberation of God's people from bondage. God's compassionate concern for his people in this endeavor is rightly seen as a motivating factor for the event.

28:22, 23, 24, 26; 29:6, 9, 16, 21; 30:8, 19, 25, 26; 32:15; 33:29; 34:27; 35:4, 9, 12, 15; 36:11, 23, 38; 37:6, 13; 38:23; 39:6, 7, 22, 28; Hosea 13:4; Joel 2:27; 3:17; Zechariah 10:6; Malachi 3:6.

[18]This jealous motive for God's own glory in the face of a challenge to that glory can be clearly seen in the following eighty three passages: Exodus 3:12; 4:23; 6:7; 7:5, 16-17; 8:1; 9:1,13-17; 10:1-2, 8; 11:9; 12:12, 26-27, 31; 13:14; 14:4, 17-18, 31; 15:11, 26; 16:12; Leviticus 10:1-3; 21:7-9; 22:1; 24:10-16; 25:17, 36, 38, 43; 27:26-30; Numbers 15:32-35, 39-41; Deuteronomy 28:58; 29:6; Joshua 4:23-24; 6:18-19; 1 Kings 20:13, 28; 1 Chronicles 15:11-13; 2 Chronicles 7:16, 19; Job chs 38-41; Psalm 50:22; Isaiah 10:12-16; 40:25; 42:8; *43:10-13*; 44:6-20; 45:5-8, 14-23; 46:5-9; 48:9-11; Jeremiah 16:19-21; Ezekiel 20:5-9, 13-14, 21-22, 44; 36:22-23; 39:25-27; Zephaniah 3:8; Haggai 1:7-9; Zechariah 14:9; Malachi 2:1-2, 5; Matthew 4:10; Mark 3:38; John 12:28-29; 17:1-5; Acts 12:21-23; 2 Corinthians 4:7, 15; Hebrews 1:4-14.

[19]Exodus 20:5 may seem like an obvious omission here, however, I believe the emphasis there is on the faithfulness of God's people and have therefore dealt with that verse in the next chapter.

[20]There are several passages in Genesis that could possibly be considered in this section: Creation itself, especially the creation of man in God's image (chs 1-2),

The LORD said, 'I have surely seen the affliction of My people who are in Egypt, and have given heed to their cry because of their taskmasters, for I am aware of their sufferings. So I have come down to deliver them from the power of the Egyptians.... Now, behold, the cry of the sons of Israel has come to Me; furthermore, I have seen the oppression with which the Egyptians are oppressing them' (Exod. 3:7-9).

When Israel *was* a youth I loved him, and out of Egypt I called My son (Hosea 11:1).

However, a careful reading of the Exodus narrative reveals that God's *primary* purpose behind the Exodus was to make himself known, and thereby display and preserve his glory.[21]

Then the LORD said to Moses, 'Go to Pharaoh, for I have hardened his heart and the heart of his servants, that I may perform these signs of Mine among them, and that you may tell in the hearing of your son, and of your grandson, how I made a mockery of the Egyptians and how I performed My signs among them, *that you may know that I am the LORD*' (Exod. 10:1-2).[22]

God wants to be known and receive glory from his creation as a proper response to that knowledge. Throughout the plagues God desires that he receive his proper honor and worship as יהוה(*Yahweh*) the God of the covenant; the name given to Moses by God himself to set himself apart from all the other gods in Exodus 3:13-15. In the Exodus he accomplishes this through his

---

The Fall and Curse (ch 3), The Flood (chs 6-8), The Tower of Babel (11:1-4), The call of Abram (Gen. 12:1-2). Although I believe these are efforts on God's part to display or preserve his glory, I have not considered them here because either his motive in these events is not explicitly stated, or, although motivated by a desire he be glorified, they are not all a jealous response *to a challenge* to God's exclusive right to be worshiped (e.g. creation and the call of Abram), which is an essential element in how I have defined jealousy.

[21]Again, recognizing that God's glory is his ultimate goal in the Exodus does not conflict with his genuine love for his people (Hos. 11:1). While God's glory is his primary purpose in the Exodus, his love is a central motivation for him as well

[22]This motive is also expressed by God in Exodus 12:12; 14:31; 15:26; 16:12; and Deuteronomy 29:6.

mighty acts which 'made a mockery' (הִתְעַלַּלְתִּי, *hit'alalĕti*) of Egypt. The hithpael perfect of עלל ('*ll*) may carry this meaning of making a mockery or a fool of someone. It is 'an action, which brings shame and disgrace on its object.'[23] This is also the description of God's dealings with Egypt in 1 Samuel 6:6. Cole shows his reluctance to allow this description of God to carry any theological meaning when he says regarding the idea of God making a mockery of Egypt:

> This last concept, as usual, represents not an emotion but the effect produced. It is an anthropomorphism, an expression of divine activity in human terms, like God's laughter in the Psalms (Ps. 2:4), and must not be unfairly pressed as a theological point.[24]

Driver agrees when he says that to take this idea as anything but an apparently meaningless anthropomorphism is to allow for an understanding of God 'which is not consonant with the higher Christian conception of God.'[25] This dismissal of a description of God's behavior as merely anthropopathic and without theological import does not do justice to God's revelation of himself. If God is not making a theological point here, what is he doing? Of course God's 'making sport' of Egypt does not carry with it the petty sinful elements that human mockery usually does. However, God has every right to make obvious Egypt's arrogant failure to acknowledge him as the LORD. Idolatry and wickedness by the creature deserve to be derisively mocked by a holy Creator,[26] and by godly people on his behalf.[27] Reluctance

---

[23]Walter C. Kaiser, *Exodus*, EBC, ed. Frank E. Gabelein, vol. 2 (Grand Rapids: Zondervan, 1990), 366.

[24]R. Alan Cole, *Exodus: An Introduction and Commentary*, TOTC, ed. D. J. Wiseman, vol. 2 (Downers Grove, Ill.: InterVarsity, 1973), 99.

[25]Samuel R. Driver, *The Book of Exodus*, The Cambridge Bible for Schools and Colleges, ed. A. F. Kirkpatrick, vol. 2 (London: Cambridge University Press, 1911), 78.

[26]Cf. 'He who sits in the heavens laughs, *the Lord scoffs at them*' (Ps. 2:4); 'I will also laugh at your calamity; *I will mock* when your dread comes' (Prov. 1:26).

[27]'It came about at noon, that *Elijah mocked them* and said, 'Call out with a loud voice, for he is a god; either he is occupied or gone aside, or is on a journey, or perhaps he is asleep and needs to be awakened' (1 Kings 18:27).

in allowing God to put idolatrous human arrogance in its place by mocking it is to fail to fully recognize God's ardent jealousy for his own glory, and the right he has to display the foolishness of man when he fails to acknowledge that glory.

God's desire for recognition as the supreme LORD in the events of the Exodus was not limited to his covenant people. God was also concerned that the Egyptians knew he was the LORD: '*The Egyptians* shall know that I am the LORD, when I stretch out My hand on Egypt and bring out the sons of Israel from their midst (Exod. 7:5).'[28] God wants to prove his presence and power to Pharaoh and his court and to 'authenticate himself by means of the mighty acts.'[29] Even the hardening of Pharaoh's heart was so that God would have more opportunity to display his mighty power and thereby be exclusively recognized as God: 'Then the LORD said to Moses, "Pharaoh will not listen to you, so that My wonders will be multiplied in the land of Egypt" ' (Exod. 11:9).

While God wants all nations to recognize his power and glory, he especially wants his covenant people to remember who he is.

> Again, as throughout the proof-of-Presence sequence, there is a difference in the intended effect of the mighty act upon the Egyptians, who are to be brought to the point where they will take Yahweh and his demands seriously, in their own territory, and upon the Israelites, who are to know by experience that he is all that he claims to be down through all the generations.[30]

The desired result of the Exodus was proper recognition and worship of God.[31] Moses' single-minded devotion to God, as expressed in Exodus 15:11, exhibits the kind of worshipful

---

[28]Cf. 7:17; 9:14-16; 14:4; 14:17; 25:36.

[29]John I. Durham, *Exodus*, WBC, ed. David A. Hubbard and Glen W. Barker, vol. 3 (Waco, Tex.: Word, 1987), 135.

[30]Durham, *Exodus*, 135. Cf. J. Phillip Hyatt, *Exodus*, NCBC, ed. Ronald E. Clements and Matthew Black, vol. 2 (Grand Rapids: Eerdmans, 1971), 123.

[31]Exodus 3:12; 4:23; 7:16; 8:1; 9:1; 9:13; 10:8; 12:26-27; 12:31; 13:14.

response God's liberating work was intended to bring about: 'Who is like You among the gods, O LORD? Who is like You, majestic in holiness, awesome in praises, working wonders?'

This recognition of Yahweh is not reserved for the generation that experienced his mighty acts. Moses is given clear instructions that he is to 'recount' (תְּסַפֵּר, *tĕsapēr*) the mighty deeds of God for generations to come. God's desire to perpetuate his glory by the retelling of his mighty acts is behind the institution of the most significant Jewish observance. Passover was to serve as a reminder of what God did for his people in the Exodus, and thus invoke the proper recognition of God for generations to come.

> And when your children say to you, 'What does this rite mean to you?' you shall say, 'It is a Passover sacrifice to the LORD who passed over the houses of the sons of Israel in Egypt when He smote the Egyptians, but spared our homes.' And the people bowed low and worshiped (Exod. 12:26-27).

The Exodus was to be remembered to instill obedience to God's commands in the lives of his people and thereby insure God would receive the glory he desires.[32]

We find God's desire that he be known and that his name be honored as the primary motive behind the Exodus in both the Wisdom and Prophetic literature as well:

> Our fathers in Egypt did not understand Your wonders; they did not remember Your abundant kindnesses, but rebelled by the sea, at the Red Sea. Nevertheless *He saved them for the sake of His name, that He might make His power known* (Ps. 106:7-8).

> But *I acted for the sake of My name*, that it should not be profaned in the sight of the nations among whom they *lived,* in whose sight

---

[32]Cf. Exodus 12:42; 13:9, 14, 16; 16:32; 23:15; 34:18; Numbers 14:19; Deuteronomy :20; 5:6; 6:12, 21; 8:14; 13:10; 16:1, 6; 26:8; Joshua 24:6, 17; Judges 2:1; 6:8, 13; 11:16; 1 Samuel 8:8; 10:18; 12:8; 2 Samuel 7:6, 23; 1 Kings 8:16, 53; 2 Kings 21:15; 2 Chronicles 5:10; Nehemiah 9:18; Psalm 114:1; Hosea 11:1; 12:9, 13; 13:4; Amos 2:10; 3:1; Haggai 2:5; and also Matthew 2:15.

I made Myself known to them by bringing them out of the land of Egypt (Ezek. 20:9).[33]

Isaiah

The clearest and most important passages in this category of God's jealousy for his own glory appear in the period of the restoration. In God's prophetic promises to restore his people and save them out of captivity, we gain vital insight into his central concern in human history. In Isaiah 48:9-11 we find one of the clearest expressions of God's self-directed jealousy as he gives assurance of his gracious restoration of Israel.

> *For the sake of*[34] *My name* I delay My wrath, and *for My praise I restrain it* for you, in order not to cut you off. Behold, I have refined you, but not as silver; I have tested you in the furnace of affliction. *For My own sake, for My own sake,* I will act; *for how can My name*[35] *be profaned?* And *My glory I will not give to another* (Isa 48:9-11).

This passage picks up on the same theme already expressed in 42:8: 'I am the LORD, that is *My name*; I will not give *My glory* to another, nor My praise to graven images.' These passages represent the main message of Isaiah, namely, the jealous preservation and presentation of God's glory.[36] Because God has entered into a covenant relationship with Israel, his name has become associated with them, and therefore, his reputation is

---

[33]This same idea is repeated in Ezekiel 20:13-14, 22.

[34]לְמַעַן שְׁמִי (*lĕmaʿan šĕmi*), contra the LXX, refers both to God's name *and* his praise. Cf. Isaiah 15:8; 28:5-6; 61:7.

[35]The NASB here (along with the KJV, RSV, ASV, NRSV, and NKJV) follows the τὸ ἐμὸν ὄνομα (to emon onoma, 'my name') of the LXX and supplies and italicizes 'My name.' The NIV chooses to follow Qa and prefers "myself" instead of 'my name.' Because of the very close connection between God's name and his very being, Moyter rightly observes that no matter which translation you choose here 'the sense remains identical.' J. Alec Motyer, *Isaiah: An Introduction and Commentary* (Downers Grove, Ill.: InterVarsity, 1993), 379. North concurs, Christopher R. North, *Isaiah 40-55* (London: SCM, 1952), 104.

[36]Oswalt, *Isaiah*, 269, links vv 9-11 with Exodus 34 and Ezekiel 36 because they carry the same theme of God's overriding concern with his own honor.

tied with their destiny. God graciously sustains his people, not because they deserve it, but primarily to maintain the honor of his name. God saves his people because he loves them and so that the world will know he is the one true God.

In Isaiah 40–48, God is confronting the rebellion of his people. In 48:1-5 he recounts this rebellion and then in verse 6 he transitions to a promise of freedom for his undeserving people and destruction of Babylon. He tells them of 'new things' he will do (v. 6). One of these 'new things' is the 'deferring of the Lord's anger for his own sake.'[37] God, unlike idols, is able to act out of his sovereign freedom and redeem his people in spite of their rebellion. God will not allow himself to be compared to idols. He withheld his wrath[38] because 'he did not want to profane his name and yield his glory to another god.'[39] To think of him as just one of the other gods or an idol would cause his name to be profaned (יֵחַל, *yēḥl*). This identity, as the one and only 'Holy One,' demands absolute loyalty from his people. He earlier affirmed this central desire in 40:25: ' "To whom then will you liken Me that I would be *his* equal?" says the Holy One.'

The patience of God in delaying his wrath, that he is אַפַּיִם אֶרֶךְ (*'erek 'apayim*, 'slow to anger') is a common affirmation of one of God's central character traits.[40] However, the primary motive behind this attribute is the jealousy of Yahweh for his own glory.[41] He delays his wrath not because Israel deserves it, but 'to satisfy a demand made upon him by his own holiness.'[42]

---

[37]Pieter A. Verhoef, 'חדש,' *NIDOTTE*, 2:34.

[38]Abraham Heschel cites this passage when he comments on the ability of God to change his course of action in spite of his genuine anger. Heschel says, 'The anger of the Lord is instrumental, hypothetical, conditional, and subject to His will.' Abraham Heschel, *The Prophets*, (New York: Harper & Row, 1962), 286.

[39]D. F. O'Kennedy, 'חלל,' *NIDOTTE*, 2:151.

[40]Other passages where God's patience is expressed as his motivating concern are, Exodus 34:6; Numbers 14:18; Nehemiah 9:17; Psalms 86:15; 103:8; 145:8; Joel 2:13; Jonah 4:2; Nahum 1:3.

[41]Psalm 79:10 and Deuteronomy 32:27 appeal to this desire of God to protect his reputation before the nations.

[42]F. Delitzsch, *Isaiah*, trans. James Martin. Commentary on the Old Testament in Ten Volumes, ed. C. F. Keil and F. Delitzsch, vol. 7. (Grand Rapids: Eerdmans, reprint 1982), 250.

Calvin says that in this situation God 'had the justest cause
for destroying this nation.'[43] However, because Israel was
associated with Yahweh, the continued existence of his
covenant people was necessary so that his glory would not be
diminished. He wanted no cause for other nations to blaspheme
his name.

In Isaiah 48:9-11, God's jealousy for his own honor is
expressed as a desire to vindicate his praise and his name.[44]
Young considers God's praise and name to be parallel ideas.[45]
When God is praised he receives the glory due him and his
name is magnified. His praise is the 'repute he would wish
for himself.'[46] God's desire to act 'for the sake of his name'
(לְמַעַן שְׁמִי, *lēma'an šēmi*) is found throughout Scripture.[47] His
concern for his glory is expressed in his concern for the vindication of his name and reputation before the nations. There
is a close connection between God's glory and his name. As
Motyer observes, his name is 'a summary statement of what
he has revealed about himself.'[48] Therefore, God's name and
glory are really 'two ways of expressing the same thing.'[49]

Even if his people did not represent the name of their God
well, he would insure that the honor of his name, which was
associated with them, was guarded.[50] It is this same foundational
desire that his name be glorified that motivates God in Ezekiel
as well.

---

[43]John Calvin, *Commentary of the Book of the Prophet Isaiah*, trans. William
Pringle (Grand Rapids: Eerdmans, 1957) 3:475.

[44]On the idea of God acting for the sake of his name see Allen P. Ross, 'שֵׁם,'
NIDOTTE, 4:148. Other passages that deal with profaning God's name are
Leviticus 22:2; Numbers 20:12; Jeremiah 34:16; Ezekiel 36:20; Amos 2:7;
Malachi 1:11-12.

[45]Edward J. Young, *The Book of Isaiah* (Grand Rapids: Eerdmans, 1972), 253.

[46]Moyter, *Isaiah*, 379.

[47]Psalms 79:9; 106:8; 143:11; Isaiah 48:9; 48:11, Ezekiel 20:9; 20:14; 20:22;
36:22; Daniel 9:19, 3 John 7.

[48]Moyter, *Isaiah*, 379.

[49]Moyter, *Name NBD*, 812.

[50]Geoffery W. Grogan, *Isaiah*, EBC, ed. Frank E. Gaebelein, vol. 6 (Grand Rapids:
Zondervan, 1986), 280-81.

Ezekiel

Ezekiel continues Isaiah's theme of God's jealousy for his own honor. In chapter 20:1-26, he compares the rebellion of his exilic audience to that of the Israelites of Moses' day and beyond.[51] He then reminds them that God preserved them, not because they deserved it, but for the sake of his name, and so he would be recognized as יְהוָה (*Yahweh*).[52] He then assures them that they will be restored for the same reason. He wants them to know that God's jealous motives do not change and that 'the principles that have governed God's dealings with them in the past continue in force into the future.'[53] We see that Yahweh's gracious saving activity on behalf of Israel is still based in his ardent desire to protect the honor of his name:

> 'And *you will know that I am the LORD*,[54] when I bring you into the land of Israel, into the land which I swore to give to your forefathers. There you will remember your ways and all your deeds with which you have defiled yourselves; and you will loathe yourselves in your own sight for all the evil things that you have done. *Then you will know that I am the LORD* when I have dealt with you *for My name's sake*,[55] not according to your evil ways or according to your corrupt deeds, O house of Israel,' declares the Lord GOD (Ezek. 20:42-44).

The attitude Israel will have after the restoration described in verses 42-43 is in stark contrast to the one Ezekiel was

---

[51]This history of apostasy has a parallel in Psalm 106.

[52]In Ezekiel 20:1-44 the phrase 'declares the Lord God,' אָמַר אֲדֹנָי יְהוִה, occurs 11 times, 'I am the Lord,' אֲנִי יְהוָה, 9 times, and 'for the sake of my name,' לְמַעַן שְׁמִי 4 times.

[53]Daniel I. Block, *The Book of Ezekiel*, NICOT, ed. R.K. Harrison and Robert L. Hubbard, vol. 1-2 (Grand Rapids: Eerdmans, 1997), 613.

[54]Ezekiel uses a form of the phrase וִידַעְתֶּם כִּי אֲנִי ('know that I am Yahweh') sixty-five times, 6:7, 10, 13, 14; 7:4, 9, 27; 11:10, 12; 12:15, 16, 20; 13:9, 14, 21, 23; 14:8; 15:7; 16:62; 17:24; 20:12, 20, 26, 38, 42, 44; 22:16; 23:49; 24:24, 27; 25:5, 7, 11, 17; 26:6; 28:22, 23, 24, 26; 29:6, 9, 16, 21; 30:8, 19, 25, 26; 32:15; 33:29; 34:27; 35:4, 9, 12, 15; 36:11, 23, 38; 37:6, 13, 28; 38:23; 39:6, 7, 22, 28.

[55]Block shows the connection between the term 'for my name's sake' and God's reputation when he translates לְמַעַן שְׁמִי as 'for the sake of my reputation,' Block, *Ezekiel*, 1:629.

confronting in his day. The knowledge of Yahweh he desires will be present and the sinfulness of her present ways will be acknowledged and she will despise them. Israel will recognize that it is not her worthiness that is the cause of God's faithfulness, rather it is because of his 'personal integrity and his jealous concern for his reputation.'[56] It is made clear to his people that their restoration is based in Yahweh's concern 'to once and for all put an end to the desecration of his name.'[57]

Ezekiel expands on this same theme in chapter 36 with a different focus—the other nations. In verses 1-16 God tells his people that his jealous wrath will strike out on behalf of Israel against the other nations who have oppressed her. In verse 16 he then reminds them of their apostasy and tells them that his wrath has been and will be restrained because he desires to protect the honor of his name among the nations:

> But *I had concern for My holy name*, which the house of Israel had profaned among the nations where they went. Therefore say to the house of Israel, 'Thus says the Lord GOD, "*It is not for your sake, O house of Israel, that I am about to act, but for My holy name*, which you have profaned among the nations where you went. *I will vindicate the holiness of My great name* which has been profaned among the nations, which you have profaned in their midst. Then *the nations will know that I am the LORD*," declares the Lord GOD, "*when I prove Myself holy among you in their sight*" ' (Ezek. 36:21-23).

Delitzsch considers this passage to be a commentary on the previously discussed Isaiah 48:11.[58] The pollution of Yahweh's people and land resulted in discrediting Yahweh himself. He would not allow his name to be dishonored among foreign nations in this way, and therefore, will turn the hearts of his

---

[56]Block, *Isaiah*, 1:657.

[57]Walther Zimmerli, *A Commentary on the Book of the Prophet Ezekiel: Chapters 1-24*, trans. Ronald E. Clements, ed. Frank Moore Cross and Klaus Baltzer (Philadelphia: Fortress, 1969), 417.

[58]Delitzsch, *Isaiah*, 251.

people back to himself (vv. 24-28), and bring them back to their land. Because Israel and her land had been desecrated, the name of Yahweh was in danger of desecration as well. Because the name of Yahweh represents his 'character and reputation'[59] he would not allow this desecration to take place and he preserves his people in order that the nations will know he is Yahweh. וָאֶחְמֹל (*w'eḥē mōl*) in verse 21 is literally 'I had compassion,' or 'I took pity.'[60] Allen rightly agrees with the NASB, RSV, NRSV, NKJV, and translates it 'I felt concerned.'[61] Motivated by this concern for his reputation among the peoples of the earth, God will act on behalf of those associated with him. This jealous, 'radically theocentric perspective'[62] forms the introduction and motivational insight for the beautiful salvation passage that follows in verses 24-38. God loves his people and is gracious and compassionate. However, the salvation that flows from this love is fundamentally motivated by his jealous pursuit of the honor of his name and this is in no way at odds with his love.

In Ezekiel 39:25-27, we see again the overriding motivation of Yahweh in his judgment and compassionate restoration of his people. Keil looks back to 36:22-23 and verse 7 of this chapter as the necessary backdrop for verses 25-27.[63] 'My holy name I will make known in the midst of My people Israel; and I will not let My holy name be profaned anymore. And the nations will know that I am the LORD, the Holy One in Israel' (Ezek 39:7). Because of this divine concern for the preservation of the integrity of his

---

[59] Block, *Ezekiel*, 2:348.

[60] Zimmerli opts for 'They I grieved,' and likes that this reading 'alleviates the sharpness of the statement that Yahweh is first concerned for his name' (Zimmerli, *Ezekiel*, 2:241). This desire to soften the self-glorifying efforts of God is an attempt to blunt the main theme of this passage and Ezekiel, and I dare say of the entire Bible.

[61] Leslie C. Allen, *Ezekiel: 20-48*, WBC, ed. Robert L. Hubbard, vol. 29 (Waco, Tex.: Word, 1990), 175.

[62] Block, *Ezekiel*, 2:351.

[63] C. F. Keil, *Ezekiel*, trans. James Martin, Commentary on the Old Testament in Ten Volumes, ed. C. F. Keil and F. Delitzsch, vol. 9 (Grand Rapids: Eerdmans, reprint 1982), 178.

name, and for accurate knowledge of who he is, God promises
to restore his people to their land.

> Therefore thus says the Lord GOD, 'Now I will restore the fortunes
> of Jacob and have mercy on the whole house of Israel; *and I will
> be jealous*[64] *for My holy name.* They will forget their disgrace and
> all their treachery which they perpetrated against Me, when they
> live securely on their *own* land with no one to make *them* afraid.
> When I bring them back from the peoples and gather them from
> the lands of their enemies, then *I shall be sanctified through them
> in the sight of the many nations*' (Ezek. 39:25-27)

God will 'restore the fortunes of Jacob'[65] because he jealously
desires that his name be publicly honored. This reversal of
fortune will not be a source of pride for Israel but will humble her
and bring her to recognition of her unfaithfulness and shame.[66]
The sin of Israel, not Yahweh's weakness, justly brought the
punishment of God on Israel (v. 23). But God's sovereign
freedom, resulting in the bestowal of unmerited favor on Israel,
brings even greater recognition of his glory and holiness as he
destroys Gog. Finally, because he restores Israel, the holiness of
Yahweh will be recognized by many nations. As Block rightly
observes, 'The primary concern of the Gog oracle is revelatory:
to make known the person and character of Yahweh, particularly
his transcendent qualities: his greatness in 38:23, his holiness
in 38:23 and his glory in 39:13.'[67] God's jealousy for his holy
name in verse 25 points to Yahweh's primary motive, not only

---

[64]Zimmerli, Keil, and every major translation except for the NIV, agree with the
NASB here in translating וְקִנֵּאתִי (*wĕqinē'ti*,'I will be jealous'). The NIV opts for
the more general and vague 'zealous.' Block's 'demonstrate passion,' and Allen's
'passionate concern,' also unfortunately sacrifice the more specific relational meaning
of וְקִנֵּאתִי (*wĕqinē'ti*) rather than risk communicating the negative understanding of
jealousy.

[65]This idiom also occurs in 16:53 and 29:14. This announcement of grace, which
reverses the judgment of Yahweh, comes as wonderfully shocking news in light of
the wrathful pronouncements found in the majority of the book.

[66]God's grace and patience leading to awareness of sin is also described in
Romans 2:4: 'Or do you think lightly of the riches of His kindness and tolerance and
patience, not knowing that the kindness of God leads you to repentance?'

[67]Block, *Ezekiel*, 2:480.

in the destruction of Gog, but in all of his acts in history. Here we see God's mercy and jealousy motivating the same action, which reveals that these concepts are not mutually exclusive, but can co-exist within godly motivation, even motivation for the same action.[68] The restoration of Israel out of exile 'would find motivation both in his affectionate love and in his zealous desire to clear his profaned name.'[69] His jealousy and mercy do not allow him to remain ambivalent in the face of infidelity, nor do they allow him to forsake his people forever. They cause him to act in such a way that all people will know that he is the only true and holy God.

The key passages we have looked at in Exodus, Isaiah, and Ezekiel lay the foundation for our understanding of God's jealousy for his own glory. We will now summarize other significant places in which this concept unfolds in the Old Testament.

The Priests

As God's representatives, priests were to keep themselves holy and obey strict codes of conduct so as to not profane God's honor. In the killing of Nadab and Abihu because of their offering of strange fire, Israel receives a severe demonstration of God's demand that the priests honor him as he requires. Moses' explanation of the divine jealousy behind God's swift judgment on them leaves their undoubtedly devastated father with no reply.

> Then Moses said to Aaron, 'It is what the LORD spoke, saying, "By those who come near Me I will be treated as holy, and before all the people *I will be honored.*" ' So Aaron, therefore, kept silent (Lev. 10:3).

The close association of the priests with the holy God demanded that they practice strict sexual purity. If the priest *or his family*

---

[68]Joel 2:18 also has this unusual combination of emotions: 'Then the LORD will be jealous for His land and will have pity on His people.'

[69]Allen, *Ezekiel*, 209.

engaged in any harlotry, the penalty was to be as swift and final as it was for Nadab and Abihu:

> They shall not take a woman who is profaned by harlotry, nor shall they take a woman divorced from her husband; for he is holy to his God. You shall consecrate him, therefore, for he offers the food of your God; *he shall be holy to you; for I the* LORD, *who sanctifies you, am holy.* Also the daughter of any priest, if she profanes herself by harlotry, she profanes her father; *she shall be burned with fire* (Lev. 21:7-9).[70]

In contrast to the corrupt priests of Malachi's day, God points to Levi as an example of proper priestly reverence:

> My covenant with him was *one of* life and peace, and I gave them to him *as an object of* reverence; *so he revered Me and stood in awe of My name* (Mal. 2:5).[71]

The Law

Fear and reverence of the Lord, and obedience to his law are closely linked.

> If you are not careful to *observe* all the words of this law which are written in this book, to *fear this honored and awesome name*, the LORD your God, then the LORD will bring extraordinary plagues on you and your descendants, even severe and lasting plagues, and miserable and chronic sicknesses (Deut. 28:58-59).

God taught his people early and swiftly that he is jealous for his honor, and obedience to his law is a primary way he is

---

[70]Regarding this specific method of execution, Harris observes, 'Burned in the fire' is a peculiar provision. The method of execution is mentioned only two other times (Gen. 38:24; Lev. 20:14). In both cases it is punishment of especially grave harlotry. Evidently this type of incest was regarded as especially reprehensible. Laird R. Harris, *Leviticus*, EBC, vol. 2 (Genesis-Numbers), ed. Frank E. Gabelein, (Grand Rapids: Eerdmans, 1990), 617.

[71]The abrupt shift from Leviticus to Malachi here is because there is no other passage between them regarding priests, where I found God's jealousy for his own honor as the focus.

to be honored. When men blasphemed the name of God or collected wood on the Sabbath they were stoned (Lev. 24:10-16; Num 15:32-36).[72] The way a person treated others was a key part of the law and reflected a person's reverence for God. 'You shall not rule over him with severity, but are to revere your God' (Lev. 25:43).

The Conquest and the Ban

As with the Exodus, the primary motive behind the conquest of Canaan was that God's people would recognize him as יְהוָה, (*Yahweh*) and ascribe to him the honor he deserves:

> For the LORD your God dried up the waters of the Jordan before you until you had crossed, just as the LORD your God had done to the Red Sea, which He dried up before us until we had crossed; that all the peoples of the earth may know that the hand of the LORD is mighty, so that you may fear the LORD your God forever (Josh. 4:23-24).[73]

God is jealous for his honor in wanting the ban to be carried out among the Canaanites. He wants to leave no doubt concerning who was responsible for the victory:

> Nevertheless, anything which a man sets apart to the LORD out of all that he has, of man or animal or of the fields of his own property, shall not be sold or redeemed. Anything devoted to destruction is most holy to the LORD.... Thus all the tithe of the land, of the seed of the land or of the fruit of the tree, is the LORD's; it is holy to the LORD (Lev. 27:28, 30).[74]

---

[72]In Numbers 15:39-40, this act of Sabbath breaking is compared to prostitution, and God reminds the Israelites that he is יְהוָה (*Yahweh*) who brought them out of Egypt. 'It shall be a tassel for you to look at and remember all the commandments of the LORD, so as to do them and not follow after your own heart and your own eyes, after which you played the harlot, so that you may remember to do all My commandments and be holy to your God. I am the LORD your God who brought you out from the land of Egypt to be your God; I am the LORD your God.'

[73]Cf., 1 Kings 20:13; 20:28.

[74]Cf., Joshua 6:18.

The Final Judgment[75]

The prophet Zephaniah warns Judah of the impending judgment
of God. In the midst of this he points to the Day of the Lord
when God will judge the entire world and his awesome jealous
wrath will be expressed:

> I will bring distress on men so that they will walk like the blind,
> because they have sinned against the LORD; and their blood will
> be poured out like dust and their flesh like dung. Neither their
> silver nor their gold will be able to deliver them on the day of
> the LORD's wrath; *and all the earth will be devoured in the fire
> of His jealousy* (קִנְאָתוֹ, *qin'ātô*) for He will make a complete
> end, indeed a terrifying one, of all the inhabitants of the earth.
> (Zeph. 1:17-18)

The Day of the Lord will bring a final assertion that Yahweh
alone is God. This passage once again points to the reality of self-
directed divine jealousy, which is 'the fierce protection of God's
unique position as sole creator and covenant God.'[76] Zephaniah
gives a jarring correction to the popular notion of Israel that the
Day of the Lord would only bring prosperity.[77] Along with all
the nations of the world, Israel will be consumed in the jealous
wrath of Yahweh. This same idea is expressed in 3:8:

> 'Therefore wait for Me,' declares the LORD, 'For the day when
> I rise up as a witness. Indeed, My decision is to gather nations, to

---

[75]The passages dealt with in this section on the Final Judgment are the only ones
I found which explicitly mentioned the self-directed jealous motive behind the final
judgment. There are a few New Testament passages, which may point to God's
jealous motive in the last days (Rev. 21:2-3, 22:14-17), but they have his people as
the main focus rather than his own glory. As stated previously, this does not mean
God's jealousy is not the ultimate goal of his actions, just that the main emphasis
of the jealousy here is his people, which are the means of gaining glory. These two
passages from Revelation will be considered in chapter 5, which deals with God's
jealousy when the emphasis is on faithfulness of his people.

[76]David W. Baker, *Nahum, Habakkuk, and Zephaniah: An Introduction and
Commentary*, TOTC, ed. D. J. Wiseman, vol. 23b (Downers Grove, Ill.: InterVarsity,
1988).

[77]Willem A. VanGemeren, *The Progress of Redemption: The Story of Salvation
from Creation to the New Jerusalem* (Grand Rapids: Baker, 1988), 292.

assemble kingdoms, to pour out on them My indignation, all My burning anger; *for all the earth will be devoured by the fire of My zeal* (קִנְאָתִי, *qin'ātô*).'[78]

God's exclusive right to be honored and worshiped as God is crucial as he carries out the events of human history. The great Day of the Lord is certainly no exception to this motivation. God's jealous nature will not rest until 'the LORD will be king over all the earth; in that day the LORD will be *the only* one, and His name *the only* one' (Zech. 14:9). This great hope and expectation of Israel sets the stage for the ministry of Jesus who declared that in his ministry the Day of the Lord had been inaugurated (Mark 1:14-15; Luke 4:16-21; 10:17-19).

The New Testament
While some may allow for jealousy to be an attribute of the God of the Old Testament, many would assume that this difficult emotion would be absent from the pages of the New Testament. Many perceive the God of the New Testament to be a kinder, gentler God who is more tolerant, passive, and less focused on his own glory. However, in the New Testament God's jealousy for his own glory is still found as a central motivation in the key events of salvation history.[79] We can still see God's jealousy for his own glory as his overriding concern in Jesus' ministry, the Early Church, and the Epistles. We now turn our attention to a survey of God's jealousy for his glory in these core sections of the New Testament.

The Purpose of Jesus' Ministry
In the central event of salvation history, the life and ministry of the incarnate God, we find the jealousy of God for his own honor and glory at the center of Jesus' mission. At the inaugural phase of Jesus' public ministry, he is tempted to deny his full calling

---

[78] For no apparent reason the translators of the NASB opt for 'zeal' here rather than 'jealous' as they did in 1:18.

[79] Passages where God's jealousy for his own glory is evident are Matthew 4:10; Mark 8:38; John 12:28-29; 17:1-5; Acts 12:21-23; 2 Corinthians 4:7, 15; Hebrews 1:4-14.

as Messiah by Satan. He offers Jesus worldly power and wealth in exchange for worship. 'Satan was offering an interpretation of the theocratic ideal that sidestepped the Cross and introduced idolatry.'[80] Jesus' response clearly asserts the exclusive right of God alone to be worshiped.[81] 'Then Jesus said to him, "Go, Satan! For it is written, 'YOU SHALL WORSHIP THE LORD YOUR GOD, AND SERVE HIM ONLY' " ' (Matt. 4:10; cf. Luke 4:8). Jesus answers Satan by quoting Deuteronomy 6:13. This chapter in Deuteronomy contains the core teaching of covenant obedience. Jesus quotes from this chapter and rebukes Satan with the jealous demands of the one true God. The context of the passage Jesus quotes from in Deuteronomy 6 is enlightening, for it explicitly states that the primary reason for covenant fidelity is God's jealousy.

> You shall fear *only* the LORD your God; and you shall worship Him and swear by His name. You shall not follow other gods, any of the gods of the peoples who surround you, for the LORD your God in the midst of you *is a jealous God* (אֵל קַנָּא יְהוָה אֱלֹהֶיךָ) otherwise the anger of the LORD your God will be kindled against you, and He will wipe you off the face of the earth (Deut. 6:13-15).[82]

Jesus would not embrace the role of kingly messiah without the suffering servant as part of his identity.[83] The price of Satan's offer, that Jesus worship him, would require the denial of God's most sacred command, that he alone is God and he alone is to be worshiped (Deut. 5:6-7). In response to this offer, Jesus quotes from a clear and uncompromising command of jealous exclusive worship from the Old Testament to reject Satan's offer.[84]

---

[80]D. A. Carson, *Matthew*, EBC, ed. Frank E. Gabelein, (Grand Rapids: Eerdmans, 1984), 8:114.

[81]For a good treatment of the parallels between idolatrous Israel and faithful Jesus in the temptation see Birgir Gerhardsson, *The Testing of God's Son: An Analysis of an Early Christian Midrash* (Lund: C. W. K. Gleerup, 1966).

[82]This passage is examined in its Old Testament context in the next chapter under God's jealousy for the faithfulness of his people.

[83]There should be little doubt that this temptation is in mind when Jesus rebukes Peter for suggesting a similar idea in Matthew 16:21-23.

At another crisis point in Jesus ministry, we gain insight into the driving motive behind his incarnate life and death—the glory of God. In John 12:20-36, Jesus explains the necessity of his death and the sober implications it will have for all who follow him. He explains a basic kingdom principle; that for him to be glorified as he desires he must die, and whoever serves him must lose his life as well (v. 25).[85] As in Gethsemane,[86] Jesus' 'soul is troubled' (ἡ ψυχή μου τετάρακται *he psuchē mou tetaraktai*) by the gravity of his own teaching and destiny. When he considers the possibility of avoiding this process, he rejects it and submits to the will of his Father so that his name will receive ultimate glory:[87]

> Now My soul has become troubled; and what shall I say, 'Father, save Me from this hour'? But for this purpose I came to this hour. 'Father, *glorify Your name.*' Then a voice came out of heaven: '*I have both glorified it, and will glorify it again*' (John 12:27-28).

Here 'the horror of death and the ardour of obedience are fused together.'[88] Father and Son of the Trinity are in agreement in fulfilling the necessary actions of Jesus' life, no matter how severe, so that the name of God be glorified.

We get another glimpse of this divine jealousy as the time for Jesus' sacrificial death approached. In his high priestly prayer in John 17 he again reflects the central theme of God's glory as the purpose of the life of the incarnate Son. He asks the Father to

---

[84]Blomberg points out the great significance of this rebuke for the deity of Christ, in light of the frequent worship Jesus receives in Matthew (e.g., 2:2; 8:2; 9:18; 14:33; 15:25; 20:20; 28:17). Craig Blomberg, *Matthew*, NAC, vol. 8, ed., David S. Dockery (Nashville: Broadman, 1992), 86.

[85]Cf. 7:18 and 8:50.

[86]Matthew 26:39; Mark 14:36; Luke 22:42.

[87]That Jesus considers the alternative to the Father's will does not mean there was any question he would obey it. As Morris says, 'It may be important that His verb is "say" rather than "choose" or the like. There was no question as to His doing the Father's will. The question was, "What is the Father's will?" ' Leon Morris, *The Gospel According to John*, NICNT, ed. F. F. Bruce, (Grand Rapids: Eerdmans, 1971), 594.

[88]Morris, *John*, quoting Bengel, note 76, p 595.

'glorify Your Son, that the Son may glorify You' (v. 1). He then points to the primary reason he took on human flesh, and asks that his pre-incarnate glory be restored: 'I glorified You on the earth, having accomplished the work which You have given Me to do. Now, Father, glorify Me together with Yourself, with the glory which I had with You before the world was' (John 17:4-5).

We have seen the jealousy of the Son for the glory of the Father and for his own glory. The author of Hebrews points us to the Father's jealousy for the honor of the Son.[89] Against the idea that Jesus is on an even plane with the angels, or any created being, the supremacy of Christ from the Father's perspective is articulated by quoting the Father's estimation of his agent, the Messiah:

> Having become as *much better than the angels*, as He has inherited a *more excellent name* than they. For to which of the angels did He ever say, 'YOU ARE MY SON, TODAY I HAVE BEGOTTEN YOU'? And again, 'I WILL BE A FATHER TO HIM AND HE SHALL BE A SON TO ME'? And when He again brings the firstborn into the world, He says, 'AND LET ALL THE ANGELS OF GOD WORSHIP HIM.' And of the angels He says, 'WHO MAKES HIS ANGELS WINDS, AND HIS MINISTERS A FLAME OF FIRE.' But of the Son *He says*, 'YOUR THRONE, O GOD, IS FOREVER AND EVER, AND THE RIGHTEOUS SCEPTER IS THE SCEPTER OF HIS KINGDOM. YOU HAVE LOVED RIGHTEOUSNESS AND HATED LAWLESSNESS; THERE-FORE GOD, YOUR GOD, HAS ANOINTED YOU WITH THE OIL OF GLADNESS ABOVE YOUR COMPANIONS.' And, 'YOU, LORD, IN THE BEGINNING LAID THE FOUNDATION OF THE EARTH, AND THE HEAVENS ARE THE WORKS OF YOUR HANDS; THEY WILL PERISH, BUT YOU REMAIN; AND THEY ALL WILL BECOME OLD LIKE A GARMENT, AND LIKE A MANTLE YOU WILL ROLL THEM UP; LIKE A GARMENT THEY WILL ALSO BE CHANGED. BUT YOU

---

[89]This fascinating concept of inter-Trinitarian jealousy, where one member of the Godhead is jealous for the glory of another is best dealt with in this chapter, for the emphasis is still divine jealousy in which the emphasis is on God's desire for his own glory.

ARE THE SAME, AND YOUR YEARS WILL NOT COME TO AN END.' But to which of the angels has He ever said, 'SIT AT MY RIGHT HAND, UNTIL I MAKE YOUR ENEMIES A FOOTSTOOL FOR YOUR FEET'? Are they not all ministering spirits, sent out to render service for the sake of those who will inherit salvation? (Heb. 1:4-14)

Seven Old Testament quotations in this passage[90] establish Jesus as superior to any created being.[91] These are quotations of the Father speaking to the Son and we are invited to listen in and recognize the divine supremacy of the Son. These passages are 'well established Messianic testimonies and were acknowledged as having met their fulfillment in Jesus.'[92] The Father is ardently concerned that his Son is recognized as (1) heir of all things, (2) creator, (3) the reflection of God's glory, (4) the image of the essence of God, (5) sustainer of all things (6) propitiation, (7) one in the place of honor. As at the announcement of his birth (Luke 1:32), his baptism (Mark 1:11), and transfiguration (Matt 17:5), the Father's declarations serve to 'exhibit the transcendent dignity of the Son of God.'[93] He will allow no rival to usurp the honor due the Son. The Father's own declarations establish the glory of the Son and demands that the hearers ascribe this glory to him as well.

The Early Church
In the Early Church, we are given an example of God's severe, jealous concern that he alone be acknowledged and worshiped as God.

---

[90]Psalm 2:7; 2 Samuel 7:14 (1 Chron. 17:13); Deuteronomy 32:43; Psalms 104:4; 45:6-7; 102:25-27; 110:1.

[91]Indeed, the theme of the entire book is to establish the superiority of Christ and his covenant over any rival. The term 'more excellent' or 'better' is used 13 times (1:4; 6:9; 7:19; 7:22; 8:6; 9:23; 10:34; 11:4; 11:16; 11:35; 11:40; 12:24) in reference to Christ and his promises, hope, sacrifice, possession, country, resurrection, blood, and covenant.

[92]F. F. Bruce, *Hebrews*, NICNT, (Grand Rapids: Eerdmans, 1990, Rev. ed.), 65.

[93]William Lane, *Hebrews: 1-9*, WBC, ed. David A. Hubbard and Glen W. Barker, vol. 47a (Waco, Tex.: Word, 1991), 17.

On an appointed day Herod, having put on his royal apparel, took his seat on the rostrum and *began* delivering an address to them. The people kept crying out, 'The voice of a god and not of a man!' And immediately an angel of the Lord struck him because *he did not give God the glory*, and he was eaten by worms and died (Acts 12:21-23).

At a prearranged meeting with the representatives from Tyre and Sidon, Herod, royal robes in full array, delivers an oration and subsequently allows himself to be praised as deity. Whether Herod was trying to portray himself as divine is uncertain.[94] Luke gives no indication that Herod intended to be considered divine. Josephus agrees, and indicates that his failure to reject their claims was what incurred his guilt when he says 'The king did not rebuke them nor did he reject their flattery as impious.'[95] However, allowing the praise to continue was worthy of a swift and final judgment. Herod's reaction to being worshiped stands in stark contrast to Paul's and Barnabas' jealousy for God's exclusive right to worship when those in Lystra worshiped them in Acts 14.[96]

But when the apostles Barnabas and Paul heard of it, they tore their robes and rushed out into the crowd, crying out and saying, 'Men, why are you doing these things? We are also men of the same nature as you, and preach the gospel to you that you should turn from these vain things to a living God, WHO MADE THE HEAVEN AND THE EARTH AND THE SEA AND ALL THAT IS IN THEM' (Acts 14:14-15).

---

[94]C. K. Barrett, *A Critical and Exegetical Commentary on the Acts of the Apostles*, ICC, ed. J. A. Emerton et al., vol. 1 (Edinburgh: T & T Clark, 1994), 590.

[95]*Ant.* 19.346. 'οὐκ ἐπέπληξεν τούτοις ὁ βασιλεὺς οὐδὲ τὴν κολακείαν ἀσεβοῦσαν ἀπετρίψατο.'

[96]Herod's reaction is similar to the King of Tyre in Ezekiel 28 who said, 'I am a god, I sit in the seat of gods In the heart of the seas' (v. 2), and who also received a rebuke from God and a reminder that, 'You are a man and not God, although you make your heart like the heart of God (v. 6).' This passage was not dealt with in the Old Testament section because the motive behind this rebuke is not explicitly stated in the passage.

The reaction of the angel in Revelation 19:10 and 22:8-9 also shows the response God desires when we receive the worship, which belongs exclusively to God:

> Then I fell at his feet to worship him. But he said to me, 'Do not do that; I am a fellow servant of yours and your brethren who hold the testimony of Jesus; worship God. For the testimony of Jesus is the spirit of prophecy' (19:10).

> I, John, am the one who heard and saw these things. And when I heard and saw, I fell down to worship at the feet of the angel who showed me these things. But he said to me, 'Do not do that. I am a fellow servant of yours and of your brethren the prophets and of those who heed the words of this book. Worship God' (22:8-9).

Paul and Barnabas and the angel recoiled from being worshiped and demanded that only God be praised.[97]

The Epistles

A primary purpose in salvation history is the redemption of mankind through the proclamation of the gospel. However, the redemption of humanity is not an end in itself. The final goal of redemption is primarily increased glory ascribed to God. This ultimate goal is in no way opposed to the good of mankind. By giving glory to God, man lives as he is intended, and is most blessed.

God jealously pursues this goal in his selection of those who proclaim the gospel. The messengers God has chosen to bring his message of salvation are not attractive or powerful from the world's perspective. Rather, his ambassadors are carefully chosen, often because of their frailty, so that God receives the glory that is rightfully his. Paul explains this in 2 Corinthians 4:7: 'But we have this treasure in earthen vessels, so that the surpassing greatness of the power will be of God and not from ourselves.'

---

[97]These passages will be dealt with in chapter 6 under the topic of godly human jealousy on God's behalf.

Paul contrasts the splendor of the gospel in verse 6 which he describes as 'the Light of the knowledge of the glory of God in the face of Christ,' with the frail 'earthen vessels' that bring this message to the world. Concerning this stark contrast, Hughes observes: 'There could be no contrast more striking than that between the greatness of the divine glory and the frailty and unworthiness of the vessels in which it dwells and through which it is manifested to the world.'[98] Paul uses ὀστρακίνοις σκεύεσιν (*ostrakinois skeusin*, 'earthen vessels') here because of their cheap, fragile, and expendable nature. They point to 'the mortal existence of himself and his apostolic associates, their humanity as it is subject to the ravages of time and adversity.'[99] Paul was aware that it was not his own power or wit that brought salvation and this 'contrast between the wealth of the Gospel and the bearers of it was intended by God.'[100] Frail messengers not only prove that God's power is sufficient to use frailty for great and eternal purposes, but they leave no doubt about the source of the salvation brought by the message. We find this same teaching in 1 Corinthians 1:18-31:

> God has chosen the foolish things of the world to shame the wise, and God has chosen the weak things of the world to shame the things which are strong, and the base things of the world and the despised God has chosen, the things that are not, so that He may nullify the things that are, so that no man may boast before God. (1 Cor. 1:27-29)

Paul makes it clear in 2 Corinthians 4:15 that God's primary purpose in salvation is to bring glory to himself: 'For all things (ta panta, τὰ πάντα) *are* for your sakes, so that the grace which is spreading to more and more people may cause the giving of

---

[98]Philip E. Hughes, *Paul's Second Epistle to the Corinthians*, NICNT, ed. F. F. Bruce (Grand Rapids: Eerdmans, 1962), 135.

[99]Victor P. Furnish, *2 Corinthians*, AB, ed. Foxwell A. Albright and David N. Freedman, vol. 32A (Garden City, N.J.: Doubleday, 1984), 278.

[100]C. K. Barrett, *A Critical and Exegetical Commentary on the Acts of the Apostles*, ICC, ed. J. A. Emerton et al., vol. 1 (Edinburgh: T & T Clark, 1994), 138.

thanks to abound to the glory of God.' τὰ πάντα (ta panta, 'all things') in this verse refers to the suffering Paul endured which was described in the previous verses.[101] Paul went through great difficulty to bring the gospel to lost people, and it was worth the cost, because God's grace is received and as a result he receives greater glory. This glory is the result of persons turning to God and fulfilling their purpose of reflecting the image of God as redeemed obedient believers.[102]

Conclusions

In this chapter we have seen the close relationship between God's glory, honor, and name. We have also seen that God's primary goal in human history, a goal for which he is intensely jealous, is his own glory and honor. God's jealousy for his glory and honor is the foundation of all godly jealousy. God desires the fidelity of his people because he loves them, but ultimately because he is most glorified when they ascribe to him the honor due his name. God's ultimate and overriding purpose in human history is the exaltation and vindication of his own glory.[103] God pursues this goal by making himself known so that people will acknowledge, fear, worship, and obey him as the one and only Lord. This goal is evident at every key stage of salvation

---

[101]Hughes, *2 Corinthians*, 151; Barrett, *2 Corinthians*, 144; Furnish, *2 Corinthians*, 287.

[102]This is the same idea in Romans 4:20 with Abraham's faith, and Romans 1:23 and 15:9 with the conversion of Gentiles.

[103]For a good summary of this theme carried out through the main events of redemptive history, see appendix 1 in John Piper's *Desiring God: Meditations of a Christian Hedonist* (Sisters, Ore.: Multnomah, 1986), 255-266. The major areas of salvation history that Piper shows as examples of God's ultimate goal of displaying his own glory are: the creation of humanity in God's image (Gen. 1:26-27); the Tower of Babel (Gen. 11:1-4); the call of Abram (Gen. 12;1-2); the Exodus (Ezek 20:6-9); the giving of the law (Exod. 20:3-5); the wilderness wanderings (Ezek. 20:21-22); the conquest of Canaan (Josh. 24:12-14); the beginnings of the monarchy (1 Sam 12:19-23); the Temple of God (1 Kings 8:41-45); the deliverance in the time of the kings (2 Kings 19:34); exile and promised restoration (Isa 48:9-11); post-exilic prophets (Zech. 2:5); Jesus' life, ministry, and death; the second coming and consummation (2 Thess. 1:9-10). Not all of these events would qualify as godly jealousy because some of them are not clearly defined as jealous responses in the Bible, and the motive for action is not necessarily in response to a challenge to God's glory within relationship.

history.[104] All godly jealousy finds its ultimate end in God's glory. God's jealousy for the fidelity of his people is based in his love and compassion, but ultimately he desires his own glory through their undivided devotion. He is jealous on behalf of his people because he has the protective heart of a father, but ultimately he desires to protect the honor of his name.

When humans share God's jealousy, they too see his glory as their ultimate goal. If humans are jealous for God's glory and honor, they will seek to know, worship, fear, and obey him in their own lives, and strive to evoke this response in others as well. This will be done not only because it is what is best for them, but primarily because they share in God's righteous, ardent desire that his own glory be recognized and magnified. God's jealousy for his own honor should cause a shift in contemporary thinking with its emphasis on obedience to God because it pragmatically benefits the individual. Rather, the connection between obedience to God's commands and the glory that gives him should be seen as the prime motive for obedience.

God's jealousy for his own glory provides the foundation for this entire study. Thus, any sub-theme in Scripture is part of the grand theme of God's ultimate purpose of glorifying himself. Because God is righteous, he values above all else what is of ultimate value. He loves most what is most worthy of being loved. This object is himself: his character, being, perfections, and glory. There is nothing morally evil in God's self-exaltation, for, 'The rules of humility that belong to a creature cannot apply in the same way to its creator.'[105] As creator, he alone is worthy of ultimate honor.[106] '*Man* may not seek glory for himself, but in this case what is wrong for man is right for God because he is

---

[104]The key events we looked at were: the Exodus, the establishment of the law and priesthood, the conquest of Canaan, the restoration from exile, Jesus' ministry, the early Church, the Epistles, and the final judgment.

[105]Piper, *Desiring God,* 47.

[106]God's exclusive right to be worshiped and honored as God is seen as being derived from his identity as the only independent, uncreated being who is creator of all. Cf., Nehemiah 9:5-6; Psalms 33:6, 9; 89:111; 148:5; Isaiah 42:5; Acts 14:15; 17:24; 1 Corinthians 4:7; Colossians 1:16; Hebrews 11:3; Revelation 4:11.

the Creator.'[107] At the root of sin is a failure to make the proper distinction between God and what he has created. Specifically because he is God,

> he is therefore rightly jealous. To concede he is something other than the center of all, and rightly to be worshiped and adored, would debase his very Godhood. He is God who, entirely rightly, does not give his glory to another.[108]

This self-directed godly jealousy is unique to God and in no way detracts from his love. God is most loving when he jealously demands the praises and honor of his name in the hearts and lives of his people. When God's creatures recognize that he is worthy of ultimate honor, and give him absolute devotion, it is the best, most fulfilling experience man can attain. God alone is able to love completely and seek his own glory at the same time.

---

[107]Grudem, *Systematic Theology*, 442.

[108]Donald A. Carson, *The Difficult Doctrine of the Love of God* (Wheaton, Ill.: Crossway, 2000), 39.

Chapter 3

God's Jealousy for the Faithfulness
of His People in the Old Testament

God is jealous for his own glory primarily as it is demonstrated through the faithfulness of his people to him. There are hundreds of instances in the Old Testament where God is jealous for the faithfulness of his people, and while we cannot treat them all here, it is important to realize how common this theme is throughout Scripture.[1] As a way of narrowing our study to the most explicit key passages, we will focus on passages where all four of the following criteria are present: (1) קנא (*qna*) or

---

[1] I found 228 passages where God either explicitly or by implication expresses jealousy for the faithfulness of his people. Passages where the קנא (*qna*)or ζῆλος (*zēlos*) word group is found are italicised. Genesis 22:12; Exodus *20:3-6*; 22:20; 23:13, 24, 32; *34:12-17*; Leviticus 18:1-5, 21, 30; 19:1-4; 20:1-8; 26:1; Numbers 18:19-20; 20:12; *25:10-13*; 33:3-4, 51-52; Deuteronomy 4:15-19; *4:23-40*; *5:7-10*; *6:13-16*; 7:2-9, 25; 8:19-20; 12:2-5; 12:29-31; 13:1-18; 14:2; 16:21-22; 17:2-7; 18:9-13, 20; 20:18; 26:16-19; 27:15; 28:36-37, 58-59, 64; *29:18-29*; 30:17-18; 31:16-18; *32:16, 19-21*; Joshua 24:2, *19*; Judges 2:1-3, 10-17; 3:6-8, 10; 8:27, 33; 10:6-7, 13-16; 1 Samuel 2:29; 8:6-8; 12:9; 1 Kings 11:1-11, 33; 14:9, *22-24*; 16:12-13, 25-26, 31-33; 19:17-18; 21:24-26; 22:52-53; 2 Kings 1:3-4; 12:2-3; 14:3-4; 15:3-4; 15:34; 16:3-4; 17:7-23, 25-41; 21:1-9, 19-22; 22:17; 1 Chronicles 5:24-25; 9:1; 10:13-14; 2 Chronicles 7:22; 21:10-13; 24:17-20; 25:14-15; 28:2-4, 24-25; 33:1-9, 21-23; 34:23-25; Psalms *78:58-59*; *79:5*; 81:8-9; Isaiah 1:21; 16:12; 17:7-8; 30:1-2; 31:1-3; 42:17; 48:5; 54:5-10; 57:3-13; 65:6-7; 65:11-12; 66:3; Jeremiah 1:16; 2:1-25; 4:1-4, 30; 5:7-11, 18-19; 7:9-11, 16-20, 30-33; 8:2-3, 19; 9:2, 13-14; 10:1-6; 11:10-15, 17; 12:16; 13:10, 25-26; 14:10; 16:10-11, 18; 17:2; 18:15; 19:4-5, 13; 22:8-9; 23:13, 27; 25:6-7; 31:20-22, 31-32; 32:29-30, 34-35; 32:38-39; 35:15; 42:11-13; 44:3-5; 44:8, 15-19, 23-25; 46:25; 49:1, 3; 50:2, 5, 38; 51:17-18; 51:44; 51:47; Ezekiel 5:8-9, *13*; 6:3-13; 7:20; *8:3-18*; 11:18-21; 14:2-8; *16:1-63*; 17:17-19; 18:3-6, 12, 15; 20:7-8, 17-20, 24, 30-33, 39; 22:3-4, 9; *23:1-31*, 36-49; 24:13; 30:13; 33:25; 37:23; 43:7-9; 44:28; Daniel 4:25; 5:20-23; Hosea 1:1-11; 2:1-23; 3:1-5; 4:1, 10-19; 5:3-4, 7; 6:4, 7, 10; 7:4-6; 8:1-6, 9, 14; 9:1, 10; 10:1-2, 5-7; 11:1-4, 8-9; 13:1-6; 14:4, 8; Joel 2:27; Amos 2:4; 3:14-15; 5:25-27; 7:9; Micah 1:7; 5:12-15; Nahum 1:14; Habakkuk 2:18-20; Zephaniah 1:4-6, 9; Malachi 1:6; 3:17-18; Matthew 10:37; Mark 8:38; Acts 7:42-43; *1 Corinthians 10:22*; Hebrews 3:10; *James 4:4-5*; Revelation 2:14, 20-22; 21:2-3; 22:14-17.

ζῆλος (*zēlos*) actually occur. (2) God is obviously the subject[2] and the faithfulness of his people is emphasized. (3) A rival to God is present as the catalyst of the jealousy (usually idolatry of some kind). (4) The passage clearly brings out a major and distinctive motif that is related to the discussion of jealousy. In other words, one or more of the key concepts that are prevalent in divine jealousy will be found in these passages. These concepts are covenant, obedience to the law, the divine name, divine wrath, the marriage metaphor, sexual imagery, and divine love. On the basis of these criteria, the representative passages that most clearly inform our analysis of divine jealousy are: Exodus 20:1-6; 34:14; Deuteronomy 4:23-24; Ezekiel 16; 1 Corinthians 10:22; and James 4:5. These six passages will be the focus of our study in this chapter and the next.

God's Jealousy in the Old Testament

The covenant that God established between himself and his people is of central importance in the Old Testament as well as all of salvation history. 'Judaism had always considered it as the most important event in its history, the ground of its faith, and the assurance of its redemption.'[3] The Decalogue stands at the heart of this covenant as the epitome of Old Testament covenant law, and therefore at the heart of the Old Testament itself.[4] God's jealous demand of covenant exclusivity is foundational to his relationship with his people.[5]

---

[2]In the prophetic literature, at times, it can be difficult to determine when the prophet is speaking from his own perspective and when he is speaking on behalf of God. I have only used instances where it is obvious that the prophet is clearly speaking the very words of God on his behalf and not just speaking about him.

[3]José Faur, 'Understanding the Covenant,' *Tradition: A Journal of Orthodox Thought* 9 (Spring, 1968): 33.

[4]Brevard S. Childs, *The Book of Exodus: A Critical, Theological Commentary*, OTL, ed. Peter Ackroyd (Philadelphia: Westminster, 1974), 397.

[5]Within the 228 passages where God's jealousy for the faithfulness of his people is expressed, the Hebrew word for covenant, בְּרִית (*bĕrit*), is found within those passages, or at least within their broader context sixty-six times: Exodus 23:32; 34:12-17; Numbers 18:19-20; Deuteronomy 4:13-19; 4:23-40; 5:7-10; 7:2-9, 25; 8:19-20; 17:2-7;

The Mosaic Covenant

> Then God spoke all these words, saying, 'I am the LORD your God, who brought you out of the land of Egypt, out of the house of slavery. You shall have no other gods before Me. You shall not make for yourself an idol, or any likeness of what is in heaven above or on the earth beneath or in the water under the earth. You shall not worship them or serve them; for *I, the LORD your God, am a jealous God*, visiting the iniquity of the fathers on the children, on the third and the fourth generations of those who hate Me, but showing lovingkindness to thousands, to those who love Me and keep My commandments (Exod. 20:1-6).

The commands found here are repeated again in Exodus 34 and Deuteronomy 4 in reaffirmations of the covenant. In the wisdom literature[6] and prophets[7] the Decalogue continues to be seen at the center of covenant adherence. There are several reasons for the central importance of the Ten Commandments.

The divinely authoritative preface to the Decalogue in Exodus 20:1, וַיְדַבֵּר אֱלֹהִים אֵת כָּל־הַדְּבָרִים הָאֵלֶּה לֵאמֹר (*wayĕdaḇēr ĕlōhim ēt kōl-hadĕ brim h'ēleh lē'mōr*, 'Then God spoke all these words, saying') is unique and carries obvious force.[8] Whenever this event at Sinai is remembered, the direct speech of Yahweh is mentioned.[9] Even the restatements of the Decalogue[10] are careful to not claim such direct divine speech. This powerful preface for the Decalogue sets it apart as a direct, unmediated word from Yahweh to Israel.

28: 64-69; 29:18-29; Judges 2:1-3, 10-17; 1 Kings 11:1-11; 2 Kings 17:7-23, 25-41; 2 Chronicles 34:23-25; Psalms 78:58-59; 79:5; Isaiah 54:5-10; Jeremiah 11:10-17; 50:5; Ezekiel 16:1-63; 17:17-19; 20:39; 30:13; 37:23, Hosea 2:1-23; 6:7; 8:1-6; 10:5-7; Malachi 3:17-18.

[6]Esp., Psalms 50:16-21; 81.

[7]Esp., Hosea 4:1-2, 6; Jeremiah 7:9.

[8]Gispen believes that the use of *Elohim* rather than Yahweh in v. 1 may point to the universal implications of the law. W. H. Gispen, *Exodus*, trans. Ed van der Mass, Bible Students Commentary (Grand Rapids: Zondervan, 1982), 188.

[9]Exodus 20:18-20; Deuteronomy 4:10-14, 32, 40; 5:4, 22-27; 9:10; Nehemiah 9:13. So, John Durham, *Exodus*, WBC (Word, 1987): 283.

[10]Exodus 34, Deuteronomy 5.

Verse 2 then begins with the standard authoritative 'auto-kerygmatic phrase'[11] אָנֹכִי יְהוָה, (*'ānôki yehwāh*, 'I am Yahweh') and interjects a personal and exclusive tone into the divine name by adding אֱלֹהֶיךָ (*ĕlōheyka*, 'your God'). The theological import of this self-introduction cannot be overstated. 'All that Yahweh is, says, and does is embodied in this one affirmation: "I am Yahweh." '[12]

God then links his divine authoritative self-introduction to his actions on behalf of Israel in the Exodus by adding that he is the God 'who brought you out of the land of Egypt, out of the house of slavery.' He reminds Israel that he is the God who has acted on behalf of Israel in history. He is not merely a god of philosophical speculation. What he has done and said as the God of the covenant is Israel's basis for knowing him,[13] and he bases his law on who he is and what he had done for Israel.[14]

Cole observes that the masculine singular object of all the commands appeals to the gratitude of individual members of the community.[15] It is amazing grace here that while God could simply demand obedience he gives a rationale based in his previous history with Israel. Although he could simply require, he chooses to persuade and convince.[16]

The first commandment is the foundational command upon which the rest of the commands, as well as the entire covenant

---

[11]Durham, *Exodus*, 283.

[12]Walter C. Kaiser, *Exodus*, EBC, ed. Frank E. Gabelein, vol. 2 (Grand Rapids: Zondervan, 1990), 422.

[13]R. A. Cole, *Exodus: An Introduction and Commentary*. TOTC, ed. Ronald Clements and Matthew Black, vol. 2 (Grand Rapids: Eerdmans, 1971), 152. Cole also points out that this kind of self-proclamation found in verse 2 was an integral part of covenant making in early Western Asia, and that this kind of covenant formula demanded exclusive loyalty. Cole, *Exodus*, 153.

[14]Gispen, *Exodus*, 189.

[15]Cole, *Exodus*, 152.

[16]While these commands put strict limits on the religious and social conduct of Israel it should be realized that the Ten Commandments are an act of grace by Yahweh in that it enables Israel to be in relationship with Yahweh. For this idea of grace in the commands see, Hyatt, *Exodus*, NCBC, eds, Ronald E. Clements and Matthew Black, vol. 2 (Grand Rapids: Eerdmans, 1971), 209.

relationship, are based. It is 'the creedal basis for all Israel's later faith.'[17] As Durham points out,

> The first of the Ten Commandments is basic to the nine that follow it and to the relationship the Decalogue is designed to insure. It sets forth an expectation of absolute priority, a first and fundamental requirement of those who desire to enter into the covenant relationship with Yahweh.[18]

This absolute priority is the essential starting point of the covenant commands. The relationship between Israel and Yahweh is to be uncompromisingly exclusive. Durham explains the exclusive grammatical thrust of the first commandment:

> The singular verbs and singular subject and indirect object, along with the plural direct object, 'gods' make the application of the command unmistakably clear. There is not to be even one other god.... Each single member of the covenant community is specifically involved, and there is no place where this expectation is invalid, since there is no place from which Yahweh's presence is barred. (so Ps. 139)[19]

The command to have no other gods is the core of the covenant community. The first command begins with the emphatic negative particle לֹא (*lō'*, 'not'). There is some debate over the exact meaning of עַל-פָּנָי (*'al-pānāya*), which most literally means 'before my face.' 'Before me' is the most common translation.[20] Other preferences are 'in my presence' (Noth), 'over against me' (Hyatt), 'in front of me' (Driver), 'besides me,' 'in preference over me' (Gispen), or 'prefer other gods to

---

[17]Cole *Exodus*, 152.

[18]Durham, *Exodus*, 284. Hyatt makes this same point, Hyatt, *Exodus*, 209, as does Noth when he says, 'The unconditional exclusiveness of the recognition and worship of the God of Israel stands rightly as *the* most important point at the beginning of the series of divine commandments.' Martin Noth, *Exodus: A Commentary*, OTL, ed. G. Ernst Wright et al. (Philadelphia: Westminster, 1962), 163.

[19]Durham, *Exodus*, 284.

[20]So the KJV, NKJV, NAS, RSV, ASV, RSV, NRS, NIV.

me' (Albright). Noth sees clear cultic implications and 'worship language' here.[21] Cole recognizes cultic meaning here but sees the primary meaning as based in God's nature and acts so that 'he will not share his worship with another.'[22] In this understanding '[b]efore me' is another way of saying I will not give my glory to another (Isa 42:8).[23]

Cole also sees the marriage metaphor, which is so central to God's understanding of his relationship with his covenant people, behind the use of עַל-פָּנָי ('al-pānāya). He believes that 'before me' 'seems also to be used of taking a second wife while the first is still alive,' and that it describes a 'breach of exclusive personal relationship.'[24] This understanding seems to fit best with the jealous motive given in the next verse. God will not tolerate any other god because he is jealous for his glory through the faithfulness of his people. One wonders why translators do not opt for the most literal translation of עַל-פָּנָי ('al-pānāya), 'before my face.' This communicates the sense that the idol is 'other than' Yahweh, and it also conveys a blatant manifestation of the idolatry and that Yahweh is fully aware of the apostasy. It also stays true to the vivid imagery of the Hebrew.

Gispen does not believe that the first commandment indicates that there are other gods but rather 'we encounter here a pure monotheism (cf. Deut. 6:4).'[25] This has profound implications for the religious and daily life of the Israelite. 'Not having other gods besides the Lord involves total surrender and consecration to the one and only God.'[26]

---

[21]Noth, *Exodus*, 162.

[22]Cole, *Exodus*, 153.

[23]Kaiser, *Exodus*, 422.

[24]Cole, *Exodus*, 153.

[25]Gispen, *Exodus*, 188. Hyatt, for example, does not believe that the command here assumes monotheism but that it assumes that other nations have gods they worship. Although the Bible acknowledges that man recognized other gods as real, it never acknowledges that other gods really existed. 'You see and hear that not only in Ephesus, but in almost all of Asia, this Paul has persuaded and turned away a considerable number of people, saying that gods made with hands *are no gods at all*' (Acts 19:26).

[26]Gispen, *Exodus*, 198.

The second, third and fourth commands expand on the first and explain how Yahweh is to be worshiped. God is not only concerned that he alone is worshiped, but that he is worshiped in the right way. The prohibition of images in the second commandment demands that God's identity and honor be protected and revered. He would not allow himself to be represented or reduced in any way that brings him to a domesticated trivialized level.

The second command of verse 4 expands and explains the first. It deals with the mode rather than the object of the worship. The keeping of this command becomes the most common gauge of the spiritual health of Israel.[27]

> You shall not make for yourself an idol, or any likeness of what is in heaven above or on the earth beneath or in the water under the earth. (Exod. 20:4)

Divine commands against idols and other gods appear frequently in the Old Testament. Almost all of the jealous expressions of God are spoken against some form of idolatry.[28] There is some

---

[27]As Curtis observes, the second commandment 'appears to be the primary basis for the evaluations of the kings of Judah and Israel in the historical books and for the pronouncements by the prophets that Israel and Judah have violated the covenant with Yahweh by following other gods and worshiping idols.' Edward Curtis, 'Man as the Image of God in Genesis in Light of Ancient Near Eastern Parallels' (Ph.D. diss., University of Pennsylvania, 1984), 246.

[28]Of the 228 Old Testament passages where God's jealousy for the faithfulness of his people is expressed, 192 of them mention some form of idolatry as the catalyst for the jealousy. The following divine jealousy passages explicitly refer to idolatry: Exodus 20:3-5, 23; 22:20; 23:13, 24, 32; 34:12-17; Leviticus 18:21, 30; 19:1-4; 20:1-8; 26:1; Deuteronomy 4:15-19; 4:23-40; 5:7-10; 6:13-16; 7:2-9, 25; 8:19-20; 12:2-5; 12:29-31; 13:1-18; 16:21-22; 17:2-7; 18:9-13, 20; 20:18; 27:15; 28:36-37, 64; 29:18-29; 31:16-18; 32:16, 19-21; Joshua 24:2, 19; Judges 2:1-3, 10-17; 3:6-8, 10; 8:27, 33; 10:6-7, 13-16; 1 Samuel 8:6-8; 1 Kings 11:1-11, 33; 14:9, 22-24; 16:12-13, 25-26, 31-33; 19:17-18; 21:24-26; 22:52-53; 2 Kings 1:3-4; 12:2-3; 14:3-4; 15:3-4; 15:34; 16:3-4; 17:7-23, 25-41; 21:1-9, 19-22; 22:17; 1 Chronicles 5:24-25; 10:13-14; 2 Chronicles 7:22; 21:10-13; 24:17-20; 25:14-15; 28:2-4, 24-25; 33:1-9, 21-23; 34:23-25; Psalms 78:58-59; 79:5; 81:8-9; Isaiah 16:12; 17:7-8; 42:17; 48:5; 57:3-13; 65:6-7; 66:3; Jeremiah 1:16; 2:1-25; 4:1-4, 30; 5:7-11, 18-19; 7:9-11, 16-20, 30-33; 8:2-3, 19; 9:2, 13-14; 10:1-6; 11:10-15, 17; 12:16; 13:10, 25-26; 14:10;

discussion as to whether the idols prohibited in the second command are those of other gods or of Yahweh, or both. The exact nature of the prohibition of verse 5 is not immediately clear. Does the 'them' referred to apply to images of Yahweh, other gods or both? Durham sees the prohibition as primarily referring to images of Yahweh[29] but allows for agreement with Zimmerli who sees it as referring to images of other gods.[30]

That God's jealousy is given as the reason for the prohibition of idols in verse 5 seems to indicate that it is primarily other gods that are being referred to. However, it is likely that God would be jealous of insufficient representations of himself as well. Any image of him will inevitably fall short of representing him and

---

16:10-11, 18; 17:2; 18:15; 19:4-5, 13; 22:8-9; 23:13, 27; 25:6-7; 32:29-30, 34-35; 35:15; 42:11-13; 44:3-5; 44:8, 15-19, 23-25; 46:25; 49:1, 3; 50:2, 5, 38; 51:17-18; 51:44; 51:47; Ezekiel 6:3-13; 7:20; 8:3-18; 11:18-21; 14:2-8; 16:1-63; 18:3-6, 12, 15; 20:7-8, 17-20, 24, 30-33, 39; 22:3-4, 9; 23:1-31, 36-49; 24:13; 30:13; 33:25; 37:23; 43:7-9; 44:28; Daniel 4:25; 5:20-23; Hosea 1:1-11; 2:1-23; 3:1-5; 4:1, 10-19; 5:3-4, 7; 8:1-6, 10; 10:1-2, 5-7; 13:1-6, 8; Amos 2:4; 3:14-15; 5:25-27; 7:9; Micah 1:7; 5:12-15; Nahum 1:14; Habakkuk 2:18-20; Zephaniah 1:4-6, 9. Kaiser notes that there are fourteen words for idols in the Old Testament. Kaiser, *Exodus*, 422.

The following works are very helpful for understanding this major Old Testament theme of idolatry: Edward Curtis, 'Man as the Image of God in Genesis in Light of Ancient Near Eastern Parallels' (Ph.D. diss., University of Pennsylvania, 1984), especially 246-98; Yehezkel Kaufman, *The Religion of Israel* (Chicago: University of Chicago, 1985); Abel Laondoye Ndjerareou, 'Theological Basis for the Prohibitions of Idolatry: An Exegetical and Theological Study of the Second Commandment' (PhD. diss., Dallas Theological Seminary, 1995); Christopher R. North, 'The Essence of Idolatry,' in *Festschrift Otto Eissfeldt*, ed. Johannes Jempel and Leonhard Rost (Berlin: Verlag, 1961), 151-60; Robert Pfeiffer, 'The Polemic Against Idolatry in the Old Testament,' *JBL* 43 (1924): 229-40; Brian S. Rosner, 'The Concept of Idolatry,' *Themelios* 24:3 (May 1999): 21-30.

[29]Durham, *Exodus*, 286.

[30]Zimmerli's study of the 'bow down and serve' found that all but one of the twenty-five occurrences of this expression outside the Decalogue has other gods as its object. It is therefore unlikely that the expression in 20:5 refers only to images but rather to both other gods of verse 3 and the images that represent them in verse 4. Walther Zimmerli, 'Das Zweite Gebot,' in *Festschrift Alfred Bertholet*, ed. Walter Baumgartner (Tübingen: J. B. C. Mohr, 1950), 553-54. von Rad concurs with this assessment when he says, 'Zimmerli has proved conclusively that the statements about jealousy in Exodus 20:5 do not refer to the commandment prohibiting images, but refer back beyond this commandment to the first commandment.' Gerhard von Rad, *Old Testament Theology: Vol. 1, The Theology of Israel's Historical Traditions*, trans. D.G.M. Stalker (NY: Harper & Row, 1962), 1:204.

therefore be a dishonoring idol. This idol, although an attempt to relate to Yahweh, becomes another god that legitimately provokes him to jealousy. It is also important to consider that '[n]either the prophets nor historiographers clearly distinguish between the first and the second commandments.'[31] This may be because worship of other gods would invariably involve idols. Worship of an image of Yahweh would incite his jealousy because 'an image of Yahweh would not be Yahweh and any worship of a Yahweh image was then by definition the worship of other gods.'[32] For these reasons, the comprehensive nature of the prohibition makes it highly likely that both images of other gods and Yahweh are excluded in this command as well as in the expansion of it in verse 5.

In verse 5 God explains the second command further and then provides the underlying reason for the first two commands when he says, 'You shall not worship them or serve them; for *I, the* LORD *your God, am a jealous God.*'[33] Yahweh, as in verse 2, grounds his commands in his character and his acts in history. As Zimmerli points out,

> We do not have a calm indicative statement of the expected recompense or payment by Yahweh (3rd and 5th commands) or a modest etiological historical backward reference (4th). Rather, there follows here a self-introduction of Yahweh, which uses the formula, which in v. 2 introduces the entire Decalogue.[34]

This 'self-introduction' of Yahweh provides a key insight into his emotive response to infidelity of any kind and it becomes

---

[31]Curtis, *Man as the Image*, 262.

[32]Ibid., 264.

[33]The hendiadys לֹא־תִשְׁתַּחֲוֶה לָהֶם וְלֹא תָעָבְדֵם (*lō tištahweh wĕhem*) means 'to offer religious worship.' Kaiser, *Exodus*, 422.

[34]Zimmerli, 'Das Zweite Gebot,' 554. 'Wir haben es in 5b.6 nicht mit einem in ruhiger Indikativaussage formulierten Hinweis auf die zu erwartende Vergeltung oder Lohnung durch Jahwe (drittes und fünftes Gebot) noch auch mit dem schlicht berichtenden ätiologischen Geschichts-Rück-verweis (viertes Gebot)zu tun. Vielmehr folgt hier eine Selbstprädikation Jahwes, die gattungsmäßig auf die Linie, der Formel zu rücken ist, die in v.2 den gesamten Dekalog einleitet.'

a basic reason for wrath on his part and due cause for fear and obedience on the part of his people. This jealous grounding for the Decalogue becomes a major distinctive in God's relationship with his people.

> We have here a not very frequent adjective bound description of the nature of Yahweh. A confessional formula of the highest importance that confronts us in other passages.[35]

Zimmerli then notes that this same self-designation of Yahweh is found in Exodus 34:14 and Deuteronomy 6:14, and observes that 'It is characteristic that the statement about the jealousy of Yahweh is both times connected with the warning about serving foreign gods.'[36]

Cole is representative of a common reluctance to allow for jealousy to be the word translated here and thinks 'zealous' would be a better translation because of the negative connotation jealousy has acquired.[37] He also thinks that,

> [l]ike 'love' and 'hate' in the Old Testament (Mal. 1:2-3) 'jealousy' does not refer to an emotion so much as to an activity, in this case an activity of violence and vehemence, that springs from the rupture of a personal bond as exclusive as that of the marriage bond.[38]

He does not think that this jealousy is to be seen as 'intolerance' but 'exclusiveness.' Why the avoidance of jealousy and the idea of emotion here? Cole gives no justification for the dismissal of the legitimate emotional jealousy that God attributes to himself. That Cole clearly recognizes the marriage metaphor here, as

---

[35]Ibid., 554-55. '[H]aben wir hier eine der nicht allzu häufigen, adjektivisch gehaltenen Wesensbeschreibungen Jahwes. Eine Bekenntnisformel von höchstem Gewicht, die uns noch an anderer, ausgezeichneter Stelle begegnet.'

[36]Ibid., 555. 'Es ist bezeichnend, daß der Hinweis auf die Eifersucht Jahwes beide Male mit der Warnung vor dem Dienst fremder Götter verbunden ist.'

[37]Noth and Hyatt also make an effort to do away with any real connection to jealousy and prefer the less specific 'zeal.' Noth, *Exodus*, 163; Hyatt, *Exodus*, 212.

[38]Cole, *Exodus*, 138.

well as the 'violence' and 'vehemence' that result from this jealousy, makes it even more odd that he fails to acknowledge an emotional element to the passage. Why he thinks that this 'zeal' is exclusive but not intolerant is difficult to understand. Does not exclusivity demand intolerance to any breach of that exclusivity? Cole beautifully expresses the loving element of the jealousy in this situation by saying that '[n]o husband who truly loved his wife could endure to share her with another man: no more will God share Israel with a rival,'[39] yet he will not support an emotional or intolerant element to this jealousy. One wonders if Cole would be as willing to dismiss the emotional facet to the love of God as well. Perhaps, but this too would be an unbiblical adherence to a too impersonal divine impassibility in light of the real and deep passion of God. To be sure, the jealousy here is not the suspicious, petty, envious kind we often see arising out of human insecurity. This jealousy is based in God's right to be exclusively worshipped and served. 'The basis for this jealousy is undiluted loyalty specified by the first commandment.'[40]

The marriage metaphor at the heart of the covenant makes any breach of covenant requirements a form of spiritual adultery, which Yahweh vehemently condemns.[41] All idolatry is spiritual adultery. The Decalogue is grounded in the exclusivity of a marriage that the first commandment establishes. 'Every form of substitution, neglect, or contempt, both public and private for the worship of God is rejected in this commandment.'[42] Yahweh desires to be the ultimate object of the affection of his people. While God's jealousy incites him to wrath and is ultimately about the preservation of his glory, divine jealousy is loving. 'He himself wants to be the object of the worship and service of the Israelites, and he wants to make himself an image (cf. e.g., the image of the Lord as Israel's Husband in the prophets, e.g.,

---

[39]Ibid.

[40]Durham, *Exodus*, 287.

[41]The marriage metaphor will be dealt with in more depth later in this chapter, as it becomes a more prominent theme in the prophetic literature.

[42]Kaiser, *Exodus*, 423.

Jer. 2:2; Hosea 1-3).'[43] In this way God's jealousy 'coincides with his love.'[44]

The Decalogue is of primary importance because of the theological grounding it provides for the faith and life of Israel. The relational nature of the covenant required clear and fundamental relational and theological parameters. The Decalogue provides these for relating to Yahweh and other people. When God establishes the Mosaic Covenant, the jealous nature of God's character is given as the primary reason for the core exclusivity behind the laws. God demands covenant fidelity from his people and institutes the Ten Commandments based on his jealousy for that exclusivity. The Decalogue, which is at the center of the relationship between Yahweh and his covenant people, begins with a clear pronouncement of God's jealous character. The primary reason for the exclusive nature of the first two commands is given by the very words of God when he says, '*for I, the* LORD *your God, am a jealous God.*' The love and holiness of Yahweh demand a jealous response to covenant infidelity. His character will allow for nothing less than complete devotion to him. Any compromise of the second command 'leads inevitably to a divided or even a redirected loyalty that Yahweh has every right, even every obligation, to punish. Yahweh's jealousy is part of his holiness (Exod. 34:14) and is demanded by what he *is*.'[45]

Exodus 34:12-17

> Watch yourself that you make no covenant with the inhabitants of the land into which you are going, or it will become a snare in your midst. But *rather,* you are to tear down their altars and smash their *sacred* pillars and cut down their Asherim for you shall not worship any other god, *for the* LORD, *whose name is Jealous, is a jealous God*, otherwise you might make a covenant with the

---

[43]Gispen, *Exodus*, 191.
[44]Ibid.
[45]Durham, *Exodus*, 287.

inhabitants of the land and they would play the harlot with their gods and sacrifice to their gods, and someone might invite you to eat of his sacrifice, and you might take some of his daughters for your sons, and his daughters might play the harlot with their gods and cause your sons *also* to play the harlot with their gods. You shall make for yourself no molten gods. (Exod 34:12-17)

Exodus 34:12-17 is another key passage in understanding God's jealousy for the faithfulness of his people. This passage will be considered in light of the examination just done of Exodus 20:1-6, which is the foundational passage from which Exodus 34:14 is principally drawn.[46] Only the distinctive contributions of this passage that are not covered in the Exodus 20 passage will be addressed. These are (1) the significant naming of God as jealous and (2) the conjugal and sexual element added by the harlot imagery in verse 16.

In Exodus 34 God is jealous within a concrete context of covenant infidelity. The Israelites demonstrated gross idolatry and broke the core covenant demands of God in worshiping the golden calf at Sinai. They broke the first and second commandments after God miraculously saved them from captivity. It seems that it was nothing more than impatience with God and Moses that led them to be unfaithful to the covenant.

Now when the people saw that Moses delayed to come down from the mountain, the people assembled about Aaron and said to him, 'Come, make us a god who will go before us; as for this Moses, the man who brought us up from the land of Egypt, we do not know what has become of him.' (Exod. 32:1)

The failure of God and Moses to be present when they wanted leads the people to create an image of Yahweh rather than allowing him to manifest his presence when and how he chooses. Far from ushering in God's presence, idolatry produces

---

[46]Albeit rearranged. So, Raymond Ortlund, *Whoredom: God's Unfaithful Wife in Biblical Theology* (Grand Rapids: Eerdmans, 1996), 29; Cole, *Exodus*, 230.

divine wrath and the threat of God removing his presence altogether.[47]

> The LORD said to Moses, 'I have seen this people, and behold, they are an obstinate people. Now then let Me alone, that My anger may burn against them and that I may destroy them; and I will make of you a great nation.' (Exod. 32:9-10)

After Moses reminds God of his covenant and of the importance of his reputation before the Egyptians, God relents and Moses goes down and confronts the people. He unleashes his own jealous anger on God's behalf and smashes the tablets and grinds the calf to powder and makes the Israelites drink it. He then sends the Levites out to slay 3,000. Moses then earnestly pleads for God to forgive his stiff-necked people, but God sends a plague (32:35) and threatens to remove his presence from them (33:3).

Moses then pleads with God to allow his presence to remain among the people. God agrees and reveals himself in a deeper way to Moses by expanding on Moses' understanding of the divine name and thereby showing him his glory. In Moses' interaction with Yahweh we once again see that God's name is a way his glory is manifested. In response to Moses' request to see God's glory, Yahweh proclaims his name to Moses.

> Then Moses said, 'I pray You, *show me Your glory*!' And He said, 'I Myself will make all My goodness pass before you, *and will proclaim the name of the LORD before you*; and I will be gracious to whom I will be gracious, and will show compassion on whom I will show compassion. (Exod. 33:18-19)

God is not trifling with Moses' earnest request to see a reassuring vision of the glory of Yahweh. Rather, he provides a glimpse of his glory through the proclamation of his name. This divine

---

[47]Curtis in *Man as the Image of God*, 291, makes this observation concerning the divine presence idea in this narrative.

description shows Moses the glory of Yahweh, not by showing him an appearance of himself, but by telling him of his character through the lens of his name.[48]

God had already used this method of encouragement when he gave Moses confidence for the initial massive challenge of confronting Pharaoh when he needed it at the burning bush. Moses realized that the identity and character of God was at the heart of accomplishing the liberation of Israel. So he asks God to tell him his name.

> Then Moses said to God, 'Behold, I am going to the sons of Israel, and I will say to them, "The God of your fathers has sent me to you." Now they may say to me, "What is His name?" What shall I say to them?' (Exod. 3:13)

God grants Moses' request and by a new and profound self-introduction reveals the divine name to Moses.

> God said to Moses, 'I AM WHO I AM'; and He said, 'Thus you shall say to the sons of Israel, "I AM has sent me to you."' God, furthermore, said to Moses, 'Thus you shall say to the sons of Israel, "The LORD, the God of your fathers, the God of Abraham, the God of Isaac, and the God of Jacob, has sent me to you." This is My name forever, and this is My memorial-name to all generations.' (Exod. 3:14-15)

So it makes perfect sense that here in Exodus 33 this name-based divine revelation would continue to be the way God encourages Moses to continue leading the people.

This name-based self-disclosure continues in chapter 34 when God renews his covenant with Moses. After having Moses chisel out new tablets to replace the ones he smashed, God further explains the meaning of his divine name with a description of himself that becomes the most important concise catalogue of God's attributes in the Old Testament.

---

[48]Durham, *Exodus*, 452.

The LORD descended in the cloud and stood there with him and *proclaimed his name, the LORD*. Then the LORD passed by in front of him and proclaimed, 'The LORD, the LORD God, compassionate and gracious, slow to anger, and abounding in lovingkindness and truth; who keeps lovingkindness for thousands, who forgives iniquity, transgression and sin; yet He will by no means leave *the guilty* unpunished, visiting the iniquity of fathers on the children and on the grandchildren to the third and fourth generations.' (Exod. 34:5-7)[49]

Then, after reaffirming his faithfulness to his covenant, and his miraculous ability to carry out the conquest of Canaan (v. 10), God again calls the people to covenant obedience. The core aspect of this obedience is once again expressed in the violent rejection of idolatry:

Watch yourself that you make no covenant with the inhabitants of the land into which you are going, or it will become a snare in your midst. But *rather*, you are to tear down their altars and smash their *sacred* pillars and cut down their Asherim. (Exod 34:12-13)

In re-establishing the covenant, Yahweh grounds it once again in uncompromising devotion to him. 'Loyalty to Yahweh must be absolutely undiluted.'[50] The reason given for this reiteration of the first and second commandments is the same as in chapter 20 – divine jealousy. 'For you shall not worship any other god, for the LORD, whose name is Jealous, is a jealous God' (Exod 34:14).[51] Cole describes this passage as 'a vivid commentary on, and explanation of, Exodus 20:5.'[52] This justification for God's exclusive demand expands on the jealousy found in the first and second commandments of Exodus 20 by deepening God's self-description by saying that not only

---

[49]The central importance of this description of God can be seen in how often it is quoted in whole or in part in the rest of the Old Testament. Cf. Joel 2:12-13; Jonah 4:1-2; Numbers 14:18; Nehemiah 9:17; Psalm 103:8; Nahum 1:3.

[50]Durham, *Exodus*, 460.

[51]קַנָּא (*qanā'*) is used twice in this verse obviously for emphasis.

[52]Cole, *Exodus*, 230.

is he jealous, but his jealousy is such a significant part of his character that his 'name is jealous.' The parallel construction of the passage gives a double meaning to 'jealous.' It is both a name and a quality.[53]

In chapter 2 we discussed the profound significance of God's name. It is worth repeating here that the name of God is a major theme of biblical theology because the name of God is a window into his character. His name reveals who he is and how he acts, and it refers to 'the total complex of God's identity and reputation.'[54] This is why David would say in Psalm 9:10: 'Those who know your name will trust in you.' God's name, his character, and his reputation are closely linked.[55] This is why Cole says that this verse defines 'God's very nature in terms of His demand for exclusive relationship with Him.'[56] The admonition to refrain from worship of other gods 'is grounded in the nature of God who is a jealous God and will not tolerate the worship of another (v. 14) and the subtle temptation to idolatry which contact with the Canaanites inevitably brings.'[57] In light of this, it would be hard to overstate the significance of God's making jealousy a proper name for himself. For God to say that his name is jealous makes jealousy a central and primary characteristic of his being and actions.[58] Any attempt to minimize or deny this attribute is antithetical to God's description of himself.[59]

---

[53]Dohmen, "Eifersüchtiger ist sein Name (Exod. 34:14)," 295.

[54]Oswalt, *Isaiah*, 270.

[55]Allen P. Ross, שׁם *NIDOTTE*, 4:148.

[56]Cole, *Exodus*, 230.

[57]Childs, *Exodus*, 613.

[58]It is worth noting that other central attributes of God that are more commonly associated with God are never given this kind of name recognition. God never says his name is 'love,' or 'grace,' or 'patience,' but he does say his name is 'jealous.' Not that these other attributes are any less important to who God is. Indeed, the unity of God demands that we consider his attributes interdependently. None of them is incidental or unessential. However, that God's jealousy is given name status demands that we recognize this emotion as a vital aspect of God's nature and his relational demands.

[59]Jealousy is central to God's nature although this attribute, like wrath, mercy, and patience, would not have had any basis for expression before creation and the fall.

Another important emphasis that Exodus 34:12-17 brings to our understanding of divine jealousy is the idea that God compares Israel's disobedience to the first and second commandments to an unfaithful, sexually promiscuous wife. He says that they must destroy the altars, sacred pillars, and Asherim or else they 'might make a covenant with the inhabitants of the land and they would "play the harlot with their gods" ' (אֱלֹהֵיהֶם וְזָנוּ אַחֲרֵי, *wezāû 'aḥĕrê 'ĕlōhêhem*), (Exod. 34:15). This concern for covenant fidelity extends to future generations as well, 'and you might take some of his daughters for your sons, and his daughters might play the harlot with their gods and cause your sons *also* to play the harlot with their gods' (v. 16).[60] The marriage and sexual imagery used here is a central emphasis within the jealousy motif.[61] This imagery points to the analogous relationship between idolatry and adultery. Idolatry within the covenant context is the equivalent of spiritual adultery.[62] Referring to the jealousy described in this passage, Thomas Watson points us to the marriage motif and jealous exclusivity that grows out of it:

In the absence of any rival, the seeds of God's jealousy lay patiently in his passion for his own glory.

[60]Before this use of 'harlot' it had only been used in reference to Diana in Genesis 34:31 and Tamar in Genesis 38:15, 24. After this occurrence it becomes a common description of unfaithful Israel, occurring in fifty-two verses used in this way. Cf. Leviticus 17:7; 20:5, 6; Numbers 15:39; 25:1; Deuteronomy 31:16; Judges 2:17; 8:27, 33; 1 Chronicles 5:25; 2 Chronicles 21:11, 13; Psalm 106:39; Isaiah 1:21; 23:15, 16, 17; Jeremiah 2:20; 3:1, 6, 8; Ezekiel 6:9; 16:15, 16, 17, 26, 28, 30, 31, 34, 35, 41; 20:30; 23:3, 5, 30, 44; Hosea 2:5; 3:3; 4:10, 12, 13, 14, 15, 18; 5:3; 9:1; Amos 7:17; Micah 1:7; Nahum 3:4.

[61]Of the 228 Old Testament passages where God is clearly jealous for the faithfulness of his people, twenty-four have explicit sexual/marriage imagery. These passages are: Exodus 34:12-17; Leviticus 20:1-8; Numbers 25:10-11; Deuteronomy 31:16-18; Judges 8:27, 33; 1 Chronicles 5:24-25; 2 Chronicles 21:10-13; Isaiah 54:5-10; 57:3-13; Jeremiah 2:1-25; 4:30; 5:7-11; 31:31-32; Ezekiel 6:1-63; 20:30-33; 22:9; 23:1-31, 36-49; 24:13; 43:7-9; Hosea 1:1-11; 2:1-23; 3:1-5. This motif will be discussed in greater detail in this chapter when is becomes more prominent in the prophetic literature.

[62]Kaiser, *Exodus*, 486. Cole prefers to translate אַחֲרֵי וְזָנוּ as 'commit adultery.' He points out that 'the metaphor is doubly appropriate, since it is in a context that also forbids literal intermarriage with the Canaanites, and also in view of the immoral nature of Baal worship (Hosea 4:13, 14) and the liaisons formed there.' Cole, *Exodus*, 230.

God will have his spouse to keep close to him, and not go after other lovers. 'Thou shalt not be for another man' (Hosea 3:3). He cannot bear a rival. Our conjugal love, a love joined with adoration and worship, must be given to God alone.[63]

Like any good husband who truly loves his wife, God demands absolute fidelity and reacts in anger in its absence. Divine jealousy is both a source of fear for those opposed to God and assurance and faith for those in devoted covenant relationship with him.

It is a horrifying thing to use your God-given life to commit adultery against the Almighty. Since God is infinitely jealous for the honor of his name, anything and any body who threatens the good of his faithful wife will be opposed with divine omnipotence. God's jealousy is a great threat to those who play the harlot and sell their heart to the world and make a cuckold out of God. But his jealousy is a great comfort to those who keep their covenant vows and become strangers and exiles in the world.[64]

In this re-establishment of the covenant with Moses we see that covenant demands are not merely a list of ethical requirements so that the Israelites would be good people. They are profoundly theological and relational. God's jealousy for the faithfulness of his people, which is so obvious in the Decalogue, demands that God alone be worshiped. This relational exclusivity points us back once again to the overriding concern of God in human history, his own glory. As John Piper says,

The Ten Commandments are not a job description for God's employees. They are the wedding vows that the peasant girl takes to forsake all others and to cleave to the king alone and to live in a way that brings no dishonor to his great name.[65]

---

[63]Thomas Watson, *The Ten Commandments* (Edinburgh: Banner of Truth, 1692, revised edition 1986), 65.

[64]John Piper, *The Lord Whose Name is Jealous (Exodus 34:10-16)*. (1998, accessed 21 September, 2000), 5; Available from http://www.soundofgrace.com/piper84/102884m.htm.

[65]Ibid.

Deuteronomy 4:23-24

Deuteronomy 4:23-24 is the next major example of God's jealousy for the faithfulness of his people.[66]

> So watch yourselves, that you do not forget the covenant of the LORD your God which He made with you, and make for yourselves a graven image in the form of anything *against* which the LORD your God has commanded you. For *the LORD your God is a consuming fire, a jealous God.*

The words of Deuteronomy are spoken to prepare the Israelites to take possession of and live in Canaan. After an historical summary of God's dealings with Israel under Moses' leadership in the wilderness, an explanation and exhortation of the law is given. Both of these serve as a solemn warning of the calamity and judgment that will follow disobedience and an encouraging reminder of the blessings that will follow obedience. God expects and demands that his people remain faithful to him. The covenant requires obedience in response to God's faithful provision and blessing. Bernard Renaud points out this divine demand at the heart of Deuteronomy when he asks, 'Is not the grand discovery of Deuteronomy the conviction that this alliance has to translate itself by a reciprocity between the two parties of the covenant?'[67]

Our first key example of God's jealousy for the faithfulness of his people in this chapter took place when the Mosaic Covenant was established at Sinai (Exod. 20:1-6), the second when it was re-established after the golden calf incident (Exod. 34:12-17), and now as Moses is seeking to renew the covenant again before entering the Promised Land we find another major reference to God's jealousy (Deut. 4:23-4). The exclusive claims of God

---

[66]Numbers 25:11 is another major passage which could be dealt with before this one because God compares Phinehas' jealousy to his own. I have left that passage for the next chapter on godly human jealousy where it will be dealt with in depth.

[67]Bernard Renaud, *Je Suis un Dieu Jaloux*, (Paris, Les Editions du Cerf, 1963), 70. 'la grande découverte du Deutéronome n'est-elle pas la conviction que cette alliance doit se traduire par une réciprocité d'amour entre les deux parties contractantes?'

in the covenant and the consequent condemnation of idolatry, which 'is tantamount to forgetting the covenant,'[68] is a central theme of Deuteronomy.[69] Indeed, divine jealousy is found often in this book:[70]

♦ 5:9: 'You shall not worship them or serve them; for *I, the LORD your God, am a jealous God.*'

♦ 6:14-15: 'You shall not follow other gods, any of the gods of the peoples who surround you, *for the LORD your God in the midst of you is a jealous God.*'

♦ 7:6: 'For you are a holy people to the LORD your God; the LORD your God has chosen you to be *a people for His own possession* out of all the peoples who are on the face of the earth.'

♦ 7:25: 'The graven images of their gods you are to burn with fire.'

♦ 8:19: 'It shall come about if you ever forget the LORD your God and go after other gods and serve them and worship them,... you will surely perish.'

♦ 12:2: 'You shall utterly destroy all the places where the nations whom you shall dispossess serve their gods.'

♦ 13:3 'The LORD your God is testing you to find out if you love the LORD your God with all your heart and with all your soul.'[71]

---

[68]Eugene H. Merrill, *Deuteronomy*, NAC, ed. E. Ray Clendenen, vol. 4 (Dallas: Broadman and Holman, 1994), 125.

[69]For the historical background of the covenant in Deuteronomy see, Meredith G. Kline, *Treaty of the Great King: The Covenant Structure of Deuteronomy* (Grand Rapids: Eerdmans, 1963).

[70]A variation of קנא (*qanā'*, 'jealous') is found seven times in Deuteronomy. In six of these God is the subject: 4:24; 5:9; 6:15; 29:20; 32:16, 21, and once God's favor toward the Gentiles is intentionally the cause of Israel's jealousy in 32:21.

[71]This 'test' of the Lord (13:1-18) is brought about by God's allowing a sign or wonder to be performed by a false prophet who tries to lead the people astray to serve other gods. This fascinating passage shows not only how deeply God hates idolatry, but even more so, how much he hates those who influence others to practice it. Even

♦ 14:2: 'the LORD has chosen you to be a *people for His own possession.*'

♦ 16:22: 'You shall not set up for yourself a *sacred* pillar which the LORD your God hates.'

♦ 17:2-3: 'If there is found in your midst...a man or a woman who does what is evil in the sight of the LORD your God, by transgressing His covenant, and has gone and served other gods and worshipped them...you shall stone them to death.'

♦ 26:18: 'The LORD has today declared you to be His people, a treasured possession.'

♦ 27:15: 'Cursed is the man who makes an idol or a molten image, an abomination to the LORD.'

♦ 29:20: 'the anger of the LORD and *His jealousy will burn* against that man.'

♦ 30:17: 'But if your heart turns away and you will not obey, but are drawn away and worship other gods and serve them... you shall surely perish.'

♦ 31:16-18: 'This people will arise and *play the harlot with the strange gods....* But I will surely hide My face in that day because of all the evil which they will do, for they will turn to other gods.'

♦ 32:16: 'They *made Him jealous* with strange gods; with abominations they provoked Him to anger.'

♦ 32:21: '*They have made Me jealous* with *what* is not God.'

♦ 32:37-39: 'Where are their gods?.... See now that I, I am He, and *there is no god besides Me.*'

---

if it were a family member who influenced his own family he was to be killed. 'So you shall stone him to death because he has sought to seduce you from the LORD your God who brought you out from the land of Egypt, out of the house of slavery' (Deut. 13:10). The idolatrous influence of Solomon's wives is soundly condemned later in 1 Kings 11. For when Solomon was old, his wives turned his heart away after other gods; and his heart was not wholly devoted to the LORD his God, as the heart of David his father *had been* (1 Kings 11:4).

Throughout Deuteronomy the exclusive relational parameters of the covenant are stated in light of God's intense jealousy for the faithfulness of his people, which is 'intolerance of rivalry or unfaithfulness.'[72] It is no wonder then, that strict fidelity to the covenant is viewed as the primary theological message of the book.

> The most important element of subjective theology in Deuteronomy is that of the absolutely unqualified, total commitment of the people to the Lord. Nothing less is acceptable. No dissimulation, no assimilation, no syncretism with other gods or religions or religious practices are to be tolerated. The people belong to the Lord alone. He is the absolute—though benevolent—sovereign, whose people uniquely and completely belong to him.[73]

Whenever the denunciation of idolatry is repeated, the first and second commandments of Exodus 20 provide the foundation. The demand of exclusive fidelity to Yahweh linked to his jealousy serves as 'a formula from the Decalogue tradition.'[74] Again we see that 'the very essence of the covenant is the truth that there is only one God, the Lord, and the recognition and worship of any other is no other than high treason, covenant violation of the grossest kind' (Deut. 6:4-5).[75]

The distinct contribution of Deuteronomy 4:23-24 to our discussion thus far is the clear linking of jealousy and the fierce wrath of God expressed in his being called 'a consuming fire.' Fire is often used to describe God, especially in relation to his wrath. However, divine wrath is the by-product of divine jealousy. The terrifying divine presence is described specifically as a 'consuming fire' seven other times in both Testaments.[76]

---

[72]Moshe Weinfeld, *Deuteronomy 1-11*, The Anchor Bible, ed. Foxwell A. Albright and David Noel Freedman, vol. 5 (New York: Doubleday, 1961, 1991), 208.

[73]Earl Kalland, S., *Deuteronomy*, EBC, ed. Frank E. Gabelein, vol. 3 (Grand Rapids: Zondervan, 1992).

[74]A. D. H. Mayes, *Deuteronomy*, NCBC, vol. 5 (Grand Rapids: Eerdmans, 1979, 1981), 155.

[75]Merrill, *Deuteronomy*, 125.

[76]Exodus 24:17; Deuteronomy 9:3; Isaiah 29:6; 30:27, 30; and Hebrews 12:29. Though not directly an act of God, the ban that he demanded be carried out against

God's judgment often comes in the form of fire.[77] He appears to Moses in the burning bush (Exod. 32), leads the Israelites in the wilderness by a pillar of fire (Exod. 13:21), and most importantly for our passage, he manifests his awesome presence on Sinai as fire.

> Now Mount Sinai *was* all in smoke because the LORD descended upon it in fire; and its smoke ascended like the smoke of a furnace, and the whole mountain quaked violently. (Exod. 19:18)

This fire at Sinai was a demonstration of God's presence that gave them a glimpse of the glory they were to acknowledge and magnify through their obedience. 'And to the eyes of the sons of Israel the appearance of the glory of the LORD was like a consuming fire on the mountain top' (Exod. 24:17).

Throughout Deuteronomy, this fire of God's presence at the establishment of the covenant at Sinai is remembered as a source of awe and reverence and motivation for undivided obedience and worship.[78] This fire concept is especially prevalent in the immediate context of Deuteronomy 4:24. Of the twenty-nine times 'fire' (אֵשׁ, *'ēš*) is used in Deuteronomy, thirteen of the occurrences are found in chapters 4 and 5.[79] There is a likely intended connection between the 'iron smelting furnace' of Egypt, out of which God brought the Israelites, and the consuming fire of Yahweh that they would face if they broke the covenant. God took them out of the oppression but if they broke covenant they would face a far greater fire found in the wrath of God.[80] However, the dominant imagery is the fire of God's presence at Sinai.

---

the Canaanites and idols included burning with fire the material representations of the things that would compete with God for worship (Deut. 12:3). The wrathful and perhaps purifying effect of fire could also be seen in Moses' burning the golden calf with fire (Deut. 9:21).

[77]For example: Genesis 19:24; Exodus 9:23; Numbers 11:1; 16:35; 1 Kings 18:23-24; 2 Kings 1:10; Matthew 3:12, 50; Mark 9:43; Acts 2:19; Revelation 14:10.

[78]Cf. 4:11, 12, 15, 24, 33, 36; 5:4, 5, 22, 23, 24, 25, 26; 7:5, 25; 9:3, 10, 15, 21; 10:4; 18:16; 32:22.

[79]These are, 4:11, 12, 15, 24, 33, 36; 5:4, 5, 22, 23, 24, 25, 26.

[80]Merrill, *Deuteronomy*, 125.

Because he has entered into covenant relationship with his people he demands covenant fidelity from them and responds with righteous wrath when they fail to worship him alone. He is holy and demands to be recognized as such. God's holiness, jealousy, and anger are closely related. 'Divine jealousy is located at the junction between the holiness, anger and love of God.'[81]

Although resisted no less than divine jealousy, divine wrath is a more commonly acknowledged characteristic of God.[82] However, God's wrath is invariably an outgrowth of his jealousy for his own glory and honor. When divine jealousy is present, it is consistently accompanied by an expression of divine wrath. This wrath is entirely just, as it is a righteous indignation in the face of an effort to deny God the honor that is his alone. As Willem VanGemeren points out,

> He tolerates no infringement on his royal authority, infraction of the covenant stipulations, detraction from his glory, and dilution of loyalty from his people. God is jealous for his own people, as they are the partakers of a special relationship with him. But if any individual detracts from his being God, he is free to discipline, judge, and remove the offender, because he is a 'consuming fire.' (Heb. 12:29)[83]

This connection between the jealousy of God and his anger is also clearly seen in Deuteronomy 6:13-16 and 32:21:

> You shall fear *only* the LORD your God; and you shall worship Him and swear by His name. You shall not follow other gods, any of the gods of the peoples who surround you, for the LORD *your God in the midst of you is a jealous God*; otherwise *the anger of the*

---

[81]Renaud, *Je Suis un Dieu Jaloux*, 153. 'La *qine'ah* divine se situe donc à la jonction de la Sainteté, de la Colère et de l'Amour de Dieu.'

[82]For a treatment of godly anger see, Sarah Chambers, 'A Biblical Theology of Godly Human Anger' (Ph.D. diss., Deerfield, Ill., Trinity Evangelical Divinity School, 1996).

[83]Willem VanGemeren, *The Progress of Redemption: The Story of Salvation from Creation to the New Jerusalem*, (Grand Rapids: Baker, 1988), 155.

LORD your God will be kindled against you, and He will wipe you off the face of the earth. You shall not put the LORD your God to the test, as you tested *Him* at Massah. (Deut. 6:13-16)

They have made Me *jealous* with *what* is not God; they have *provoked Me to anger* with their idols. (Deut. 32:21)

God responds with jealous anger when his people play the harlot with other gods. 'Where disloyalty to the only God brings forth a holy wrath that destroys the sinner from off the earth. He himself becomes a consuming fire that accomplishes that task. Cf. Lev. 10:2; Num. 16:35.'[84]

This intimidating picture of God's awesome and angry fire is the complement of Deuteronomy 4:31: 'For the LORD your God is a compassionate God; He will not fail you nor destroy you nor forget the covenant with your fathers which He swore to them.' This covenant demand is in line with the deep love God has for his people and the language of jealousy is an expression of this love that is at the heart of the covenant.[85] And 'to construct images would be to indicate that the first love of the Israelites had been forgotten.'[86] Divine jealousy and wrath are not the opposite of love but grow out of true love, and 'does not represent a change in God, but is, as it were, the reverse of the coin of love; it was the people who were prone to change and forgetfulness, and from outside the relationship of love, God was indeed awesome like a *consuming fire.*'[87]

Passages in the Old Testament Historical and Wisdom Literature
God's jealousy for the faithfulness of his people remains a consistent response to any rival to him throughout the rest

---

[84]Merrill, *Deuteronomy*, 125.

[85]Duane L. Christensen, *Deuteronomy 1-11*, WBC, ed. David A. Hubbard, vol. 6A (Waco, Tex.: Word, 1991), 87; Mayes, *Deuteronomy*, 155; Peter C. Craigie, *The Book of Deuteronomy*, NICOT, ed. R.K. Harrison, vol. 5 (Grand Rapids: Eerdmans, 1976), 138.

[86]Craigie, *Deuteronomy*, 138.

[87]Ibid.

of the historical books and wisdom literature of the Old Testament.[88]

♦ Joshua 24:19: You will not be able to serve the LORD, for He is a holy God. *He is a jealous God.*

♦ Judges 10:13-14: You have *forsaken Me and served other gods*; therefore I will no longer deliver you. Go and cry out to the gods which you have chosen; let them deliver you in the time of your distress.

♦ 1 Samuel 8:8: They have forsaken Me and served other gods.

♦ 1 Samuel 12:9: But they forgot the LORD their God.

♦ 1 Kings 14:22: Judah did evil in the sight of the LORD, *and they provoked Him to jealousy* more than all that their fathers had done.

♦ 2 Chronicles 34:25: Because *they have forsaken Me and have burned incense to other gods*, that they might provoke Me to anger with all the works of their hands; therefore My wrath will be poured out on this place and it shall not be quenched.

♦ Psalm 78:58-59: For they provoked Him with their high places and *aroused His jealousy with their graven images*. When God heard, He was filled with wrath and greatly abhorred Israel.

♦ Psalm 79:5: How long, O LORD? Will You be angry forever? *Will Your jealousy burn like fire?*

♦ Psalm 81:9: Let there be no strange god among you; Nor shall you worship any foreign god.

---

[88]Joshua 24:2, 19; Judges 2:1-3, 10-17; 3:6-8, 10; 8:27, 33; 10:6-7, 13-16; 1 Samuel 2:29; 8:6-8; 12:9; 1 Kings 11:1-11, 33; 14:9, 22-24; 16:12-13, 25-26, 31-33; 19:17-18; 21:24-26; 22:52-53; 2 Kings 1:3-4; 12:2-3; 14:3-4; 15:3-4; 15:34; 16:3-4; 17:7-23, 25-41; 21:1-9, 19-22; 22:17; 1 Chronicles 5:24-25; 9:1; 10:13-14; 2 Chronicles 7:22; 21:10-13; 24:17-20; 25:14-15; 28:2-4, 24-25; 33:1-9, 21-23; 34:23-25; Psalms 78:58-59; 79:5; 81:8-9.

Divine jealousy is usually a response to typical pagan idolatry, but even members of one's own family can become rivals to God. Speaking of Eli's failure to do anything about the irreverence and immorality of his sons, the Lord says, 'Why do you kick at My sacrifice and at My offering which I have commanded *in My* dwelling, and *honor your sons above Me*?' (1 Sam. 2:29).

The frequent evaluations of the reigns of the kings of Israel and Judah in the historical books were primarily based on how well they led the people into greater faithfulness to God. When they led them into idolatry they were heartily condemned by God.[89]

♦ 1 Kings 11:4: For when Solomon was old, his wives turned his heart away after other gods; and *his heart was not wholly devoted to the LORD his God*, as the heart of David his father *had been.*

♦ 1 Kings 14:9: (God speaking to Jeroboam through Ahijah) You also have done more evil than all who were before you, and have gone and *made for yourself other gods and molten images to provoke Me to anger, and have cast Me behind your back.*

♦ 2 Kings 16:3-4: But he (Ahaz) walked in the way of the kings of Israel,... He sacrificed and burned incense on the high places and on the hills and under every green tree.

Even if a king was personally faithful, God criticized his reign for not being active enough in stamping out idolatry. Personal holiness was not enough; God's people were required to influence faithfulness to God as well as jealous distain for anything that competes with God for his honor.

---

[89]The following instances of God's jealousy for the faithfulness of his people are condemnations of leaders of Israel and Judah for their involvement in idolatry. 1 Kings 11:4 (Solomon); 14:9 (Ahijah); 16:12-13 (Elah); 25-26 (Omri); 31-33, 21:24-26, 22:51-53(Ahaziah); 2 Kings 21:1-9 (Manasseh); 21:19 (Amon); 1 Chronicles 5:24 (Heads of households); 2 Chronicles 21:10-12 (Libnah, Asa); 25:14-15 (Amaziah); 28:2-4, 24-25 (Ahaz); 33:1 (Manasseh); 33:21-23 (Amon).

♦ 2 Kings 12:2-3: Jehoash did right in the sight of the Lord.... *Only the high places were not taken away.*

♦ 2 Kings 14:3-4: He (Jehoahaz) did right in the sight of the Lord,... *Only the high places were not taken away.*

♦ 2 Kings 15:3: He (Azariah) did right in the sight of the Lord,... *Only the high places were not taken away.*

♦ 2 Kings 15:34-35: He (Jotham) did what was right in the sight of the Lord;... *Only the high places were not taken away.*

The main cause of the exile was unfaithfulness to God. Once in the Promised Land, his people disregarded the absolute exclusive devotion God instituted at Sinai and his jealous demands brought his judgment resulting in the exile. God expected his people to worship him alone, *and in the way* he desired to be worshiped, or else forfeit his blessings.

♦ 2 Kings 17:11ff.: and there they burned incense on all the high places as the nations *did* which the Lord had carried away to exile before them; and they did evil things *provoking the Lord.* [12]*They served idols,...* [15]*They rejected His statutes and His covenant* which He made with their fathers... [23]*So Israel was carried away into exile* from their own land to Assyria until this day.

♦ 1 Chronicles 9:1: And Judah was carried away into exile to Babylon for their unfaithfulness.

♦ 2 Chronicles 7:22: And they will say, 'Because they forsook the Lord, the God of their fathers who brought them from the land of Egypt, and they adopted other gods and worshipped them and served them; therefore He has brought all this adversity on them.'

We have seen the foundational place divine jealousy has in the historical and wisdom literature. However, divine jealousy is expressed most frequently and clearly in the prophetic literature. We now turn our attention there.

The Prophets
Within the hundreds of passages that could be examined in this category of God's jealousy for the faithfulness of his people, the most vivid and numerous occur in the prophetic literature.[90] Throughout this study I have sought to focus on the passages where God's jealousy is most evident (usually when the actual word is used), and where an important theme within the topic is brought out. These passages serve as representative examples of the major subcategories within God's jealousy. Choosing a representative prophet or passage within one of them proves a formidable task.

Isaiah
Isaiah shows us God's jealousy where his people are the focus as he speaks with the jealous voice of a husband who has been betrayed by an adulterous wife:

♦ 1:21: How the *faithful city has become a harlot*, She *who* was full of justice!

♦ 54:5-6: '*For your husband is your Maker*, whose name is the LORD of hosts; and your Redeemer is the Holy One of Israel, who is called the God of all the earth. For *the LORD has called you, like a wife forsaken* and grieved in spirit, even like a wife of *one's* youth when she is rejected,' says your God.

♦ 57:3: But come here, you sons of a sorceress, offspring of an *adulterer and a prostitute*.

---

[90]Isaiah 1:21; 16:12; 17:7-8; 30:1-2; 31:1-3; 42:17; 48:5; 54:5-10; 57:3-13; 65:6-7; 65:11-12; 66:3; Jeremiah 1:16; 2:1-25; 4:1-4, 30; 5:7-11, 18-19; 7:9-11, 16-20, 30-33; 8:2-3, 19; 9:2, 13-14; 10:1-6; 11:10-15, 17; 12:16; 13:10, 25-26; 14:10; 16:10-11, 18; 17:2; 18:15; 19:4-5, 13; 22:8-9; 23:13, 27; 25:6-7; 31:20-22, 31-32; 32:29-30, 34-35; 32:38-39; 35:15; 42:11-13; 44:3-5; 44:8, 15-19, 23-25; 46:25; 49:1, 3; 50:2, 5, 38; 51:17-18; 51:44; 51:47; Ezekiel 5:8-9, 13; 6:3-13; 7:20; 8:3-18; 11:18-21; 14:2-8; 16:1-63; 17:17-19; 18:3-6, 12, 15; 20:7-8, 17-20, 24, 30-33, 39; 22:3-4, 9; 23:1-31, 36-49; 24:13; 30:13; 33:25; 37:23; 43:7-9; 44:28; Daniel 4:25; 5:20-23; Hosea 1:1-11; 2:1-23; 3:1-5; 4:1, 10-19; 5:3-4, 7; 6:4, 7, 10; 7:4-6; 8:1-6, 9, 14; 9:1, 10; 10:1-2, 5-7; 11:1-4, 8-9; 13:1-6; 14:4, 8; Joel 2:27; Amos 2:4; 3:14-15; 5:25-27; 7:9; Micah 1:7; 5:12-15; Nahum 1:14; Habakkuk 2:18-20; Zephaniah 1:4-6, 9; Malachi 1:6; 3:17-18.

♦ 57:8: Indeed, far removed from Me, *you have uncovered yourself*, and have gone up and made your bed wide. And you have made an agreement for yourself with them, *you have loved their bed*, you have *looked on their manhood*.

The root קָנָא (*qna*) appears eight times[91] in Isaiah with God as the subject in six of those occurrences.[92] There are no examples where I decided that the faithfulness of his people was the main focus of קָנָא (*qna*).[93]

Jeremiah

Although the קָנָא (*qna*) root does not appear in Jeremiah, it has almost twice as many passages as any other prophet where the concept of God's jealousy for the devotion of his people is present.[94] He also strongly uses the marriage metaphor and speaks with great passion about Israel's unfaithfulness.

♦ 2:2: I remember concerning you the devotion of your youth, *the love of your betrothals*.

♦ 3:20: Surely, *as a woman treacherously departs from her lover*, so you have dealt treacherously with Me.

♦ 31:32: My covenant which they broke, although *I was a husband to them*.

Jeremiah was written during one of Judah's darkest times of her history when her harlotry was greatest. When the pressures of the world closed in, she fled to the arms of other gods. The marriage motif and sexual imagery of the harlotry metaphors are in full use as the prophet uses sexually graphic and jealous language to describe this apostasy.

---

[91] 9:7; 11:13(2x); 26:11; 37:32; 42:13; 59:17; 63:15.

[92] 9:7; 26:11; 37:32; 42:13; 59:17; 63:15.

[93] 9:7; 26:11; 37:32; and 63:15 are God's zeal on behalf of his people. 42:13 and 59:17 are his jealousy for his own glory.

[94] I found fifty examples in Jeremiah, twenty-eight in Ezekiel, twenty-three in Hosea and twelve in Isaiah.

How can you say, 'I am not defiled, I have not gone after the
Baals'? Look at your way in the valley! Know what you have
done! You are a swift young camel entangling her ways, a wild
donkey accustomed to the wilderness, that sniffs the wind in her
passion. In *the time of* her heat who can turn her away? All who
seek her will not become weary; in her month they will find her.
Keep your feet from being unshod and your throat from thirst.
But you said, 'It is hopeless! No! For I have loved strangers, And
after them I will walk.' (Jer. 2:23-25)

Her breach of God's exclusive demands at the center of the
covenant is described by Jeremiah not just as ethical failure but
as spiritual adultery. This offensive image of animals in heat
is intended to show the people of God the disgusting nature
of seeking God in other religions. Her pitiful condition was
'faddish and insecure, nervously searching the latest offerings
from neomania, for they do not grasp the true meaning and
abiding claim of the covenant.'[95]

Hosea

While there is no occurrence of the קנא (*qna*) root in Hosea, he
too provides a vivid and passionate picture of God's jealousy
as the prophet himself lives out the jealous love of God as he
knowingly marries a prostitute and deals with her harlotry. This
minor prophet is packed with jealous descriptions of Israel's
unfaithfulness. The marriage metaphor, sexual imagery, and
language of betrayal abound in this passionate denunciation
of idolatry.[96]

♦ 2:2-3: Contend with your mother, contend, for she is not my
  wife, and I am not her husband; and *let her put away her
  harlotry from her face and her adultery from between her
  breasts*, or I will strip her naked and expose her as on the
  day when she was born.

---

[95]Ortlund, *Whoredom*, 87.
[96]A form of the root זנה (*znh*, 'harlot') occurs twenty times in Hosea. Hosea contains
thirteen percent of the occurrences of this word in the entire Old Testament.

- 2:5: For their mother has played the harlot; she who conceived them has acted shamefully. For she said, *'I will go after my lovers.'*

- 2:10: And then *I will uncover her lewdness In the sight of her lovers*, and no one will rescue her out of My hand.

- 2:13: 'I will punish her for the days of the Baals.... *When she used to follow her lovers, so that she forgot Me,'* declares the LORD.

- 2:20: And I will *betroth you to Me in faithfulness*. Then you will know the LORD.

- 3:1: Then the LORD said to me, 'Go again, love a woman *who* is loved by *her* husband, yet an *adulteress*, even as the LORD loves the sons of Israel, though *they turn to other gods* and love raisin cakes.'

- 3:3: Then I said to her, 'You shall stay with me for many days. *You shall not play the harlot*, nor shall you have a man; so I will also be toward you.'

- 4:10: They will eat, but not have enough; *they will play the harlot*, but not increase, because they have stopped giving heed to the LORD.

- 4:12: My people consult their wooden idol, and their *diviner's* wand informs them; for a spirit of harlotry has led *them* astray, and they have *played the harlot, departing from their God.*

- 5:3-4: O Ephraim, you have played the harlot, Israel has defiled itself. Their deeds will not allow them to return to their God. For *a spirit of harlotry* is within them, and they do not know the LORD.

- 6:4: What shall I do with you, O Ephraim? What shall I do with you, O Judah? For *your loyalty is like a morning cloud* and like the dew which goes away early.

- 6:7: But like Adam they have *transgressed the covenant*; there they have dealt treacherously against Me.

- 8:9: For they have gone up to Assyria, *like a wild donkey all alone*; Ephraim has *hired lovers*.

- 8:14: For Israel has *forgotten his Maker*.

♦ 9:1: Do not rejoice, O Israel, with exultation like the nations! *For you have played the harlot, forsaking your God.* You have loved *harlots'* earnings on every threshing floor.

♦ 9:10b: *But* they came to Baal-peor and devoted themselves to shame, and *they became as detestable as that which they loved.*

♦ 10:2: Their *heart is faithless*; now they must bear their guilt. The LORD will break down their altars *and* destroy their *sacred* pillars.

♦ 11:3 Yet it is I who taught Ephraim to walk, I took them in My arms; but *they did not know that I healed them.*

♦ 13:6: As *they had* their pasture, they became satisfied, and being satisfied, their heart became proud; therefore *they forgot Me.*

In Hosea, the fickle wanton infidelity of God's people is explained in a sober and painful way that shows the irrationality of sin. 'What one observes in Hosea's historical situation is the admixture of contrary theologies made congenial not by logic of principle but by fashion and feeling.'[97]

Ezekiel

The messages of Isaiah, Jeremiah and Hosea clearly portray a jealous God. Ezekiel has perhaps the most vivid and powerful portrayal of the God who is jealous for the faithfulness of his people.[98]

A form of קנא (*qna*) occurs in Ezekiel thirteen times, and eleven of these refer to God's jealousy, which is more than any other book of the Bible.[99] Seven of these express God's angry jealousy for the faithfulness of his people in response to idolatry.[100]

---

[97]Ortlund, *Whoredom*, 48.

[98]This prophet has many instances of God's jealousy for the faithfulness of his people clearly displayed: 5:8-9, 13; 6:3-13; 7:20; 8:3-18; 11:18-21; 14:2-8; 16:1-63; 17:17-19; 18:6, 12, 15; 20:7-8, 17-20, 24, 30-33, 39; 22:3-4, 9; 23:1-31, 36-49; 24:13; 30:13; 33:25; 37:23; 43:7-9; 44:28.

[99]Ezekiel 5:13; 8:3, 5; 16:38, 42; 23:25; 36:5, 6; 38:19; 39:25 are the eleven occurrences of קנא (*qna*) when God is subject. The other two occurrences are 31:9

♦ 5:13: Thus shall my anger spend itself, and I will vent my fury upon them and satisfy myself; and they shall know that *I, the* LORD, *have spoken in my jealousy*, when I spend my fury upon them.

♦ 8:3: The Spirit lifted me up between earth and heaven, and brought me in visions of God to Jerusalem, to the entrance of the gateway of the inner court that faces north, where was the seat of the *image of jealousy*, which *provokes to jealousy*.

♦ 8:5: So I lifted up my eyes toward the north, and behold, north of the altar gate, in the entrance, was this *image of jealousy*.

♦ 16:38: And I will judge you as women who break wedlock and shed blood are judged, and bring upon you *the blood of wrath and jealousy*.

♦ 16:42: So will I satisfy my fury on you, and *my jealousy shall depart from you*; I will be calm, and will no more be angry.

♦ 23:25: '*I will set My jealousy against you*, that they may deal with you in wrath....and your survivors will be *consumed by the fire*.

In addition to the frequency of קנא (*qna*), Ezekiel has graphic and emotive descriptions of Israel's shameless, ungrateful spiritual adultery, which incurs God's angry jealousy.[101] It is no wonder, then, that Ezekiel is seen as the key biblical writer in regard to divine jealousy.

---

and 35:11 and refer to a national envy of another nation. Deuteronomy is second for number of times the קנא (*qna*) is used with God as the subject, with seven.

[100]These are Ezekiel 5:13; 8:3, 5; 16:38, 42; 23:25; 36:5, 6, and 38:19 are God's jealousy (or zeal) on behalf of Israel. 39:25 is God's jealousy for the honor of his holy name.

[101]A form of the root זנה (*znh*, 'harlot') occurs forty-three times in Ezekiel. Ezekiel contains thirty percent of the Old Testament occurrences of this word. The word group translated as some form of 'idol' is found forty-six times in Ezekiel, which represents twenty-seven percent of the Old Testament uses. Isaiah is second in the uses of idol with seventeen occurrences, which is twelve percent of the Old Testament occurrences.

Thus, by his frequent use of the word but most of all by the enrichment that he brought to the notion, Ezekiel plays a premiere role in the history of jealousy. One could not expect less from the prophet who preached with the insistence on the transcendence and holiness of God.[102]

Because of his heavy emphasis on God's jealousy we look to Ezekiel to find the main representative passage of God's jealousy for the faithfulness of his people. Within Ezekiel three passages stand out as particularly stark examples of God's jealousy for the faithfulness of his people; chapters 8, 16 and 23.

Ezekiel 8 increasingly describes the abominable idolatry that had overtaken Jerusalem. The 'idol of jealousy which provokes to jealousy' (Ezek. 8:5) at the entrance of the north altar gate was the first example the Lord showed Ezekiel. This idol is 'an emphatic reference to the passion that the object ignites in Yahweh's heart.'[103] This chapter is a clear example of God's jealousy, but does not necessarily add a major distinctive contribution to our previous discussion to the nature of idolatry and God's jealous response to it.

Chapters 16 and 23 are quintessential examples of the prophetic denunciation of unfaithfulness to God. They are shocking descriptions of the depth of Jerusalem's infidelity and ingratitude. The harlot wife of Yahweh in 16 and the prostitute sisters in 23 give sexually graphic, disgusting portrayals of the gross sin of trusting in any god, nation, or possession instead of the true God of the covenant. The personal and covenantal nature of the betrayal of idolatry comes across clearly in these powerful chapters. They show that breaking God's law is a personal breach of a personal relationship that incurs a deeply personal judgment. While the word jealousy occurs only twice

---

[102]Renaud, *Je Suis un Dieu Jaloux*, 90. Ainsi par l'emploi fréquent du mot, mais surtout par l'enrichissement qu'il apporte à la notion, Ézéchiel joue dans l'histoire de la *qine'ah* un rôle de premier plan. On ne pouvait pas attendre moins du prophète qui a prêché avec tant d'insistance la Transcendance et la sainteté de Dieu.

[103]Daniel Block, *The Book of Ezekiel*, NICOT, ed., R.K. Harrison and Robert Hubbard, vol. 1 (Grand Rapids: Eerdmans, 1997), 282.

in chapter 16 (38, 42) and once in 23:25, every verse of these stories drips with divine jealousy. The basic presentation of these chapters is similar; allegorical stories of shameless whores who spurn God's provision and love for other 'lovers.' These whores represent the people of Israel (specifically Jerusalem in 16 and Samaria and Jerusalem in 23). These chapters both deepen our understanding of divine jealousy in their use of the marriage metaphor, sexual/harlot imagery, and the wrathful judgment and shame produced by the infidelity. Because they are so similar, looking closely at both of these chapters would not yield significantly different understanding to our discussion on divine jealousy. I've chosen chapter 16 to focus our study on because, unlike chapter 23, it is more comprehensive in that it shows the final outcome of divine jealousy: repentance and restoration. Another less significant reason for choosing 16 is that the קנא (*qna*) root occurs twice in 16 opposed to once in 23.

Ezekiel 16
It is important to begin by noting the strong connection between the passages we have already focused on, and those in the Prophets. In the prophetic literature, the first and second commandments, which are at the center of Old Testament religion, remain the foundation of God's jealousy. When Ezekiel accuses Israel of spiritual adultery, the exclusive claims of the covenant law in Exodus and Deuteronomy are the basis for that accusation. Yahweh's 'arousal at the "image of jealousy" in Ezekiel 8:3, 5, and his response to Israel's infidelity in chapters 16 and 23 must be interpreted in the light of Moses' warning in Deuteronomy 4:15-24.'[104]

> So watch yourselves, that you *do not forget the covenant* of the LORD your God which He made with you, and make for yourselves a graven image in the form of anything *against* which the LORD your God has commanded you. '*For the LORD your God is a consuming fire, a jealous God.* (Deut. 4:23-24)

---

[104]Block, *Ezekiel*, 14 n.24.

Near the conclusion of Ezekiel 16 we are pointed back to the covenant demands as the core issue of the harlotry of Jerusalem. For thus says the Lord GOD, 'I will also do with you as you have done, you who have *despised the oath by breaking the covenant* (Ezek. 16:59). As the apostasy of God's people increased so did the warnings and condemnations of that apostasy.

> The essential difference between Ezekiel's historical surveys and Deuteronomy's sermonic reflecting lies only in the extent of the imagery. Both are the theological reflections of profound and creative minds motivated by a passionate concern, seeking to reach their audiences by extreme means which, while bordering on the excessive as in Deut. 7:7 or 9:4-7, or as in Ezekiel 16, still demonstrate the power of theology to become proclamation.[105]

Ezekiel spoke primarily to the exiles in Babylon as a watchman, warning of Judah's impending judgment as Jeremiah was simultaneously proclaiming the same message to those in Jerusalem and Judah. The overall structure of Ezekiel reflects the historical transitions that occur within the book. Chapters 1–24, which are prior to the fall of Jerusalem in 586 BC, tell of the coming judgment on Jerusalem, and 25–32 declare the coming judgments on foreign nations. A shift takes place in chapters 33–48, which take place after the fall of Jerusalem, and speaks primarily of the covenant faithfulness of God and the blessings and restoration that he would bring.

Chapter 16 is within a collection of oracles alternating their focus between Judah's sin and the judgment coming through Babylon.[106] Through his shocking imagery, Ezekiel hopes to 'transform his audience's perception of their relationship with Yahweh, exposing delusions of innocence and offering a divine understanding of reality.'[107]

---

[105]Ronald M. Hals, *Ezekiel*, FOTL, ed. Rolf P. Knierim and Gene M. Tucker, vol. 19 (Grand Rapids: Eerdmans, 1989), 112.

[106]Block, *Ezekiel*, 522.

[107]Ibid., 14.

In Ezekiel 16:1-43 we have a vivid portrayal of the unfaithfulness of God's people expressed in an 'extended metaphor'[108] of an unfaithful wife. The prophecy of the vine in chapter 15 fell on deaf ears. The people were not convinced of their useless, detestable condition, so Ezekiel tells them this story in order to show them their utter dependence upon God for their very existence, and their utter failure in being true to him. The story goes through the history of Jerusalem in light of her destitute beginnings. From her birth through her courtship and marriage to Yahweh, to her prostitution, judgment, and future restoration, the sixty-three verses of this chapter illustrate not only the history of Jerusalem, but all of humanity.

Ezekiel is told by God to make known Jerusalem's 'vile deeds' (תּוֹעֲבֹתֶיהָ, *tô'ăbōteyah*) to her. The root of תּוֹעֲבֹתֶיהָ (*tô'ăbōteyah*) is used eleven times in this chapter describing cultic practices that violate the first and second commandments. At times these abominations can be political alliances that often result in religious syncretism, as in chapters 22 and 23. But here the abominations are religious pagan idolatry.

The pitiful description of the birth of Jerusalem in verses 2-5 as an abandoned baby girl squirming in her own blood reveals her helpless, hopeless condition from God's perspective. 'No eye looked with pity on you to do any of these things for you, to have compassion on you. Rather you were thrown out into the open field, for you were abhorred on the day you were born' (Ezek. 16:5). Exposing unwanted newborns, especially girls, to the elements to let them die was a widespread custom in the Ancient Near East.[109] This reference to Jerusalem, which had a heathen origin and was neglected by her Canaanite founders, shows that God's miraculous intervention was needed for her to

---

[108]Hals prefers 'extended metaphor' rather than 'allegory' to describe chapter 16 because no interpretation section is provided and many of the elements of the story have no allegorical meaning, Cf. Hals, *Ezekiel*, 109. The story does however fit the definition of allegory in its symbolic representation of human existence and it teaches basic truth without a strict literal history.

[109]Ralph H. Alexander, *Ezekiel*, EBC, ed. Frank E. Gabelein, vol. 6 (Grand Rapids: Eerdmans, 1986), 811.

become what she now was in Ezekiel's time. 'When I passed by you and saw you squirming in your blood, I said to you *while you were* in your blood, "Live!" Yes, I said to you *while you were* in your blood, "Live!"'(Ezek. 16:6).

When the girl had come of age she still remained 'naked and bare.' God then sent David to rescue the city from her exposed condition and Yahweh made a covenant with her and made her his wife by spreading his garment over her (cf. Ruth 3:9):

> 'Then I passed by you and saw you, and behold, you were at the time for love; so I spread My skirt over you and covered your nakedness. I also swore to you and entered into a covenant with you so that you became Mine,' declares the Lord GOD. (Ezek. 16:8)

He then protected, cleansed, and gave her beautiful marriage gifts (vv. 9-14). These descriptions of God's free and gracious salvation and marriage of the woman set the stage for the harlotry that follows. God's initiative in saving the life of the infant, establishing covenant with her, and lavishing her with gifts, are intended to stand in stark contrast to her shameless infidelity in the verses that follow.

> Every part of the chapter's development is directed toward the construction of a pattern of the absolute contrast between God's unmotivated graciousness and his people's shameless apostasy. Israel's sin appears all the more offensive as the betrayal of such amazing, freely given love. (ch 20)[110]

The gracious, life-giving God deserves unlimited devotion, for he is the source of life and prosperity. Far from absolute devotion, Jerusalem became prideful in her beauty and riches and prostituted herself. 'But you trusted in your beauty and played the harlot because of your fame, and you poured out your harlotries on every passer-by who might be *willing*' (Ezek 16:15). 'Jerusalem the ingrate is the overarching theme

---

[110]Hals, *Ezekiel*, 111.

that gives cohesion to the whole allegory.'[111] Zimmerli points out the hubris at the heart of Jerusalem's sin: 'The root of the sin of the woman who had been so lavishly favored by Yahweh lies in her false trust in her own beauty and the reputation gained from this. The gift replaces the giver.'[112]

Hosea and Isaiah condemned foreign involvements but she carried on with them anyway. God's wife became a licentious, promiscuous whore as she attracted and paid her lovers with the very gifts bestowed upon her by her groom (vv. 17-19). In the descriptions of the adulterous wife in verses 15-34, we hear echoes of Hosea and Jeremiah. Even the children given to her by God were sacrificed in her idolatrous adultery (vv. 20-21).[113] She forgot her destitute and vulnerable state before God rescued her, and her lewdness only increased, as did her lovers. Her devotion was given to Egypt, the Philistines, Assyrians, and Babylonians. True to the nature of sexual promiscuity, her lewdness was never satiated. Her idolatry was worse than prostitution because she did not even get paid for her services; rather, she gave her riches away in the process.[114]

God warned his people to not forget him when they were prospering in the Promised Land.

> Then it shall come about when the LORD your God brings you into the land which He swore to your fathers, Abraham, Isaac and Jacob, to give you, great and splendid cities which you did not build, and houses full of all good things which you did not fill, and hewn cisterns which you did not dig, vineyards and olive trees which you did not plant, and you eat and are satisfied, then watch yourself, that you *do not forget the LORD* who brought you from the land of Egypt, out of the house of slavery. (Deut. 6:10)

---

[111]Block, *Ezekiel*, 240.

[112]Walther Zimmerli, *Ezekiel*, Hermeneia (Philadelphia: Fortress, 1979), 1:342.

[113]This infanticide was common in the worship of the pagan deity Molech (2 Kings 16:3; 21:6; 23:10; Jer. 32:35). This was boldly contrary to the Mosaic covenant (Lev. 18:21). Cf. Alexander, *Ezekiel*, 813.

[114]In verse 17 she melts down the gold and silver jewelry given to her by God and makes them into male images. This is reminiscent of the golden calf incident at Sinai. Cf. Block, *Ezekiel*, 488.

Verse 15 tells us Jerusalem's main problem that led to adultery: she trusted in her beauty rather than her God. She became self-centered and self-satisfied rather than continually recognizing her utter dependence on Yahweh. She not only participated in pagan practices but also became an outspoken advocate of them. This made her beauty detestable.

The apostasy began with Solomon's taking foreign wives and incorporating their religions into the life of Israel (1 Kings 11:1-10):

> It was customary to seal international treaties with a marriage. Solomon's many foreign wives lead him to rely on these treaties rather than on the Lord. This led to his worship of the foreign gods of his wives. The emphasis came to be on externals and material objects. The very gifts God had given to Jerusalem had become the means of her downfall, for she loved the gifts rather than the giver.[115]

The sexual imagery used to describe Jerusalem's sin is as graphic and intentionally offensive as the Bible gets.[116] It is obvious that Ezekiel hopes to shock his hearers into an awareness of their apostate condition. 'Driven by a passion for the glory of God, he challenges his contemporaries with symbols designed to shock their stony hearts.'[117] The goal is repentance. Her vile condition is held up before her with the hope that 'all the props on which their smug sense of security were based will be smashed.'[118]

One cannot help but feel the visceral sting of jealousy as the gross sexual betrayal of Yahweh's wife is described.

♦ 15: you poured out your harlotries on every passer-by who might be *willing*.

♦ 25: You built yourself a high place at the top of every street and made your beauty abominable, and you spread your legs[119] to every passer-by to multiply your harlotry.

---

[115]Alexander, *Ezekiel*, 813.

[116]For an excellent treatment of the motive and method of this offensive sexual imagery see Block, *Ezekiel*, 466-467.

[117]Block, *Ezekiel*, 470.

[118]Ibid., 462.

♦ 26: You also played the harlot with the Egyptians, your lustful[120] neighbors, and multiplied your harlotry to make Me angry.

♦ 27: The daughters of the Philistines, who are ashamed of your lewd conduct.

♦ 28: Moreover, you played the harlot with the Assyrians because you were not satisfied;

♦ 32: You adulteress wife, who takes strangers instead of her husband!

♦ 31: When you built your shrine at the beginning of every street and made your high place in every square, in disdaining money, you were not like a harlot.

♦ 36: Because your lewdness was poured out[121] and your nakedness uncovered through your harlotries with your lovers and with all your detestable idols.

♦ 37: So I will gather them against you from every direction and expose your nakedness to them that they may see all your nakedness.

Harlotry is the major concept in the chapter. Some form of זנה (*znh*), 'to play the harlot' or 'harlotry' is used forty-three times in Ezekiel,[122] and 'functions as the *Leitwort* of the oracle.'[123] Twenty-one of the forty-three occurrences of the harlot

---

[119] וַתְּפַשְּׂקִי אֶת־רַגְלַיִךְ literally means 'you spread apart your feet,' the opening of something that is usually closed This is only one of many graphic expressions that show how utterly despicable was Jerusalem's conduct. Alexander, *Ezekiel*, 814. The 'offering your body' of the NIV or 'offering yourself' of the RSV, NRSV, and NKJV wrongly domesticate this intentionally disturbing image.

[120] 'Of great flesh' is a more literal and accurate translation of בָּשָׂר וַתַּרְבִּי. This same imagery is intensified in 23:20 in comparing the penis of Judah's sexual partners to that of a donkey. This is one example where most English translations mute the intentionally graphic and offensive message of Scripture.

[121] Because of an Akkadian cognate of נְחֻשְׁתֵּךְ meaning 'abnormal genital discharge,' Block believes this expression הִשָּׁפֵךְ נְחֻשְׁתֵּךְ ('lewdness was poured out') refers to an erotic image of 'female genital distillation produced at sexual arousal.' Block, *Ezekiel*, 500.

[122] Cf. 6:9; 16:15, 16, 17, 20, 22, 25, 26, 28, 29, 30, 31, 33, 34, 35, 36, 41; 20:30; 23:3, 5, 7, 8, 11, 14, 17, 18, 19, 27, 29, 30, 35, 44; 43:7, 9.

[123] Block, *Ezekiel*, 465.

word group in Ezekiel are in chapter 16, and eighteen are in chapter 23. The basis of the harlotry metaphor is in the jealous God of the Decalogue who allows for no rivals. One would think that because of the marriage motif 'adultery' would be the primary word used to describe the infidelity of Jerusalem in this allegory. It seems that even the vile word 'adultery' was not strong enough for Ezekiel. According to Block, the use of 'harlotry' instead of נאף (*n'p̄*, 'adultery'), can be attributed to four factors.[124]

(1) The habitual nature of a professional prostitute. While adultery can take place in one incident, harlotry is an ongoing seemingly insatiable activity. (2) The motive of personal gain. Professional prostitution perverts the intent of sexual intercourse even more than adultery because it turns it into a commodity to be sold. (3) The involvement of multiple partners. While adultery can take place with only one rival, harlotry involves many. (4) The female sense of harlotry.

The marriage metaphor with Yahweh as husband is kept consistent with a term unique to females rather than נאן which could apply to either gender. The use of 'harlot' serves to intensify and deepen the shameless ungrateful nature of the adultery of Jerusalem. The gut-wrenching reality of a wife who has spurned the love and covenant of her husband is the tragic condition of God's people in Ezekiel's day. God speaks this allegory through his prophet and describes his jealous feelings as a betrayed husband to awaken his people to their depraved condition. Ezekiel sought to describe Jerusalem's rebellion in such a way that it 'might move *via* its emotional dimensions beyond the sphere of the purely intellectual into the deepest levels of self-understanding.'[125] It appears that God's people had rationalized their infidelity, or had become so calloused to it that they were oblivious of how far they had strayed from the demands of the covenant. Calvin's assessment of this far too common human folly still rings true. 'Men are often so blinded

---

[124]These factors are taken from, Block, *Ezekiel*, 465.
[125]Hals, *Ezekiel*, 111.

by their vices that they do not perceive what is sufficiently evident to every one else.'[126]

After setting the stage with a description of Jerusalem's harlotry, God then warns of the brutal judgment and punishment that she has incurred. 'Thus I will judge you like women who commit adultery or shed blood are judged; and I will bring on you *the blood of wrath and jealousy*' (Ezek. 16:38). Adultery (Deut. 22:20-24) and child sacrifice (Lev. 20:2) were both offenses warranting capital punishment,[127] and Ezekiel has left no doubt that Jerusalem is guilty of these capital offenses. But notice that her offense is not merely the breach of an ethical demand. Her punishment is the result of very personal emotions, wrath and jealousy, for they are in response to very personal transgressions. To break the law of God, which reflects his character, and play the harlot with other 'lovers' beside Yahweh, is to commit spiritual adultery and incur his jealous wrath.

The humiliating punishment she receives for her infidelity and murder would return her to the destitute state she was in before Yahweh saved her and made her his wife.

> I will gather all your lovers with whom you took pleasure, even all those whom you loved *and* all those whom you hated. So I will gather them against you from every direction and expose your nakedness to them that they may see all your nakedness. (Ezek. 16:37)

God renders her 'naked and bare' (v. 39), shamefully displayed in front of the very nations with whom she prostituted herself. God then turns her over to these nations and they ravage her.[128]

---

[126]John Calvin, *Commentaries of the Book of the Prophet Ezekiel*, trans. Thomas Myers (Grand Rapids: Eerdmans, 1948), 93.

[127]William H. Brownlee, *Ezekiel 1-19*, WBC, ed. David A. Hubbard, vol. 28 (Waco, Tex.: Word, 1986), 237.

[128]For an excellent response to accusations of misogyny and wife abuse in this chapter, see Block, *Ezekiel*, 467-71.

I will also give you into the hands of your lovers, and they will tear down your shrines, demolish your high places, strip you of your clothing, take away your jewels, and will leave you naked and bare. They will incite a crowd against you and they will stone you and cut you to pieces with their swords. They will burn your houses with fire and execute judgments on you in the sight of many women. Then I will stop you from playing the harlot, and you will also no longer pay your lovers. (Ezek. 16:39-41)

This brutal punishment of the harlot foreshadows the impending exile and destruction of Jerusalem. God's people had forgotten their absolute dependence on God, and he would do whatever was necessary to shatter their pride so that repentance and reconciliation would take place. 'Jerusalem's remembering is the only element Ezekiel describes as a link between her grievous past and her forgiven future.'[129]

Stuart points out that עֵירֹם ('*êrōm*, 'naked') and גָּלוּת (*gālût*, 'exile') have basically the same meaning in Hebrew which is to be exposed, or taken away from protection.[130] God would abandon her for a time and turn her to the abuse of the 'lovers' she preferred over her one true husband. 'You adulteress wife, who takes strangers instead of her husband!' (Ezek. 16:32). The judgments of God in the exile and destruction of Jerusalem 'demonstrated God's faithfulness to his holy character (cf. Lev 26; Deut. 28-30) as revealed in his covenants.'[131]

The judgment of God that falls on Jerusalem is motivated by his jealous anger, which is appeased in the destruction of the city and exile of the people. 'So I will calm My fury against you and *My jealousy will depart from you*, and I will be pacified and angry no more' (Ezek. 16:42). The idea of appeasing God's wrath is perceived by some as characteristic of pagan and primitive religion or at least something relegated to the capricious God of the Old Testament alone.[132] However, this is

---

[129]Hals, *Ezekiel*, 112.

[130] Douglas Stuart, *Ezekiel*, The Communicators Commentary, ed. Lloyd J. Ogilvie, vol. 18 (Waco, Tex.: Word, 1989), 141.

[131]Alexander, *Ezekiel*, 743.

a central teaching of the atonement in both Testaments, and a necessary reality when the personal natures of God and sin are taken seriously.[133]

God's jealousy is the very real response he has to the infidelity of his people, the primary motive for his wrath and harsh judgment. But it is also the emotion and motive behind his inability to allow his wayward loved-one to stray from his side forever. His jealousy is the catalyst for the process that insures the restored relationship with his people, and the great blessings they receive as a result of that restoration. There is a profound relationship between jealousy and love.

Because of his great love for his wife, Yahweh will bring judgment on her from her lovers; his angry jealousy will be satisfied and he will restore her and bless her. His jealous love will insure that she fulfills her covenant role.

> Jerusalem had forgotten God. In order that she might remem-ber him once again, God would bring this discipline on her. Though mankind may forget God, his love prevents him from forgetting his own (v. 43). God takes his commitments in personal relationships seriously.[134]

It is the depth of his love for his people that will not allow for ambivalence when they are unfaithful. 'Divine jealousy was a result of divine love betrayed.'[135] Jealousy could even be defined as 'the anger of betrayed love.'[136] Because the marriage

---

[132]For this view see, C. H. Dodd, *The Bible and the Greeks* (London: Hodder & Stoughton, 1935).

[133]Cf. Leon Morris, *The Apostolic Preaching of the Cross* (Grand Rapids: Eerdmans, 1965, 2000 3rd revised); 'The Meaning of "*Hilastarion*" in Romans 3:25,' *New Testament Studies*, 2 (Spring 1955): 33-43; and 'The Use of "*Hilaskesthai*" etc. in Biblical Greek,' *The Expository Times*, 62 (May 1951): 227-333; R. V. G. Tasker, *The Biblical Doctrine of the Wrath of God* (London: Tyndale, 1951); Vincent Taylor, *The Atonement in New Testament Teaching* (London: Epworth, 1950, 1963 3rd edition); *The Cross of Christ* (London: Macmillan, St. Martin's Press, 1956); *Forgiveness and Reconciliation* (London: Macmillan, 1956, 1960 2nd edition).

[134]Alexander, *Ezekiel*, 816.

[135]Renaud, *Je Suis un Dieu Jaloux*, 70. 'La jalousie divine était une conséquence de l'amour divin trahi.'

[136]Ibid., 90. 'La colère de l'amour trahi.'

metaphor is at the foundation of God's covenant, jealousy is the natural and expected response of the spurned husband. Because of this, 'instead of treating *qin'â* ("jealousy") cynically, one should hear in the word the legitimate, nay amazing passion of God for one whom he loves.'[137]

The jealous love of God we find in Ezekiel 16 ensures the fulfillment of the covenant promises and restoration of his people. It is this same jealous love of a husband that Isaiah speaks which will bring the return from exile:

> 'For *your husband is your Maker*,... In an outburst of anger I hid My face from you for a moment, but with everlasting lovingkindness I will have compassion on you,' says the LORD your Redeemer.... For the mountains may be removed and the hills may shake, but My lovingkindness will not be removed from you, and *My covenant of peace will not be shaken*,' says the LORD who has compassion on you. (Isa 54:5, 8, 10)

It is this same love that Jeremiah speaks of as he promises his covenant faithfulness:

> 'Behold, days are coming,' declares the LORD, 'when I will make a new covenant with the house of Israel and with the house of Judah, not like the covenant which I made with their fathers in the day I took them by the hand to bring them out of the land of Egypt, My covenant which they broke, *although I was a husband to them*,' declares the LORD. (Jer. 31:31-32)

And it is in this same love that Hosea bases his assurance that the people of God will remain his people.

> *I will betroth you to Me forever*; yes, I will betroth you to Me in righteousness and in justice, in lovingkindness and in compassion, and I will betroth you to Me in faithfulness. Then you will know the LORD. (Hosea 2:19-20)

---

[137]Block, *Ezekiel*, 13.

The other side of God's jealous love is his compassionate undying commitment to his covenant promises. Israel was to remember that 'the intensity of his wrath at threats to this relationship is directly proportional to the depth of his love.'[138] While Israel may have dreaded the anger of God's jealousy, the prophets always reminded her that this same jealousy ensured that her rebellious heart would not triumph. The sovereign jealous love of her faithful divine husband would.

---

[138]Block, *Ezekiel*, 14.

Chapter 4

God's Jealousy for the Faithfulness
of His People in the New Testament

God remains intensely jealous for the faithfulness of his people in the New Testament as well as in the Old.[1] In the New Testament, the Kingdom of God is ushered in through the person and work of Christ. God's presence and character are no longer shrouded in the fire of Sinai. He is now veiled in flesh, walking the shores of Galilee and preaching the good news of the Kingdom to the poor. The New Testament records the decisive events of salvation history that accomplish the redemption of wayward mankind. As Jesus brings the Kingdom of God to bear on the world, he is reclaiming that which is rightfully his. His atoning life of perfect obedience, and his atoning death enable the restoration of what was lost in the fall. God demands that he be known as God, and reconciled with his lost creation, and Christ made this possible. He is the object of the faith that God jealously demands. Unwavering allegiance to Christ is the demand of the New Testament and idolatry is putting anything above him or equal to him. Obeying Jesus is the way one gives evidence of love and faithfulness (John 14:15).

In chapter 2 we saw that the central purpose of Jesus' life and ministry was to glorify his Father (Matt. 4:10; John 17). We saw inter-Trinitarian jealousy where the Father and Son are concerned for each other's glory (John 17; Heb. 1:4-13). We saw that in the early Church God struck down Herod for accepting glory that only God deserves (Acts 12:21-23), and

---

[1]New Testament passages where God is seen to be jealous for the faithfulness of his people are Matthew 10:37; Mark 8:38; Acts 7:42-43; 1 Corinthians 10:22; Hebrews 3:10; James 4:5; Revelation 2:14, 20-22; 21:2-3; 22:14-17.

that God entrusts his gospel to 'earthen vessels' so that he will receive the glory, not the vessels (2 Cor. 4:7).

What then is the New Testament evidence that God is jealous for the faithfulness of his people? The two important passages for this idea, as we noted in the previous chapter, are 1 Corinthians 10:22 and James 4:4-5. We will examine those in detail and summarize the other passages that show us God's jealous demand for devotion.

The Gospels

In the Gospels, Jesus demands that his followers love him more than anyone or anything. Even members of one's own family can become rivals to God. 'He who loves father or mother more than Me is not worthy of Me; and he who loves son or daughter more than Me is not worthy of Me' (Matt. 10:37).

Jesus' teaching can seem harsh and unloving, as if love for Christ and love for family are somehow in competition with one another. However, as we shall see in our study of James 4:4-5, love for the world and God are antithetical, and at times honoring one's own family can require denying Christ. While this is not necessarily the case, at times in this fallen world some of the greatest adversaries to devotion to Christ can come from one's own family. Jesus recognized this hard reality:

> Do not think that I came to bring peace on the earth; I did not come to bring peace, but a sword. 'For I came to SET A MAN AGAINST HIS FATHER, AND A DAUGHTER AGAINST HER MOTHER, AND A DAUGHTER-IN-LAW AGAINST HER MOTHER-IN-LAW; and *A MAN'S ENEMIES WILL BE THE MEMBERS OF HIS HOUSEHOLD*. (Matt. 10:34-36)

When a choice must be made between honoring Christ and honoring one's family, Jesus demands that he reign supreme. God responds with this same jealousy in the Old Testament when Eli puts devotion to family members above devotion to God. Eli's failure to do anything about the irreverence and immorality of his sons, caused the Lord to say, 'Why do you kick at My sacrifice and at My offering which I have commanded in My dwelling, and honor your sons above Me?' (1 Sam. 2:29).

Jesus realized the difficulties that following him would bring, for he knew how foolish and offensive the gospel is to those who are perishing.[2] Following Christ without compromise can cause great strife in relationships and there is a powerful temptation to put human relationships above one's relationship with Christ. Jesus demands that he have no rival in the heart of the believer. Confessing Christ before a sinful world can require great courage, which is why Jesus said,

> For whoever is ashamed of Me and My words in this adulterous and sinful generation, the Son of Man will also be ashamed of him when He comes in the glory of His Father with the holy angels. (Mark 8:38)

Jesus uses the well-known Old Testament prophetic metaphor of adultery to describe the faithless and wicked generation of his day. This statement comes in the context of some of Jesus' most demanding teaching. He predicted his death and Peter rebuked him for suggesting such an idea. Jesus calls Peter 'Satan' for suggesting the same 'kingdom without a cross' idea that Satan did at Christ's temptation (Matt. 4:10). 'But turning around and seeing His disciples, He rebuked Peter and said, "Get behind Me, Satan; for you are not setting your mind on God's interests, but man's" ' (Mark 8:33). God's interests must rule in the believer's life, not those of the world.

Christ then teaches the necessity of denying self and bearing one's cross for anyone who would follow him. Recognizing the sobriety of the challenge, he tells his disciples that nothing less than absolute devotion to him, expressed through confessing him before a culture opposed to him, would be necessary to

---

[2]Cf.,Matthew11:6,13:57;Mark 6:3-4;Luke 7:23;Romans9:33;1 Corinthians 1:18-25; 1 Peter 2:8.

be accepted by Jesus on Judgment Day. Acceptance before men can become an idol when that acceptance prevents bold confession of Christ.

The Epistles

In the Epistles, we get our two most important passages where God is jealous for the faithfulness of his people. 1 Corinthians 10:22 and James 4:4-5 teach that the jealous God of the Old Testament has not changed in his demand of absolute devotion to him expressed through obedience to his commandments.

1 Corinthians 10:22

'Or do we *provoke the Lord to jealousy*? We are not stronger than He, are we?' In chapters 8 and 10 of 1 Corinthians, Paul addresses the believer's Christian liberty versus his responsibility to his Christian brother. The test case for this larger issue is eating food sacrificed to idols. Some of the Corinthians were partaking in pagan feasts and apparently encouraging others to do the same.

In chapter 8 Paul specifically addresses the issue of eating food sacrificed to idols and gives a reaffirmation of the core monotheism of the *Shema* and the Decalogue when he says,

> Therefore concerning the eating of things sacrificed to idols, we know that there is no such thing as an idol in the world, and that there is no God but one. For even if there are so-called gods whether in heaven or on earth, as indeed there are many gods and many lords, yet for us there is but one God, the Father, from whom are all things and we exist for Him; and one Lord, Jesus Christ, by whom are all things, and we exist through Him. (1 Cor. 8:4-6)

In chapter 10 Paul returns to the issue of idolatry in the history of Israel and tells the Corinthians to not follow their bad example, and stay faithful to the one true God. 'Do not be idolaters, as some of them were; as it is written, "THE PEOPLE SAT DOWN TO EAT AND DRINK, AND STOOD

UP TO PLAY"' (1 Cor. 10:7). Here we see a reference to Exodus 32:1-6, and the golden calf incident at Sinai. He then refers to another major act of idolatrous infidelity in Israel's history at Baal Peor in Numbers 25. 'Nor let us act immorally, as some of them did, and twenty-three thousand fell in one day. Nor let us try the Lord, as some of them did, and were destroyed by the serpents' (1 Cor. 10:8-9). This reference, like most of those dealing with idolatry, has sexual immorality in it because the two were often intertwined. Mare points out that the Moabite worship of Baal-Peor involved the prostitution of virgins and therefore 'idolatry and fornication were in that case inseparable.'[3] Paul repeats this charge to break from the bad example of Israel's idolatry when he responds to the issues of idol feasts and the Lord's Supper. 'Therefore, my beloved, flee from idolatry' (1 Cor 10:14).

He then returns to the issue of eating food sacrificed to idols that he spoke of in chapter 8. He assures his audience that the pagan 'gods' have no reality apart from human invention or demonic activity:

> What do I mean then? That a thing sacrificed to idols is anything, or that an idol is anything? No, but I say that the things which the Gentiles sacrifice, they sacrifice to demons and not to God; and I do not want you to become sharers in demons. You cannot drink the cup of the Lord and the cup of demons; you cannot partake of the table of the Lord and the table of demons. (1 Cor. 10:19-21)

The Corinthians were right in believing that the idol had no existence of its own, but Paul would not allow for them to be treated 'as if they were nothing more than so many blocks of wood and stone.'[4] Although the inanimate object of an idol has no existence in itself and 'does not correspond to any spiritual

---

[3] Harold Mare, *First Corinthians*, EBC, ed. Frank E. Gabelein, vol. 10 (Grand Rapids: Zondervan, 1986).

[4] Leon Morris, *The First Epistle of Paul to the Corinthians*, Tyndale New Testament Commentaries, ed. R. V. G. Tasker (Grand Rapids: Eerdmans, 1958, 2002 2nd edition), 147.

reality,'[5] the meaning humans attached to it is not to be taken lightly. Man has a great capacity to become enamored with the work of his own hands to the point of deifying it and straying from the one true God as he 'worships and serves the creature rather than the creator' (Rom. 1:25). The worship of images is foolish, but even worse, it dishonors God, for they inevitably obscure his glory and convey false ideas about him.

In addition to the folly of inventing meaning around idols is the danger of opening oneself to demonic influence that come through participation in idolatry. Paul makes it clear that a sacrifice made to an idol is not 'some neutral activity that has no meaning...to share food is to establish fellowship.'[6]

> No, but I say that the things which the Gentiles sacrifice, *they sacrifice to demons and not to God* ;[7] and I do not want you to become sharers in demons. You cannot drink the cup of the Lord and the cup of demons; you cannot partake of the table of the Lord and the table of demons. (1 Cor. 10:20-21)

Paul is saying that although an idol has no spiritual reality of its own, demons use the avenue of idolatry as an *entrée* into men's lives to lead them away from God. Paul wants them to know that '[t]he devils make use of men's readiness to worship idols.'[8]

---

[5]C. K. Barrett, *The First Epistle to the Corinthians*, Harper's New Testament Commentaries, ed. Henry Chadwick (New York: Harper & Row, 1968), 236.

[6]Morris, *First Corinthians*, 147.

[7]There is some debate as to whether the θεω (*theō*, 'God') of v. 20 is speaking of the true God or false gods. Grosheide believes the absence of the definite article means it should be translated 'a god.' F. W. Grosheide, *Commentary on the First Epistle to the Corinthians*, NICNT, ed. F. F. Bruce (Grand Rapids: Eerdmans, 1974), 235. It was obvious to Paul's audience that it was not the true God to whom they were sacrificing. In light of the jealousy he refers to in the next verse he may have merely been emphasizing what they already knew to make their infidelity obvious. I agree with all of the major translations, contra Grosheide, in their decision to render qew, 'God,' rather than 'god.'

[8]Morris, *First Corinthians*, 147.

It is likely that the pagan feasts Paul was dealing with were held entirely in honor of a sponsoring deity.[9] The cup of demons Paul refers to in verse 21 may refer to libation poured at the end of a meal in honor of the god being honored.[10] His point is that to partake in pagan idolatry is to be a partaker with demons. He had just said in verse 16 that to participate in the Lord's supper is to have fellowship (κοινωνία, *koinōnia*) with Christ. 'Is not the cup of blessing which we bless a sharing in (κοινωνία, *koinōnia*) the blood of Christ? Is not the bread which we break a sharing (κοινωνία, *koinōnia*) in the body of Christ?' (1 Cor. 10:16). If partaking of the Lord's Supper is to have fellowship with him, then to partake in pagan feasts is to have fellowship with them. Paul is pointing out the impossibility of fellowshipping with both the Lord and his arch adversaries. Malachi 1:6-7 was probably in Paul's mind here as one of those 'Scriptures written down for our instruction' he refers to in 10:11.[11]

A son honors his father, and a servant his master. Then if I am a father, where is My honor? And if I am a master, where is My respect? says the LORD of hosts to you, O priests who despise My name. But you say, 'How have we despised Your name?' You are presenting defiled food upon My altar. But you say, 'How have we defiled You?' In that you say, 'The table of the LORD is to be despised.' (Mal. 1:6-7)

Paul has made it clear that partaking in idolatrous feasts is antithetical to a devoted Christian life. To engage in worship of anything besides God is to violate the first and second commandments and to arouse the jealousy warned of in the Decalogue, and thereby incur his wrath. No doubt Paul had in mind the awesome direct command of Yahweh from Sinai.

---

[9]R. C. H. Lenski, *The Interpretation of The First Epistle to the Corinthians* (Minneapolis: Augsburg, 1937), 416.

[10]F. F. Bruce, *1 Corinthians*, NCBC, ed. Matthew Black (Grand Rapids: Eerdmans, 1971), 97.

[11]Barrett, *First Corinthians*, 97.

You shall not worship them or serve them; for I, the LORD your
God, am a jealous God, visiting the iniquity of the fathers on the
children, on the third and the fourth generations of those who
hate Me. (Exod. 20:5)

Paul warns his people to worship God alone and not incite
God's jealousy: 'Or do we[12] provoke the Lord to jealousy?[13]
We are not stronger than He, are we?' (1 Cor. 10:22).

The ἤ ('or')[14] that begins this sentence indicates that we are
getting an option to the previous verse. The option is either,
you stop partaking in idolatry or you incite Almighty God to
jealous wrath. Considering the context a good paraphrase may
be, 'Or will you continue eating at both meals, and thus arouse
the Lord's jealousy as Israel did in the desert?'[15]

Paul is warning them of God's jealous nature and the power
and wrath that back up that jealousy. 'Do not be deceived,
God is not mocked; for whatever a man sows, this he will also
reap' (Gal. 6:7). The Corinthians need to be reminded that
'God watches jealously over his honor (Deut. 32:21)'[16] and
to engage in any form of idolatry would 'incite him to action

---

[12]Paul's identification with his people and pastor's heart come out in his switch
to the first person, thereby including himself in the question even though he would
never have personally partaken of the pagan feast. Gordon D. Fee, *The First Epistle
to the Corinthians*, NICNT, ed. F. F. Bruce (Grand Rapids: Eerdmans, 1987), 473.

[13]The present indicative active verb parazhlou/men ('provoke to jealousy') is a
strong question. It is also the same verb used of God in Deuteronomy 32:21 in the
LXX. Paul continues with his reference to the Song of Moses begun in verses 4
and 20. Ibid.

[14]Found in better manuscripts.

[15]Fee, *1 Corinthians*, 473. Robertson's paraphrase is, 'Is that what we are engaged
in—trying whether the Lord will suffer Himself to be placed on a level with
demons?' Archibald Robertson, *A Critical and Exegetical Commentary on the First
Epistle to the Corinthians*, ICC, ed. Samuel Driver (Edinburgh: T & T Clark, 1911),
218. Barrett's is, 'Do we suppose that we can play fast and loose with our loyalty to
him (as some in Corinth were disposed to do), and get away with it?' C. K. Barrett,
The First Epistle to the Corinthians, Harper's New Testament Commentaries, ed.
Henry Chadwick (New York: Harper & Row, 1968), 238.

[16]Hans Conzelmann, *1 Corinthians: A Commentary on the First Epistle to the
Corinthians*, trans. James W. Leitch, Hermeneia, ed. George MacRae, vol. 46
(Philadelphia: Fortress, 1975), 174.

in his hatred of sin and for mixed allegiance (Deut. 32:21; Ps. 78:58).'[17]

The basis for Paul's warning about God's jealous response to the Corinthian's idolatry is firmly grounded in the Old Testament understanding of God's character.

> The belief of Paul and Deuteronomy 32 that idolatry arouses God's jealousy is, of course, a sturdy Old Testament theme with a long history.... [T]he conviction that God's jealousy inevitably leads him to stern action is also deeply rooted in the Old Testament.'[18]

As we have seen, Paul begins this chapter with an historical sketch of Israel's failures in the wilderness, and it is Moses' summary and prophecy of Israel's idolatrous history in Deuteronomy 32 that serves as the backdrop for 1 Corinthians 10.

> They *sacrificed to demons who were not God*, to *gods whom they have not known*, new *gods* who came lately, whom your fathers did not dread. *You neglected the Rock* who begot you, and *forgot the God who gave you birth*. The LORD saw *this,* and spurned *them* because of the *provocation* of His sons and daughters. Then He said, 'I will hide My face from them, I will see what their end *shall be*; for they are a perverse generation, sons in whom is *no faithfulness. They have made Me jealous* with *what* is not God; they have *provoked Me to anger* with their idols. So I will make them jealous with *those who* are not a people; I will provoke them to anger with a foolish nation.' (Deut. 32:17-21)

There is so much overlap between Deuteronomy 32:17-21 and 1 Corinthians 10:14-21 that it has been suggested that Paul's words are a 'Christian midrash' of Moses' Song.[19] Paul's familiarity with Deuteronomy 32 is obvious as we see

---

[17]Mare, *First Corinthians*, 273.

[18]Brian S Rosner, 'Stronger Than He?: The Strength of 1 Corinthians 10:22b,' *Tyndale Bulletin* 43, no. 1 (1992), 178.

[19]A. T. Hanson, *Studies in Paul's Technique and Theology* (London: SPCK, 1974), 15, 167.

him later quote Deuteronomy 32:21 in Romans 10:19, and
Deuteronomy 32:35 in Romans 12:19.[20] As Moses predicts
Israel's future unfaithfulness he tells them that this unfaith-
fulness will provoke God's jealousy and wrath. 'They have
made Me jealous with what is not God; they have provoked
Me to anger with their idols' (Deut. 32:21). The major Old
Testament theme of God's jealous response to any rival finds
itself in the New Testament as the core reason for absolute
devotion to him. Charles Hodge comments on the jealousy of
God in 1 Corinthians 10:22:

> Jealousy is the feeling which arises from wounded love, and is
> the fiercest of all human passions. It is therefore employed as an
> illustration of the hatred of God towards idolatry. It is when a
> bride transfers her affections from her lawful husband, in every
> way worthy of her love, to some degraded and offensive object.
> This illustration, feeble as it is, is the most effective that can
> be borrowed from human relations, and is often employed in
> Scripture to set forth the heinousness of the sin of idolatry. [21]

The most used description for the Lord in Deuteronomy 32 is
the 'Rock.'[22]

♦ 4: *The Rock*! His work is perfect, for all His ways are just;
  a God of faithfulness and without injustice, righteous and
  upright is He.

♦ 15: Then he forsook God who made him, and scorned *the
  Rock of his salvation*.

♦ 18: *You neglected the Rock* who begot you, and *forgot the
  God who gave you birth*.

Paul picks up on this title of strength and applies it to Christ in
1 Corinthians 10:4: 'and all drank the same spiritual drink, for

---

[20]Rosner, 'Stronger Than He?' 174.

[21]Charles Hodge, *An Exposition of the First Epistle to the Corinthians* (Grand
Rapids: Eerdmans, 1857, 1976), 195.

[22]Cf. 32:4, 13, 15, 18, 30, 31, 37.

they were drinking from a spiritual *rock* which followed them; and the *rock was Christ.'*

Although the צוּר (*ṣûr,*'rock') of Deuteronomy 32 is יְהוָה, (*yĕhwăh,* 'LORD') Paul applies this same nomenclature to Jesus. The rock that followed and provided for the Israelites in the wilderness in the old covenant was the Christ who provides for the Corinthian believers in the new covenant. The Lord of 10:22 is the Lord of the table, cup and bread.

Perhaps the most significant contribution of this passage to our discussion thus far is that the Lord who is being provoked to jealousy in 10:22 is Christ.

> The 'Lord' refers to Jesus for it is his table that was forsaken. Christ is therefore our Jehovah. He is our husband, to whom our supreme affection is due, and who loves us as a husband loves his wife.[23]

The Lord, with whom believers have fellowship in the Lord's Supper, is the one who is provoked to jealousy because of idolatry and whose strength is not to be trifled with. We have seen the inter-Trinitarian jealousy of the Father and the Son for each other's glory (John 12:27-28; 17:4-5; Heb. 1:1-14). Here we have an example of God the Son's jealousy for the undivided devotion of his people. The Son's jealousy that desires the Father's glory is in no way contradicted by his jealousy for the absolute faithfulness of his people to himself. The Father is glorified when his Son is, for the Son is the image of the invisible God (Col. 1:15).

God's strength ('You neglected the Rock'), and Israel's utter dependence on him for her very existence ('and forgot the God who gave you birth'), are themes on which Paul bases his charge to remain faithful in 1 Corinthians 10.

---

[23]Hodge, *1 Corinthians*, 195-96. Robertson (216) and Barrett (238) agree with Hodge, that contextually 'The Lord' must refer to Jesus. This is contra Grosheide who believes that because it is a quotation it must refer to God.

Paul's question is designed not only to underscore the impotence of believers (the view of most commentators), but also to stress the omnipotence of God. Paul sees the provocation of God's jealousy as arousing his power, a discernable theme of Deuteronomy 32.[24]

Sin is always irrational, and the sin of overt idolatry is especially so. Paul warns the Corinthians of the peril they risk in partaking of the table of Christ and of his enemy. In his rhetorical question, 'Or do we provoke the Lord to jealousy? We are not stronger than He, are we?,' he gives a final warning,

> God's jealousy cannot be challenged with impunity. Those who would put God to the test by insisting on challenging him by their actions, daring him to act. Secure in their own foolhardiness, they think of themselves as so 'strong' that they can challenge Christ himself.[25]

God's power and strength are commonly given in the Old Testament as reasons to obey and submit to him.

♦ Job 9:32: For He is not a man as I am that I may answer Him, that we may go to court together.

♦ Job 37:23: The Almighty—we cannot find Him; He is exalted in power and He will not do violence to justice and abundant righteousness.

♦ Ecclesiastes 6:10: Whatever exists has already been named, and it is known what man is; for he cannot dispute with him who is stronger than he is.

♦ Isaiah 55:9: For as the heavens are higher than the earth, so are My ways higher than your ways and My thoughts than your thoughts.

♦ Ezekiel 22:14: Can your heart endure, or can your hands be strong in the days that I will deal with you? I, the LORD, have spoken and will act.

---

[24]Rosner, 'Stronger Than He?' 177.
[25]Fee, *First Corinthians*, 474.

Because of God's awesome power he is to be feared and obeyed and no rival to him should be entertained in the life of the Christian. 'Only if we were stronger than he could such an attempt be made with impunity; as it is, it is madness to act in such a way as deliberately to court the wrath of the Almighty.'[26] Paul is saying that once the Corinthians realized that partaking in pagan feasts was idolatry, and therefore guaranteed to incite God's jealousy and wrath, the only way they could continue to partake in them was to actually think they were stronger than God. Rosner again points us to Deuteronomy 32 as the foundation of Paul's words and explains the connection between Israel's self-perception of her own strength and her disobedience to God in the Old Testament.

> In Deuteronomy 32, especially in the Targumim, the question of Israel's participation in idolatry and the Lord's jealousy and discipline is set in terms of strength and power. Israel follows other gods when they feel strong.'[27]

A proper understanding of God's jealous nature and strength, and the consequent understanding of humanity's relative frailty motivate a life of uncompromising obedience and devotion. The God of the New Testament remains intolerant of idolatry.

> Paul is convinced that the God of the Jewish Scriptures is unchanged in his attitude to idolatry.... Amidst the pressures to be open, tolerant and accommodate other faiths of the early Empire some Corinthian Christians were quite unaware of the real danger of becoming guilty of idolatry by association.[28]

Humility in light of God's power results in fear of the Lord and obedience to his covenant requirements. 'Therefore let him who thinks he stands take heed that he does not fall' (1 Cor. 10:12).

---

[26]Barrett, *First Corinthians*, 97.
[27]Rosner, 'Stronger Than He?' 177.
[28]Ibid., 179.

James 4:4-5

The second of the two primary New Testament passages on
our topic occurs in James 4:4-5.

> You adulteresses, do you not know that friendship with the world
> is hostility toward God? Therefore whoever wishes to be a friend
> of the world makes himself an enemy of God. Or do you think
> that the Scripture speaks to no purpose: '*He jealously desires the
> Spirit which He has made to dwell in us?*'

James was the leading elder of the Jewish church and his letter
is written to a Christian Jewish audience. He speaks to the
spiritual and ethical difficulties that were facing his readers
as he shepherds them from afar. This epistle is in many ways
a theological bridge between the Old and New Testaments as
James speaks as a 'Christian Prophet.'[29]

Because of its practical orientation, James could be thought
of as a non-theological book. However, the doctrine of God is
vital to the teaching of the letter. There is a significant emphasis
on monotheism and the oneness of God. 'You believe that God
is one. You do well; the demons also believe, and shudder'
(James 2:19).[30]

Directly related to, and as a consequence of his emphasis
on monotheism, another main theological concern of James is
God's jealousy.

> To be sure, this characteristic is mentioned in only one verse of
> James, 4:5, and the sense of the verse is hotly contested. But we
> think it very probable that James here cites the scriptural teaching
> about the jealousy of God for his people as substantiation for
> his call to them to abandon their flirtation with the world. And
> although James refers to this attribute of God in only this one
> verse, it is central to the argument of the letter.[31]

---

[29]Ortlund, *Whoredom*, 140.

[30]Cf. 1:5, 17; 2:11; 4:11.

[31]Douglas J. Moo, *The Letter of James*, PNTC, ed. D. A. Carson (Grand Rapids:
Eerdmans, 2000), 29.

James 4:4-5 comes in a discussion of worldly attitudes which are the root cause of fights and quarrels among the believers. These attitudes were internal greed and selfishness in the pursuit of worldly pleasure. 'You lust and do not have; *so* you commit murder. You are envious (ζηλοῦτε, *zēloute*) and cannot obtain; *so* you fight and quarrel' (James 4:2a). This pursuit of pleasure is sinfully and selfishly motivated. 'You ask and do not receive, because you ask with wrong motives, so that you may spend *it* on your pleasures' (James 4:3). Rather than seeing fellow believers as created in God's image (James 3:9), and persons for whom Christ died, many in James' audience were viewing others as competition for the pleasures of this world. These selfish motives lead to worldly lifestyles.

> But if you have bitter envy (ζῆλον, *zēlon*) and selfish ambition in your hearts, do not be boastful and false to the truth. Such wisdom does not come down from above, but is earthly, unspiritual, devilish. For where there is envy (ζῆλος, *zēlos*) and selfish ambition, there will also be disorder and wickedness of every kind. (James 3:14-16)

In James' view, this worldly way of living is not incidental to one's relationship with God. It is rebellion against God that amounts to spiritual adultery: 'You adulteresses, do you not know that friendship with the world is hostility toward God? Therefore whoever wishes to be a friend of the world makes himself an enemy of God' (James 4:4).

For James, the κόσμος (*kosmos*) is not merely the earth or the originally good, yet fallen creation. It is the evil system that dominates human existence. It is the same system that Paul recognizes as controlled by Satan:

> And you were dead in your trespasses and sins, in which you formerly walked according to the course of this world (κόσμος, *kosmos)*, according to the prince of the power of the air, of the spirit that is now working in the sons of disobedience. (Eph. 2:1-2)

Life under worldly satanic dominance is indicative of the lifestyle of those still in bondage to sin.

> The world for James denotes in general the values of human society as against those of God, and hence the man who pursues pleasure aligns himself with the world and compromises or actually denies his relationship with God, he appoints himself an enemy of God.[32]

Pagan idolatry that the Old Testament prophets railed against was mostly demonstrated by Assyrian and Babylonian cultic worship practices. In the New Testament, idolatry 'is lifted to the level of the axiomatic, with "the world" as the enemy of God in the hearts of his people.'[33] Worldly lifestyles are antithetical to being God's people and the options are not ambiguous. Either one loves God or the world, there is no middle ground. Loving the world to James means not only that you don't love God, it means you are his enemy. 'He who determines to be a friend of the world becomes an enemy of God, not because God hates him but because he hates God.'[34]

Friendship in much of our contemporary culture has been trivialized, and calling someone friend requires little meaningful relationship. Friendship in the Hellenistic context was not the shallow idea it often is today.[35] In James' context being a friend meant 'sharing all things in unity, both spiritual and physical.'[36] With this deeper understanding of friendship, it becomes obvious why for James 'love for God and love for

---

[32]Sophie Laws, *A Commentary on the Epistle of James* (Peabody, Mass.: Hendrickson, 1980), 174.

[33]Ortlund, *Whoredom*, 140.

[34]James B. Adamson, *The Epistle of James*, NICNT (Grand Rapids: Eerdmans, 1976), 170-71.

[35]See, Julia Annas, *The Morality of Happiness* (Oxford, 1993), 249-90 and Craig Keener, 'Friendship,' *Dictionary of New Testament Background*, eds., Craig A. Evans & Stanley E. Porter (Downers Grove: IVP, 2000), 380-88.

[36]Luke Timothy Johnson, *The Letter of James: A New Translation with Introduction and Commentary*, Anchor Bible, ed. Foxwell A. Albright, vol. 37A (New York: Doubleday, 1995), 279.

the world are mutually exclusive.'[37] Jesus taught this same message of non-compromising devotion to God which rules out any flirtation with worldly values:

> No servant can serve two masters; for either he will hate the one and love the other, or else he will be devoted to one and despise the other. You cannot serve God and wealth. (Luke 16:13)[38]

To spurn God, is not a neutral or passive activity. It is active, personal rebellion. To be a friend of the world is to be God's hostile *enemy*. This perspective is especially sobering when we realize that the offenses of James' audience were not gross pagan revelry, but behaviors that are routinely dismissed or rationalized as minor. Discrimination (2:1-13), slander (3:1-12), envy and selfish ambition (3:13-18), and seeking selfish pleasure (4:1-3) are the cause of this strong accusation of spiritual adultery.[39] These self-centered offenses, which are often encouraged by contemporary attitudes and marketing campaigns, are considered rebellious harlotry by James.

Because 'the sin of adultery is tantamount to apostasy,'[40] James begins his stern rebuke and call to repentance by addressing his audience as 'You adulteresses' (μοιχαλίδες *moichalides*). This feminine plural noun is a Greek vulgarism that should not be taken literally, but as a figurative description drawing from the Old Testament prophetic denunciation of idolatry that portrayed God's people as his wife.[41] 'It is very likely that the text has the OT idea in view that God is married to his people and that his bride has proven unfaithful.'[42]

---

[37]Martin Dibelius, *A Commentary on the Epistle of James*, trans. Williams Michael, Hermeneia, ed. Helmut Koester, vol. 59 (Philadelphia: Fortress, 1975), 220.

[38]Cf. 1 John 2:15-16; Matthew 6:24.

[39]Moo, *James*, 187.

[40]Ralph P. Martin, *James*, WBC, ed. David A. Hubbard, vol. 48 (Waco: Word, 1988), 148.

[41]James B. Adamson, *The Epistle of James* (Grand Rapids: Eerdmans, 1976), 170-71. Tasker, 88; Moo, 186; Kistemaker, 134; Ropes, 260; Ross, 77 all agree with this interpretation.

[42]Martin, *James*, 148.

Taking the address 'adulteresses' literally has caused scribes and translators to wonder why it only refers to women and why the focus of sinful behavior so abruptly turns from selfish motives and envy to sexual immorality. This has caused translation and scribal inaccuracies, probably due to a failure to appreciate the strong connection between James' words and the Old Testament idea of God's unfaithful wife.[43]

The church is considered the Bride of Christ,[44] and Jesus also used this marriage metaphor when he rebuked the worldly attitudes of his day by calling them μοιχαλίδες (*moichalides*).

♦ Mark 8:38: For whoever is ashamed of Me and My words in this *adulterous and sinful* generation, the Son of Man will also be ashamed of him when He comes in the glory of His Father with the holy angels.

♦ Matthew 12:39: But He answered and said to them, 'An *evil and adulterous* generation craves for a sign; and *yet* no sign will be given to it but the sign of Jonah the prophet.[45]

It is likely James had these words of his brother in mind, or perhaps Gomer, when he used μοιχαλίδες (*moichalides*) to rebuke his audience.[46] As Gomer was unfaithful to Hosea, so too the Jewish Christians to whom James was writing had become 'renegades to their vows.'[47]

---

[43]The KJV and NKJV have 'Ye adulterers and adulteresses,' which is the result of a probable scribal emendation in the Byzantine mss from which the KJV was translated. See, Bruce Metzger, *A Textual Commentary on the Greek New Testament*, corrected ed. (London: United Bible Societies, 1975), 683. The 'unfaithful creatures' (RSV), 'adulterers' (NRSV), 'adulterous people' (NIV), all miss the intended Old Testament prophetic imagery of the address.

[44]2 Corinthians 11:2; Ephesians 5:24-28; Revelation 19:7; 21:9.

[45]Cf., Matthew 16:14; Revelation 2:22.

[46]R. V. G. Tasker, *The General Epistle of James: An Introduction and Commentary* (Grand Rapids: Eerdmans, 1975), 88. Oddly, even though Tasker clearly sees the unfaithful wife metaphor here he still prefers the 'unfaithful creatures' of the RSV.

[47]James Hardy Ropes, *A Critical and Exegetical Commentary on the Epistle of St. James*, ICC, ed. Alfred Plummer, vol. 59 (Edinburgh: T & T Clark, 1968), 260.

Contend with your mother, contend, for she is not my wife, and I am not her husband; and let her put away her harlotry from her face and her adultery from between her breasts. (Hosea 1:2)

When the marriage metaphor is seen as the basic image of God's relationship with his people, and love of the world is viewed as adultery, the jealous reaction of a personal God is to be expected:

What husband permits his wife to have an illicit affair with another man? And what do you think of a wife who forsakes marital love by engaging in adulterous relations? What do you think is God's reaction when a believer becomes enamored with the world? God is a jealous God (Exod. 20:5; Deut. 5:9). He tolerates no friendship with the world.[48]

Love of the world is treason toward God. His reaction to this is the jealousy of a betrayed husband.

Spiritual adultery consists in the lingering wish to retain the world's favour even as one also wishes to enjoy the benefits of redemption. Such hypocrisy provokes God to jealousy, as James goes on to explain in verse 5.[49]

God's jealous response to adulterous love of the world is Scriptural teaching that is well known by James' audience. He phrases his statement of God's jealousy as a rhetorical question, 'Or do you think that the Scripture speaks to no purpose?' If it is a direct quotation that follows this question, the source is unknown. However, based on the context of the passage where divine jealousy is evident, it is likely that the γραφὴ (*graphē*, 'scripture') is a summary statement of familiar Old Testament passages such as Exodus 20:5 and 34:14.[50] This idea

---

[48]Simon J. Kistemaker, *Exposition of the Epistle of James and the Epistles of John* (Grand Rapids: Baker, 1986), 134.

[49]Ortlund, *Whoredom*, 143.

[50]While most commentators agree with this assessment, two notable exceptions are Davids and Dibelius. Davids thinks the author is quoting an unknown apocryphal

that 'he is expressing the theme of God's jealousy as contained in the OT,'[51] fits well with the context, especially if verse 5 speaks of divine jealousy, as I believe it does.

I believe the best translation of James 4:5b (πρὸς φθόνον ἐπιποθεῖ τὸ πνεῦμα ὃ κατῴκισεν ἐν ἡμῖν (*pros epipothei to pnuema ho katōkisen en hēmin*)) is, 'He yearns jealously over the spirit which He has made to dwell in us' (RSV). It is based on several conclusions that are much debated among commentators.[52] Two conclusions that support this translation are based on the context and grammar of the verse:

(1) The immediate context of the sentence favors the divine jealousy translation. The ἤ ('or') at the beginning of verse 5 links it closely with the preceding verse, which has clearly set up the clear options between loving God and the world. God's jealous response to any rival is a well-known concept in Jewish thought. In the face of infidelity expressed by his beloved, God is a jealous lover. 'This obviously suits perfectly the preceding context.'[53] When exegetical difficulties exist, we must lean heavily on context, and the context of our verse 'provides strong, and, in our opinion, decisive, support for the 'divine jealousy' interpretation.'[54]

(2) The grammar of the sentence supports the divine jealousy translation. Grammatically, it makes the most sense to take God as the subject of both ἐπιποθεῖ (*epipothei*, 'jealously

---

work. Peter H. Davids, *The Epistle of James: A Commentary on the Greek Text*, New International Greek Testament Commentary (Grand Rapids: Eerdmans, 1982), 162. Dibelius thinks that the jealousy passages of the Old Testament are too different from James 4:5 in structure and content to allow for a summary statement of Old Testament teaching on divine jealousy. Martin Dibelius, *A Commentary on the Epistle of James*, trans., Michael Williams, Hermeneia, ed. Helmut Koester, vol. 59 (Philadelphia: Fortress, 1975), 223.

[51]Martin, *James*, 149.

[52]For excellent summaries of the key issues and differing perspectives on them see, Moo, *James*, 186-91 and Johnson, *James*, 280-81. Most commentators take the subject to be God and prefer the 'divine jealousy' translation. Cf. Hort, 93; Davids, 164; Mayor, 142; Ropes, 264; Tasker, 91; Dibelius, 224; Martin, 145; Moo, 188-90.

[53]Ropes, *James*, 264.

[54]Moo, *James*, 190.

desires') and κατῴκισεν (*katōkisen*, 'caused').[55] This best fits the common subject-verb-object word order of Greek grammar. Further, in this sentence it is easier to supply the subject than the object.[56]

The major issue that causes some commentators to conclude that the 'divine jealousy' translation has 'severe and perhaps fatal problems,'[57] involves the translation of φθόνον (*phthonon*) as the jealousy of God. They point out that in Greek usage the meaning of φθόνος (*phthonos*) is never positive and is never used to translate קנא (*qna*) in the Septuagint. Therefore, '[a] writer of James' familiarity with the LXX is highly unlikely to write of God's jealousy in a way that neglects the usual terms and adopts language unprecedented and unsuitable in this context.'[58] Therefore, God cannot be the unspecified subject of ἐπιποθεῖ (*epipothei*, 'jealously desires') and therefore, πνεῦμα (*pneuma*, 'spirit') must be. This means πνεῦμα (*pneuma*, 'spirit') must refer to the human spirit, and the verse refers to the envious longing of the human spirit. The translation of the 4:5b then should read something like 'the spirit God caused to live in us tends toward envy.'[59]

In response to this problem, it should be noted that although it would be exceptional, a positive use of φθόνος (*phthonos*) is not impossible. While acknowledging the notorious difficulty of translating James 4:5, Field allows for the possibility that it 'may provide the only example of *phthonos* used in a good sense.'[60] The possibility is increased when one realizes that φθόνος (*phthonos*) and ζῆλος (*zēlos*) are used interchangeably

---

[55]God as the subject of κατῴκισεν ('caused') is a *hapax legomenon* (a unique occurrence in the New Testament).

[56]Joseph B. Mayor, *The Epistle of St. James* (Minneapolis: Klock and Klock, 1892), 142.

[57]Johnson, *James*, 281.

[58]Laws, *James*, 178.

[59]Commentators supporting this view are Adamson, 170; Laws, 178; and Johnson, 281.

[60]D. H. Field, 'Envy,' in *NIDNTT*, ed. Colin Brown, vol. 3 (Grand Rapids: Zondervan, 1978), 558. BAGD also indicates that this phrase was a Greek adverbial idiom meaning 'jealously,' *BAGD*, 857.

in Greek.[61] Another possible reason James may have chosen this unusual usage is because he has already used ζῆλος (*zēlos*) negatively (3:14, 3:16) and therefore 'may deliberately select φθόνον (*phthonon*) as a synonym not yet used.'[62]

Another usage issue that affects our passage is that ἐπιποθεῖ (*epipothei*) is never used with reference to God in the New Testament. However, this is offset by the fact that it always has a positive meaning elsewhere in the New Testament (Rom. 1:11; Phil. 1:8; 1 Pet. 2:2).[63]

Considering the context and grammar clearly favoring God as the subject of the verbs, and the possibility, however rare, of φθόνος (*phthonos*) being used positively, I agree with Moo when he says, 'On the whole, this issue is most naturally resolved in favor of the "divine jealousy" interpretation.'[64]

The last question to answer concerning the translation of our verse is whether πνεῦμα (pneuma, 'Spirit') is the Holy Spirit or the life-giving human spirit that God has given to each person. It is difficult to answer this question definitively because there is nothing in the passage that helps determine the specific definition of *pneuma*.[65] I agree with Laws when she says, 'It is certainly more probable that James writes of the spirit imparted to man at creation; his only other reference to *pneuma* is to the spirit which vivifies the body (2:26).'[66] That God has bestowed this spirit in his creative act[67] gives him possession over all men. 'If the spirit turned toward the world, God's jealousy would be aroused. Such a threat clearly supports James 4:4.'[68] The most important issue concerning

---

[61] 1 Maccabees 8:16; *T. Simeon* 4:5; *T. Gad* 7:2.

[62] Davids, *James*, 164. Mayor adds more support to this idea by pointing out that fqo,noj is often used of the feeling towards a rival. Joseph B. Mayor, *The Epistle of St James* (Minneapolis: Klock and Klock, 1892), 141.

[63] Moo, *James*, 189; Alexander Ross, *The Epistles of James and John*, NICNT (Grand Rapids: Eerdmans, 1974), 78.

[64] Ibid.

[65] Dibelius, 220 ('the human heart'); Laws, 177; and Davids, 164 opt for 'the human spirit.' Ross, 78; and Tasker prefer 'the Holy Spirit.'

[66] Laws, *James*, 177.

[67] Genesis 6:3 LXX; 6:17; 7:15; Psalm 104:29-30; Ezekiel 37.

this spirit, whether it be the human or Holy Spirit in the final analysis, is that 'the phrase reminds us that God has a claim on us by virtue of his work in our lives.'[69]

Verse six tells us that those who humbly submit to God will receive his grace for living the Christian life. 'But He gives a greater grace. Therefore *it* says, "GOD IS OPPOSED TO THE PROUD, BUT GIVES GRACE TO THE HUMBLE." ' In light of God's jealousy James pleads for his flock to submit to God. But he assures them that God's jealous demands will be attainable through his grace.[70]

> In his holy jealousy, God demands the exclusive devotion of his people—a potentially fearsome and unattainable requirement. So James assures his readers that the same God who makes such stringent and all-encompassing demands also 'gives us more grace.' (James 4:6)[71]

Assuming the divine jealousy understanding of this passage, we have in James a 'passionate summons to his readers to turn away from their worldly ways and submit themselves wholeheartedly once again to their gracious but jealous God.'[72] As he follows in the steps of the Old Testament prophets, James emphasizes God's character as he calls God's people to obedience. He does not offer pragmatic rationale or assurance that their lives will be easier or more fulfilling as motivation for obedience to God. Rather, he reminds them of God's jealous character.

> Verse 5 explains why flirtation with the world is so serious a matter by bringing to mind the jealousy of the Lord, which demands total,

---

[68]Davids, *James*, 164.

[69]Moo, *James*, 190.

[70]This assurance is quite different than Joshua's words after he gave a charge much like James' to the Israelites. 'Then Joshua said to the people, "You will not be able to serve the LORD, for He is a holy God. He is a jealous God; He will not forgive your transgression or your sins." '

[71]Moo, *James*, 29.

[72]Ibid., 186.

unreserved, unwavering allegiance from the people with whom he has joined himself.[73]

The jealous character of God demands that man choose to love him or the world that is opposed to him.

> He longs for the wholehearted undivided love of His people with an intensity which is often present in human jealousy, but, at the same time, with a purity which is, in most cases, absent from human jealousy.... God is a jealous Lover, and He will tolerate no rival in His child's heart; no spiritual adultery and no alien friendship can be tolerated for a moment by Him.[74]

James calls his readers to lives of radical obedience and devotion to God. This call is not a legalistic demand based on earning God's love. It is a call to faithfulness to the jealous God of the covenant who demands that his beloved remain in his love. 'Here if anywhere we find the heart of James's letter.'[75]

Conclusions

We saw in chapter 2 that God's glory is the ultimate goal of everything he does. In chapters 3 and 4 we saw that his jealousy is most often expressed in wrath when his glory is not displayed through the faithfulness of his people. Faithfulness to God in the covenant is expressed through obedience to the commandments of God. The Decalogue, which begins with the exclusive demands of the covenant, is always in the background whenever idolatry of any kind is denounced in the Bible. God responds with righteous anger whenever any rival arouses his jealousy. The exclusive demands of the Decalogue allow for no other gods or idolatry of any kind.

While God's jealousy is legitimate cause for fear by those who reject his love, it is also a great source of comfort for those

---

[73]Ibid., 189.
[74]Ross, *James*, 78.
[75]Moo, *James*, 186.

who are his beloved. God's jealousy prevents him from ever being ambivalent about the adultery of his people. It insures that his people, who are prone to wander, will not stray from his side for long. God's jealous love will not allow for it. The jealousy of God should be a cause of great humility and awe.

The marriage metaphor that describes God's relationship with his people in Scripture is central to understanding God's jealous love. This marriage imagery at the heart of the covenant is the reason biblical writers see idolatry of any kind as spiritual adultery. The sexual imagery that accompanies this metaphor intensifies the jealous denunciation of spiritual adultery. The harlotry of God's people is graphically portrayed in the Bible.

That God compares his relationship with his people to a marriage should engender a great appreciation for how completely he has entered into time, space, and human relationship. When we consider that God is entirely self-sufficient and independent, it is staggering that he has, nevertheless, chosen to enter into intimate relationship with his people to the point that he is moved to intense loving jealousy when they spurn him. We can understand why Augustine would in wonder ask God how this could be so. 'What am I to you, that you should command me to love you and, if I do not, you should be angry with me and threaten great miseries?'[76]

The difficulty we often have with ascribing emotions to God is part of the deeper and more foundational issue of reconciling God's transcendence and immanence. While the limitations of this study do not allow for a thorough examination of these issues, it is important to note that when divine emotions are discussed they must be considered with a healthy understanding of God's transcendence, sovereignty, and immutability as well as his immanence and personal nature. To slight the former will inevitably open the door for open or process theism, to slight the latter results in a deistic or even pantheistic understanding of God, both of which fail to adequately consider the complete

---

[76]Augustine, *Confessions*, I,5.

Biblical data.[77] God is both transcendent and immanent. He is both the eternal sovereign Creator and the intimately involved jealous husband of his people. This astounding reality is at the core of the unique character of the God of the Bible. No other religion has a God who is truly transcendent and immanent, almighty and personal. This central aspect of the God of the Bible is profoundly intensified when the great I AM not only enters into covenant at Sinai, but takes on human flesh in a manger. Yahweh entered into intimate covenant relationship with his people in the Old Testament and into humanity itself in the New. The transcendent eternal Son of God took on temporal physical humanity and thereby identified with man as completely as possible.

The marriage metaphor used to describe the covenant and the sexual imagery used to describe the idolatry of God's people provide the foundation for the sacredness of marriage and sex. In addition to invoking an appreciation for the depth of God's love for his people, it should also instill a deep reverence and respect for human marriage and sexual relations. Because these gifts from God illustrate the spiritual relationship God has with his people, they should not be trivialized or perverted in any way.

One of the greatest contemporary theological implications of these chapters is in regard to religious pluralism.[78] The uniqueness of Christ, and the necessity of exclusive submission to him as Savior and Lord in our pluralistic, relativistic age, is seen as an arrogant, ignorant, and narrow religious perspective. Religious pluralism, which rejects the supremacy of God's self-revelation in Jesus Christ, is perhaps the greatest challenge to any Christian wanting to communicate the gospel to contemporary society.

However, this challenge is not only found in non-Christian circles. A pluralistic mind-set is infiltrating the church as well.

---

[77]This issue will be discussed in more depth in chapter 7 when theological implications of divine jealousy are dealt with.

[78]This implication will be dealt with in greater depth in chapter 7.

The ecumenical movement and culture wars have stressed the need for unity within religious communities, often at the expense of truth. There is a desire to get beyond doctrinal barriers to unity and reduce the Christian faith to the least common denominator. Unity, rather than truth, is now the most important value—even if this unity is around a theologically vapid faith. Christianity without conflict hardly seems like the faith in Christ that he warns will cause division, even in families (Matt. 10:34-36).

Chapter 5

Godly Human Jealousy in the Old Testament

As we have seen, God is intensely jealous for his own glory and for the faithfulness of his people. In this chapter we will turn our attention to godly human jealousy. There are hundreds of examples in the Bible where persons express a jealousy that reflects God's jealousy.[1]

---

[1] I found 246 passages where godly human jealousy is present (passages in italics have either the קנא (*qna*) or ζῆλος (*zēlos*) word group in them). I have included both Old and New Testament references, although in this chapter I will consider the Old Testament only. Several New Testament passages will be dealt with in the next chapter. Genesis 14:22-23; 34:7, 31; 35:2-4; Exodus 15:11; 18:11; 32:19-20, 25-29; 39:9; 48:17; 49:3, 5; Numbers *5:14*; *11:29*; 12:13; 14:13-19, 16-22; *25:1-18*; 31:14-18; Deuteronomy 3:24; 4:23-40; 9:16-21; 10:12-16; 11:16, 28; 32:12, 15-18, *21*; Joshua 22:10-23; 23:7-8, 16; 24:14-16, 19-27; Judges 5:7; 6:27-28; 8:23; 1 Samuel 2:1-2; 7:3-4; 12:20-22; 15:22-26, 32-33; 17:26, 36, 45-51; 31:11-13; 2 Samuel 1:14-15; 7:22-24; 8:11-12; 1 Kings 1:17; 8:23; 15:11-15; 18:18, 21, 27, 39-40; *19:10-14*; 2 Kings 9:22; *10:16*, 25-31; 11:17-18; 18:1-6; 19:3-4, 14-19; 23:1-25; 1 Chronicles 10:11-12; 16:25-26; 17:20-22; 29:18-19; 2 Chronicles 2:5; 6:14; 14:2-5, 11; 15:7, 16-17; 16:7-9; 17:6; 19:1-3; 23:16-17; 30:13-14; 31:1; 33:15, 19; 34:1-7; 34:33; Ezra 9:1-6, 10-15; Nehemiah 9:5-6, 17-18; 13:7-8, 17, 23-27; Esther 3:1-4; Job 12:6; 31:9-12, 26-28; 36:13-14; Psalms 4:2-3; 9:17; 16:4; 24:3-4; 31:6; 35:10; 44:20-21; *69:8-9*; 71:19; 73:25-26; 79:9-10; 83:18; 86:8-10; 89:6-8; 95:3; 96:5; 97:7, 9; 106:19-22, 28-40; 109:21; 115:1-8; *119:139*; 135:5, 15-18; 136:3-4; 138:1; 143:11; 148:13; Proverbs 2:16; 5:15-20; *6:34*; 7:1-21; *23:17*; Song of Songs 2:16; 6:3; *8:6*; Isaiah 2:6-8, 18, 20; 19:1; 22:11; 26:3; 27:9; 30:22; 31:6-7; 37:14-20; 38:2-3; 40:18-20; 41:21-29; Jeremiah 14:20-22; 16:19-21; Lamentations 1:2; Daniel 1:8; 3:12, 16-18, 28; 6:10; Hosea 1:1-11; 2:1-23; 3:1-5; Jonah 2:8-9; Micah 7:18; Malachi 2:10-11, 13-16; Matthew 4:10; 6:24; 14:3-5; 16:23; 19:4-9; 21:12-13; 22:21, 37-40; 24:15-20; Mark 6:18; 7:9-13; 8:33; 10:11; 11:15-18; 12:17, 29-31; 13:14; Luke 1:16-17; 3:19-20; 4:5-8; 9:62; 16:13; 19:45-46; John 2:13-17; 3:29-30; 12:27-28; 17:1-5; Acts 4:18-20; 5:28-30; 7:39-43; 10:25-26; 13:8-12; 14:14-15; 17:16, 29-30; 19:26-27; Romans 1:21-25; 7:1-4; 11:2-6; 12:10-11; 1 Corinthians 3:3-9; 4:18-21; 6:18-20; 7:1-4, 23, 32-35; 8:4-5; 10:6-8; 10:14, 18-21; 2 Corinthians 6:14-18; 7:11; *11:1-4*; 12:14; Galatians 1:6; 5:11-12; Philippians 2:20-21; 3:2-3; 1 Thessalonians 1:9-10; Hebrews 3:3-6; James 4:4; 1 Peter 2:9; 4:3; 2 Peter 2:1, 22; 1 John 5:21; Jude 1:10; Revelation 9:20-21; 15:3-4; 17:5; 19:1, 9-10; 21:8; 22:8-9. 212 of the 246 passages are godly human jealousy on behalf of God for his glory.

There are instances when persons express godly jealousy for the faithfulness of another person.[2] In these passages human beings jealously desire the faithfulness from another person that rightfully belongs to them. In Numbers 5, the ritual to determine whether a husband's jealousy is legitimate, assumes there is a jealousy that is righteous in the face of a wife's infidelity. Solomon also acknowledges the legitimate jealousy of a husband whose wife commits adultery (Prov. 6:24-35; 7:1-22; Song 8:6), as well as the proper desire a spouse should have to be exclusively favored (Song 2:16, 6:3). In the New Testament, Paul jealously desires that the Corinthians remain faithful and loyal to both God and himself (2 Cor. 11:1-4; 12:14).[3]

There are also passages where humans are jealous on behalf of another person.[4] When the faithfulness or honor due an individual is threatened or denied, godly men express jealousy on behalf of that individual. Although they expressed their jealousy for Dinah's honor in an ungodly way (Gen. 49:5-7), her brothers were rightly jealous for her honor when she was raped (Gen. 34:7, 31). Joseph fears God and is jealous for Potipher's marriage, and thus refrains from committing adultery (Gen. 39:9). Joshua is jealous for Moses' honor as God's supreme spokesman and he reacts against a perceived challenge to his authority (Num. 11:28). The inhabitants of Jabesh-gilead and David are jealous for Saul's honor as King, and they act to protect his honor (1 Sam. 31:11; 2 Sam. 1:14).

---

[2]Genesis 49:3; Numbers 5:12-31; Proverbs 6:24-35; 7:1-27; Song of Songs 2:16; 6:3; 8:6; 2 Corinthians 11:1-4; 12:14.

[3]Paul's primary desire in these passages is that the Corinthians will remain faithful to God by believing only the true gospel. However, Paul's life is so linked to the gospel and he so deeply loves those he shepherds, that he is also personally jealous for their love and devotion as well. I believe jealousy on behalf of God and jealousy for the faithfulness of other humans is present in 2 Corinthians 11:1-4. However, Paul's jealousy on behalf of God is the dominant idea.

[4]Genesis 34:7, 31; 39:5-7; 39:9-10; 48:17-18; Numbers 11:28-29; 1 Samuel 31:11-13; 2 Samuel 1:14-15; 1 Kings 1:17-18; 1 Chronicles 10:11-12; Job 31:9-12; Proverbs 2:16-17, 5:15-20; Malachi 2:13-16; Matthew 14:3-5, 19:4-9; Mark 6:18, 7:9-13, 10:11-12; Luke 3:19-20; John 3:29-30; Romans 7:1-4; 1 Corinthians 7:1-4.

In the wisdom literature Solomon is jealous for faithfulness within a young man's marriage (Prov. 2:16-17, 5:15-20). The prophet Malachi is also jealous for marital fidelity among the Israelites (Mal. 2:13–16). In the New Testament John the Baptist is jealous for fidelity within Herod's marriage and it cost him his life (Matt. 14:3-5; Mark 6:18; Luke 3:19). He is also jealous for the Messiah's exclusive right to devotions as the husband of his people (John 3:29). Jesus expresses this same jealousy for marital faithfulness as he outlaws divorce (Matt. 19:4). He also jealously demands the honor due parents that the Decalogue requires (Matt. 19:19). Paul is also jealous for fidelity in the marriages of others within the church (Rom. 7:1-4; 1 Cor. 7:1-4).

Godly human jealousy for God's honor represents the highest form of human jealousy. It is always clearly linked to God's ultimate goal in all he does—his own glory and honor. This is by far the most common kind of godly human jealousy we find in Scripture.[5] This emotion earnestly desires that God

[5]Of the 246 passages where godly human jealousy is found, 212 are jealousy on behalf of God's honor. They are: Genesis 14:22-23, 35:2-4; Exodus 15:11, 18:11, 32:19-20, 25-29; Numbers 12:13, 14:13-19, 16-22, 25:1-18, 31:14-18; Deuteronomy 3:24, 4:23-40, 9:16-21, 10:12-16, 11: 16, 28, 32:12, 15-18; Joshua 22:10-23, 23:7-8, 16, 24:14-16, 19-27; Judges 5:7, 6:27-28, 8:23; 1 Samuel 2:1-2, 7:3-4, 12:20-22, 15:22-26, 32-33, 17:26, 36, 45-51; 2 Samuel 7:22-24, 8:11-12; 1 Kings 8:23, 15:11-15, 18:18, 21, 27, 39-40, 19:10-14; 2 Kings 9:22, 10:16, 25-31, 11:17-18, 18:1-6, 19:3-4, 14-19, 23:1-25; 1 Chronicles 16:25-26, 17:20-22, 29:18-19; 2 Chronicles 2:5, 6:14, 14:2-5, 11, 15:7, 16-17, 16:7-9, 17:6, 19:1-3, 23:16-17, 30:13-14, 31:1, 33:15, 19, 34:1-7, 34:33; Ezra 9:1-6, 10-15; Nehemiah 9:5-6, 17-18, 13:7-8, 17, 23-27; Esther 3:1-4, Job 12:6, 31:26-28, 36:13-14; Psalm 4:2-3, 9:17, 16:4, 24:3-4, 31:6, 35:10, 44:20-21, 69:8-9, 71:19, 73:25-26, 79:9-10, 83:18, 86:8-10, 89:6-8, 95:3, 96:5, 97:7, 9, 106:19-22, 28-40, 109:21, 115:1-8, 119:139, 135:5, 15-18, 136:3-4, 138:1, 143:11, 148:13; Proverbs 23:17; Isaiah 2:6-8, 18, 20, 19:1, 22:11, 26:3, 27:9, 30:22, 31:6-7, 37:14-20, 38:2-3, 40:18-20, 41:21-29; Jeremiah 14:20-22, 16:19-21; Lamentations 1:2; Daniel 1:8, 3:12, 16-18, 28, 6:10; Hosea 1:1-11, 2:1-23, 3:1-5; Jonah 2:8-9, Micah 7:18; Malachi 2:10-11; Matthew 4:10, 6:24, 16:23, 21:12-13, 22:21, 37-40, 24:15-20; Mark 8:33, 11:1518, 12:17, 29-31, 13:14; Luke 1:16-17, 4:5-8. 9:62, 16:13, 19:45-46; John 2:13-17, 3:29-30, 12:27-28, 17:1-5; Acts 4:18-20, 5:28-30, 7:39-43, 10:25-26, 13:8-12, 14:14-15, 17:16, 29-30, 19:26-27; Romans 1:21-25, 7:1-4, 11:2-6, 12:10-11; 1 Corinthians 3:3-9, 4:18-21, 6:18-20, 7:23, 32-35, 8:4-5, 10:6-8, 10:14, 18-21; 2 Corinthians 6:14-18, 7:11, 11:1-4; Galatians 1:6, 5:11-12; Philippians 2:20-21, 3:2-3; 1 Thessalonians 1:9-10; Hebrews 3:3-6; James 4:4; 1 Peter 2:9, 4:3;

be recognized for who he is, and that he be worshiped and obeyed as he should be. It is to take God's side and represent his case before man. Many of the great leaders of God's people have exhibited this emotion. A godly perspective causes one to act on his behalf to bring about justice and covenant fidelity. This emotion is a primary basis for the courage, boldness, and integrity with which great leaders of God's people lived their lives.[6]

Whether it is Moses smashing tablets and grinding the golden calf to make the Israelites drink it, Phinehas killing Zimri and Cozbi for their insolent disregard for God's commands, Samuel killing Agag before the Lord, David taking the challenge of the giant who dared challenge the armies of the living God, Elijah taking on the prophets of Baal, or the God-man overturning tables in the temple, we can clearly see godly jealousy as the motivating emotion behind the actions of the greatest leaders in the Bible. Godly human jealousy is evident whenever religious reform and revival took place in Israel. Jealousy on behalf of God, for his exclusive right to be worshiped and obeyed is at work when Hezekiah smashes the sacred pillars and cuts down Asherah poles (2 Kings 18:3-4; 19:15-19a), Jehoiada tears down the house and altars of Baal (2 Kings 11:17), or when Josiah removes the high places (2 Kings 23:19). Jealousy is always the proper response when there is a perceived violation of fidelity in relationship.

---

2 Peter 2:1, 22; 1 John 5:21; Jude 1:10; Revelation 9:20-21, 15:3-4, 17:5, 19:1, 9-10, 21:8, 22:8-9.

[6]The following fifty-two persons are the subjects of the 212 passages which express godly human jealousy on behalf of God's honor: Abraham, Jacob, Moses, Miriam, Jethro, *Phinehas*, the people of Judah, Joshua, Deborah, Gideon, Hannah, Samuel, *David*, Solomon, Asa, *Elijah*, Jehu, Jehoiada, Hoshea, Hezekiah, Josiah, Jehoshaphat, Manasseh, Ezra, the Levites, Job, Elihu, Korah (the psalmist), Asaph, Ethan, *unknown psalmists*, Isaiah, Jeremiah, Daniel, Shadrach, Meshach, Abednego, Hosea, Jonah, Micah, *Jesus*, John the Baptist, Peter, John, Stephen, *Paul*, Barnabas, James, Jude, those who had been victorious over the Beast and the Image, a Righteous Multitude, an Angel. Persons who have the קנא (*qna*) or ζῆλος (*zēlos*) word group actually used to describe them (in italics above) are Phinehas, David, Elijah, an unknown psalmist, Jesus, and Paul.

While the limitations of this study do not allow for a treatment of them all, we will consider the examples that most clearly represent godly human jealousy.[7] We will therefore focus on godly human jealousy where God's honor is the object of that jealousy. Of the hundreds of examples where godly human jealousy on behalf of God is present, there are five individuals that stand out as most clearly possessing this emotion. These are: Phinehas, David, Elijah, Jesus, and Paul. When we consider the godly jealousy of these men, there are key passages that epitomize this attribute for each of them. These are Numbers 25 (Phinehas), Psalm 69:9 (David), 1 Kings 19:10-14 (Elijah), John 2:13-17 (Jesus), and 2 Corinthians 11:1-4 (Paul). Each of these passages use either קנא (*qna*) or ζῆλος (*zēlos*) to describe these men, and they all clearly show us their intense desire for the preservation of God's honor in the face of a challenge to that honor. We now turn our attention to the first of these key examples.

Phinehas

The clearest example of godly human jealousy in the Bible is found in Numbers 25:11 where God says,

> Phinehas the son of Eleazar, the son of Aaron the priest, has turned away My wrath from the sons of Israel in that he was jealous with My jealousy among them, so that I did not destroy the sons of Israel in My jealousy.

The people had fallen into sexual immorality with Moabite women, which led to worshipping Baal. As a result, God's jealous anger went out against Israel in the form of a plague. In the midst of the tears of repentance, an Israelite sins with a Midianite woman in sight of the Tent of Meeting.

> Then behold, one of the sons of Israel came and brought to his relatives a Midianite woman, in the sight of Moses and in the

---

[7]Please see appendix 3 for a diagram of where some of the key examples of godly human jealousy occur throughout salvation history.

sight of all the congregation of the sons of Israel, while they were weeping at the doorway of the tent of meeting. (Num. 25:6)

With the jealous anger of God, Phinehas carries out justice by killing the guilty parties. Phinehas represents God before the people in his reaction to the gross public affront to God's covenant requirements that had just occurred. His action stops the plague and God rewards him with a covenant of peace and an everlasting right to the priesthood.

> Behold, I give him My covenant of peace; and it shall be for him and his descendants after him, a covenant of a perpetual priesthood, because he was jealous for his God and made atonement for the sons of Israel. (Num. 25:12-13)

This righteous action, motivated by his godly jealousy, caused Phinehas to stand as a type of Christ in that his action atoned for the sin of God's people and he therefore stood in the line of the everlasting priesthood of the Great High Priest.

Phinehas the man

So who was this jealous hero of the faith who foreshadowed the Priest who would overturn tables in the temple with a jealousy for the House of the Lord? While Phinehas is not well known today, and children seldom, if ever, learn about him in Sunday school, he is an important and revered figure in the Old Testament and Jewish tradition. His most important role is played in Numbers 25, but he is mentioned at other key times as well, usually jealously defending God's honor.[8]

Phinehas was the son of Eleazar, the high priest, and the grandson of Aaron (Exod. 6:25). His role as a Levite not only required outward action, it required inward godliness. 'Priests, such as Phinehas, were God's representatives among Israel and

---

[8]Other places where Phinehas is mentioned are Exodus 6:25; Numbers 31:6; Joshua 22:13-33; 24:33; Judges 20:28; 1 Chronicles 6:4, 50; 9:20; Ezra 7:5; 8:2, 33; and Psalm 106:30-31.

were to symbolize God's character in their behaviour.'⁹ This character was evident as he acted on behalf of God at Baal-peor.

Among other things, the Levites were responsible for protecting the tabernacle from defilement. Phinehas had the job of protecting the sanctuary of the Tabernacle, as the leader of the gatekeepers. Speaking of the gatekeepers, the Chronicler says, 'Phinehas the son of Eleazar was ruler over them previously, *and* the LORD was with him' (1 Chron. 9:20).

After his defining event at Baal-peor, which occurred when he was a young man, he commanded the army that fought the Midianites (Num. 31:6-8). This seems only appropriate seeing that his killing of Cozbi insured that this war would occur.

He continued to protect proper worship in Israel once the Jordan had been crossed. In the Promised Land, when the Reubenites, the Gadites, and the half-tribe of Manasseh built a large altar, the rest of the nation was prepared to go to war with them for this apparent rebellion against the covenant demands (Josh. 22:12). It was Phinehas who led the party to investigate the situation. It is likely that we have his words, as he speaks to these tribes on behalf of the nation. His speech reflects his well-known jealousy for God's honor, and refers back to the apostasy at Baal-peor.

> Thus says the whole congregation of the LORD, 'What is this *unfaithful act* which you have committed against the God of Israel, *turning away from following the LORD* this day, by building yourselves an altar, to rebel against the LORD this day? *Is not the iniquity of Peor enough for us*, from which we have not cleansed ourselves to this day, although a plague came on the congregation of the LORD, that you must turn away this day from following the LORD? If you rebel against the LORD today, He will be angry with the whole congregation of Israel tomorrow. (Josh. 22:16-18)

As the tragic period of the Judges comes to a close with one of the most degenerate events in Israel's history, Phinehas is

---

⁹Gordon J. Wenham, *Numbers*, TOTC, ed. D. J. Wiseman, vol. 4 (Downers Grove, Ill.: InterVarsity, 1981), 185.

there, defending God's honor in the war with the Benjamites.
The horrible murder of the Levite's concubine at Gibeah led
to civil war among the Israelites. Phinehas served as the main
advisor in this war with the Benjamites.

> The sons of Israel inquired of the LORD (for the ark of the covenant
> of God *was* there in those days, and Phinehas the son of Eleazar,
> Aaron's son, stood before it to *minister* in those days), saying,
> 'Shall I yet again go out to battle against the sons of my brother
> Benjamin, or shall I cease?' And the LORD said, 'Go up, for
> tomorrow I will deliver them into your hand.' (Judg. 20:27-28)

Perhaps we see the importance of Phinehas' influence in Eli's
naming one of his sons after him. This may have been an
attempt by Eli to legitimize his priesthood. Tragically, Eli's
son Phinehas greatly lacked his namesake's revered trait
of jealousy for God's honor, and it cost him and his family
severely (1 Sam. 2:12-36).

In the wisdom literature, Phinehas' jealousy is seen as the
basis of his righteousness. In Psalm 106, the Psalmist proclaims God's lovingkindness, even in the midst of the history
of Israel's unfaithfulness. The Psalmist remembers Phinehas'
atoning act as a demonstration of God's grace, and Phinehas
and his progeny are considered righteous because of his jealous action.

> They joined themselves also to Baal-peor, and ate sacrifices
> offered to the dead. Thus they provoked *Him* to anger with their
> deeds, and the plague broke out among them. Then Phinehas
> stood up and interposed, and so the plague was stayed. And it
> was reckoned to him for righteousness, to all generations forever.
> (Ps. 106:28-31)

In the intertestamental period, when syncretism and temptation
to forfeit the distinctive elements of the covenant was great,
Phinehas continued to be revered as an example of jealous
conviction. In the Apocrypha he receives high honor and is

spoken of as a man of glory on a level with Moses, Aaron, and David.

> Phinehas the son of Eleazar is the third in glory, for he was zealous (ζηλῶσαι, *zēlōsai*) in the fear of the Lord, and stood fast, when the people turned away, in the ready goodness of his soul, and made atonement for Israel. (Sir 45:23-24)

In the apocryphal tradition, when Mattathias responded with violent anger against the apostasy of Jerusalem, he did so in the tradition of Phinehas. When offered a bribe to go along with the leaders who had betrayed the covenant, Mattathias refused in no uncertain terms. Following this refusal he has an experience compared with that of Phinehas at Baal-Peor.

> When he had finished speaking these words, a Jew came forward in the sight of all to offer sacrifice on the altar in Modein, according to the king's command. When Mattathias saw it, *he burned with zeal* (ἐζήλωσεν, *ezēlōsen*) and his heart was stirred. He gave vent to righteous anger; he ran and killed him on the altar. At the same time he killed the king's officer who was forcing them to sacrifice, and he tore down the altar. Thus *he burned with zeal* (ἐζήλωσεν, *ezēlōsen*) *for the law, just as Phinehas did against Zimri son of Salu.* Then Mattathias cried out in the town with a loud voice, saying: 'Let every one who is *zealous* (ζηλῶν, *zēlon*) for the law and supports the covenant come out with me!' (1 Macc. 2:23-27)

When Mattathias gave his dying farewell speech he encouraged his people to 'show zeal for the law (ζηλώσατε τῷ νόμῳ, *zēlōsate tō nomō*) and give your lives for the covenant of our fathers' (1 Macc. 2:50). He then gives Phinehas as an example, along with Abraham, Joseph, Joshua, Caleb, David, Elijah, Hananiah, Azariah, Mishael, and Daniel, of ones who were jealous for God's honor. 'Phinehas our father, because he was deeply zealous (ζηλῶσαι ζηλον, *zēlōsai zēlon*) received the covenant of everlasting priesthood' (1 Macc. 2:54).

Mattathias' son Judas was the greatest military hero of the intertestamental period. And according to Jewish tradition, like Phinehas, he purged evildoers from the land and thereby appeased God's wrath. 'He went through the cities of Judah; he destroyed the ungodly out of the land; thus *he turned away wrath from Israel* ' (1 Macc 3:8).

Phinehas stands as a revered symbol of godly jealous for God's honor in the Old Testament and intertestamental literature. We will now turn our attention to the key event in Phinehas' life that won him this exalted status.

The Incident at Baal-peor

Most structuring of Numbers has been done according to geography. The usual sections are divided into three parts: (1) Mt. Sinai (1:1-10), (2) at and around Kadesh-barnea (10:11-19:22), (3) on the plains of Moab (20:1–36:13). Within this structure are two travel sections, one from Sinai to Kadesh-barnea, and the other from Kadesh-barnea to the plains of Moab. Given this structure, chapter 25 falls within the plains of Moab section. This is the time where the nation remained at Shittim, just east of the Jordan River, on the brink of the Promised Land. It was a time to learn key final lessons and purge evil from the camp as preparation for entering Canaan.

Numbers 25 takes place within the Oracles of Balaam. It follows on the heels of Balaam's wonderful prophecies about the future of Israel. Noth sees a major break in tradition and content between Balaam's oracles and chapter 25 and therefore assumes that a redactor inserted the Phinehas story later. He thinks it too unusual for Israel to have such a sharp shift from victory to apostasy.[10]

However, far from being uncharacteristic for Israel, it was certainly not uncommon for her to act in this way. Not long after God brought Israel out of captivity in Egypt, they were worshipping the golden calf. After miraculous provision of

---

[10]Martin Noth, *Numbers: A Commentary*, OTL, ed. James D. Martin (Philadelphia: Westminster, 1966), 195.

manna the people ungratefully complain. Moral laxity and temptation often follow spiritual victory. To place the failure of Baal-peor after victory shows the contrast between God's consistency and faithfulness and the weakness and infidelity of his people. God was blessing at Sinai while his people strayed, and he was blessing at Baal-peor when his people played the harlot on the plains of Moab. Noth assumes this jarring contrast means different sources and traditions rather than the shocking contrast between almighty God and his frail creatures. The Bible often juxtaposes God's glorifying events with the horrible reality of human sinfulness. 'In this way Scripture tries to bring home to us the full wonder of God's grace in face of man's incorrigible propensity to sin.'[11]

Another reason it is assumed that we are dealing with the compilation of two stories is that the intermarrying was with Moabites, and Cozbi was a Midianite. However, Moabites and Midianites are related in the Balaam story (22:4, 7), and 'it is possible to understand that some Midianites lived under Moabite hegemony.'[12] This seems to have resulted in the two nations worshiping at the same shrine.[13]

Structurally, this chapter fits together well when we consider that there are many parallels between the apostasy at Baal-Peor and the apostasy at Sinai in Exodus 32. The time in the wilderness is established and ended with similar gross ingratitude and idolatry by Israel. In both of these instances the core covenant demands are broken, a census is taken, laws are given, God's wrath is appeased by the Levites' killing the chief offenders, and a priesthood is set apart for the Lord.

The message of Numbers 25 is the same as Exodus 32, and much of the Bible—God alone is to be worshipped. Speaking of Numbers 25 Levine says,

---

[11]Wenham, *Numbers*, 184.

[12]Katharine D. Sakenfeld, *Journeying with God*, International Theological Commentary, ed. Fredrick C. Holmgren and George A. F. Knight (Grand Rapids: Eerdmans, 1995), 136.

[13]Wenham, *Numbers*, 185.

In the larger context of Numbers, its principal message is that just as the Israelites brought their own unique religion with them to Canaan, they also had been made aware, before entering the Promised Land, of its unique challenge. Unlike other peoples, they dared not tolerate the worship of other gods.[14]

Sadly, Israel's history was continually marked by apostasy. God's chosen people often failed to worship him as their only God.

'Ironically, yet justifiably, the *coup de grâce* to the generation of the Exodus is executed when they commit apostasy for the second time. In a real sense, Baal-peor is but an extension of the golden calf.'[15]

Verses 1-3a: An Adulterous People

While Israel remained at Shittim, the people began to play the harlot with the daughters of Moab. For they invited the people to the sacrifices of their gods, and the people ate and bowed down to their gods. So Israel joined themselves to Baal of Peor, and the LORD was angry against Israel. (Num. 25:1-3)

On the threshold of Canaan, Israel fell into the exact apostasy God had warned them would bring their downfall once in the land. He had given this prophetic warning when he renewed the covenant after the apostasy at Sinai:

for you shall not worship any other god, for the LORD, whose name is Jealous, is a jealous God — otherwise you might make a covenant with the inhabitants of the land and they would play the harlot with their gods and sacrifice to their gods, and someone might invite you to eat of his sacrifice, and you might take some of his daughters for your sons, and his daughters might play the

---

[14]Baruch A. Levine, *Numbers 21-36*, The Anchor Bible, ed. William F. Albright and David N. Freedman, vol. 4A (New York: Doubleday, 2000), 303.

[15]Jacob Milgrom, *Numbers*, JPS Torah Commentary (Jerusalem: Jewish Publication Society, 1990), 211.

harlot with their gods and cause your sons *also* to play the harlot with their gods. (Exod. 34:14-16)

This jealous warning, at the heart of the demands of the covenant, goes unheeded before the Jordan is even crossed. At Shittim, Israel encountered 'a foretaste of the same kind of depraved cultic practices they would encounter in the Promised Land.'[16] They intermarried with foreign women and began to 'play the harlot' with their gods. They offered sacrifice to, and prostrated themselves before, the gods of Moab. Milgrom translates לִזְנוֹת *'liznût,* whoring after.'[17] He points out that this is the only time in Scripture that זנה, when taken literally, takes a masculine subject הָעָם, *hā'ām.* This is most likely indicative of the apostasy's being a direct result of intermarrying with foreign women.[18]

They 'bound' (וַיִּצָּמֶד, *wāyṣamed*) themselves to the Baal of Peor. צמד (*ṣmd,* 'bound') is the key word in the apostasy here. The only other time this verb occurs is in Psalm 106:28, where this same event is described with added insight into the cultic nature of the offense which involved offering sacrifice to the dead: 'They joined themselves also to Baal-peor, and ate sacrifices offered to the dead.'

The idea that they 'bound' or 'joined' themselves to Baal shows that this worship was not merely a passing fancy for Israel; she had joined herself through personal loyalty and affection to this pagan god;[19] Baal of Peor, the Canaanite god of fertility. The Canaanites believed they were dependent on Baal for the fertility of the land, which led to gross sexual immorality as part of the worship of this cult. 'Canaanite religion was doubtless the most depraved and morally corrupt of any cultic system the world has ever known.'[20] It is likely that the Israelite

---

[16]R. K. Harrison, *Numbers: An Exegetical Commentary* (Grand Rapids: Baker, 1992), 335.

[17]Milgrom, *Numbers,* 211.

[18]Ibid., 212.

[19]Levine, *Numbers 21-36,* 284.

[20]Harrison, *Numbers,* 335.

men were involved with the temple prostitutes of the heathen temples. This was a direct violation of the first (polytheism), second (idolatry), and seventh (adultery) commandments. It was physical *and* spiritual adultery. God does not allow for any other gods, or alternative ways of worshipping him. They broke their marriage covenants, both with God and their wives. They defiled the sacred relationship between the holy God and the people he set apart for his glory.

While historical background can perhaps shed light on the nature of the sexual immorality of the Israelites, the text does not go any further than simply telling us that the men were engaging in sexual immorality with Moabite women (v. 1) and this led them to worship Baal-Peor (v. 5). There is little doubt that when the most sacred of all human relating is shared with someone who worships another god, spiritual adultery will follow.[21] This is clearly in line with the prophetic warning of Exodus 34:14-16.

For Israel, the immoral apostasy of Baal-peor served as a warning for centuries to come. As Moses exhorts Israel to stay faithful to Yahweh, he reminds them of God's jealous wrath at Shittim: 'Your eyes have seen what the LORD has done in the case of Baal-peor, for all the men who followed Baal-peor, the LORD your God has destroyed them from among you' (Deut. 4:3). Joshua recalls this event upon entering the Promised Land. 'Is not the iniquity of Peor enough for us, from which we have not cleansed ourselves to this day, although a plague came on the congregation of the LORD?' (Josh. 22:17). Hosea remembers the sin of Baal-peor as he rebukes the Israelites of his day for their apostasy. 'But they came to Baal-peor and devoted themselves to shame, and they became as detestable as that which they loved' (Hosea 9:10b). And this shameful event

---

[21]Levine doubts, *contra* most commentators, that Israel's 'playing the harlot' and 'being joined' to Baal involved sexually immoral orgiastic rites of the cultic worship of Baal. Levine, *Numbers*, 296. Although the text is not overtly graphic about the nature of Israel's sin in Numbers 25, the sexual implications of involvement in Canaanite idolatry are unavoidable.

also became an example to be avoided in the New Testament church. 'Nor let us act immorally, as some of them did, and twenty-three thousand fell in one day' (1 Cor. 10:8).[22]

Verses 3b-5: God's Jealous Judgment

> The LORD was angry against Israel. The LORD said to Moses, 'Take all the leaders of the people and execute them in broad daylight before the LORD, so that the fierce anger of the LORD may turn away from Israel.' So Moses said to the judges of Israel, 'Each of you slay his men who have joined themselves to Baal of Peor.' (Num. 25:3-5)

God responds to Israel's sin in accordance with his character and promises. Jealous anger is always his normative response to unfaithfulness. He burned with anger (וַיִּחַר־אַף, *wayiḥar-'ap̄*) and expressed fierce anger against the apostasy. אַף (*'ap̄*, 'wrath') always refers to God's anger in the Bible, and always has drastic consequences (e.g., Exodus 32:12; Joshua 7:26; 1 Samuel 28:18; Job 20:23; Psalm 78:49).[23] Anyone familiar with the Old Testament is not surprised when Paul says 'the wages of sin is death' (Rom. 6:23). Once again, Yahweh showed Israel that he demands covenant exclusivity. 'He is a jealous God who is in the midst of his people but he does not tolerate any infringement on his holiness and glory.'[24]

In response to the sin of intermarrying, God demands the execution of the leaders of people. Milgrom maintains that it was all the leaders, because the leaders of the people were responsible for the behavior of the nation and the whole nation was corporately involved in the sin.[25] If this were the

---

[22]Paul has 1000 less in his number of those who lost their lives. Perhaps he knew somehow that 2300 died in one day but Numbers 25:9 reports another 1000 who died later.

[23]Ashley, *Numbers*, 518.

[24]Willem A VanGemeren, *The Progress of Redemption: The Story of Salvation from Creation to the New Jerusalem* (Grand Rapids: Baker, 1988), 175.

[25]Milgrom, *Numbers*, 212.

case, Moses disobeyed God and reduced the sentence to only
require that the actual Baal worshipers were killed. It has even
been suggested that it was Moses' failure to carry out the full
extent of God's judgment that brought about the plague.[26]
However, the precedent God set in previously dealing with
apostasy at Sinai was to have only those involved in the sin
punished (Exod. 32:25-29). One wonders who was to carry out
the command if all the leaders were to be killed. Considering
these observations and Moses' response to the command,
I agree with Levine who says, 'the sense is that all involved
with pagan worship were to be put to death.'[27]

The exact mode of death is uncertain. The hifil imperative
of יָקַע (*yq'*) seems to suggest that they were to be hanged in
some manner, perhaps impaled, and in public. It was to be
done 'before the Lord' (לַיהוָה, *layhwāh*). God is the object
of this propitiation. It was also to be done נֶגֶד הַשָּׁמֶשׁ (*nened
hašāmeš*), literally 'against the sun,' or 'in broad daylight.'
The executions were intended to publicly demonstrate the
serious nature of violating the covenant. This method of
representative public execution is similar to that suffered by
seven of Saul's descendents at the hands of the Gibeonites
(2 Sam. 21:1-14). Refusal to bury the victims in this way was
a great disgrace. God provided a powerful and brutal lesson
in covenant obedience for the people about to enter Canaan.
He wanted his people to know that the covenant demands had
not changed since Sinai. His jealousy is still operative. 'While
God is a God of love, He is jealous to maintain His rights under
the covenantal agreement—namely, the worship of His chosen
people, the observance of His enacted laws, and obedience to
His revealed will.'[28]

The sin, executions, and plague caused the people to weep
in apparent repentance and mourning at the entrance of the tent

---

[26]W. H. Gispen, *Het Boek Numeri* (Kampen: J. H. Kok, 1964), 147, as cited by
Wenham, *Numbers*, 147.

[27]Levine, *Numbers 21-36*, 285.

[28]Harrison, *Numbers*, 337.

of meeting. 'This action, because of its cultic locale, probably describes a formal lament of the community such as is found, e.g. in the Psalter.'[29]

Verse 6: An Adulterous Man

In the midst of this tragic national crisis, and in sight of the leaders at the tent of meeting, an Israelite commits a bold-faced violation of the covenant demands.

> Then behold, one of the sons of Israel came and brought to his relatives a Midianite woman, in the sight of Moses and in the sight of all the congregation of the sons of Israel, while they were weeping at the doorway of the tent of meeting. (Num. 25:6)

Commentators have emphasized one of three aspects of Zimri's sin: (1) immoral sex, (2) foreign marriage, or (3) cultic worship. The exact details of Zimri's offense are not clear in the text, but it seems that all three offenses were likely present.[30] In spite of the lack of detailed description of the offense, commentators have spent much effort trying to figure out what exactly the offense must have been. As Levine observes, '[t]he admixture of sexual allusions and pagan cultic practices and the ambiguities of language that characterize Numbers 25 have given free rein to the interpretive imagination.'[31]

One of the difficulties is the precise definition of the tent in which the killing took place. קֻבָּה (*qubāh*) means a large vaulted tent. Some have argued that he took her into the Tabernacle compound, which would have been a violation of Levitical law (Mendenhall, Reif). Others believe it was the inner part of Zimri's personal family tent (Wenham, Harrison). Reif maintains that the tent was a cult shrine of Baal.[32] I agree

---

[29]Ashley, *Numbers*, 519. For community laments, see Psalms 12, 44, 58, 60, 74, 79, 80, 83, 85, 89:38-51, 90, 94, 123, 126, 137.

[30]Ibid., 518.

[31]Levine, *Numbers 21-36*, 181.

[32]S. C. Reif, 'What Enraged Phinehas,' *JBL* 90 (1971): 200-06.

with Wenham who says this possibility is unlikely.[33] That Zimri brought Cozbi before his family implies it was his personal tent. However, while the text is not specific it seems that the central location (in sight of all the community), and the reaction of Phinehas, meant it was part of the Tabernacle precinct, and he was most likely engaging in a cultic ritual performed for Baal. Before this, the immorality had taken place outside of the city; now we have apostasy and sexual immorality in the worship setting.

Mendenhall suggests that Zimri was trying to halt the plague through his cultic sexual activity. He says, 'it is quite possible that the Simeonite Zimri was very sincerely convinced that his ritual conduct with the Midianite princess was the best way to secure the welfare of his group.'[34] He does not excuse his conduct however, and goes on to say, '[t]he fact remains that he was acting in conscious rebellion against that which he had promised to obey—if he were not, he would not have been identified with the infant community of ancient Israel.'[35]

This open and full defiance of God not only took place in the sacred area, but in sight of the weeping leaders and congregation, who had gathered to lament the national crisis in front of the tent of meeting. This act flagrantly repudiated the heart of the covenant.[36] The sin of Zimri was not only sexual immorality but at its core it was a spiritual and religious apostasy. This ritual 'constituted a breach of covenant, in that it either created or presupposed a relationship to a pagan god.'[37] Because Zimri showed his contempt for the covenant, the jealous anger of God burned against him, and so did the jealous anger of a godly man.

---

[33]Wenham, *Numbers*, 187.

[34]George E. Mendenhall, 'The Incident at Bet Baal Peor (Nu. 25),' in *The Tenth Generation* (Baltimore: Johns Hopkins University Free Press, 1973), 115.

[35]Ibid., 116.

[36]For in depth discussions of the nature and cultic significance of the sin of Zimri, see Mendenhall, 'The Incident at Bet Baal Peor,' and S. C. Reif, 'What Enraged Phinehas.'

[37]Mendenhall, 'Incident at Beth Baal Peor,' 112.

Verses 7-8: The Killing

> When Phinehas the son of Eleazar, the son of Aaron the priest,
> saw it, he arose from the midst of the congregation and took a
> spear in his hand, and he went after the man of Israel into the
> tent and pierced both of them through, the man of Israel and the
> woman, through the body.[38] So the plague on the sons of Israel
> was checked. (Num. 25:7-8)

Phinehas arose from the community as a lone voice of divine
jealousy. It has been speculated that Moses' apparent lack of
response to Zimri's sin may have resulted from Moses having
taken a Midianite wife himself from the family of Jethro.[39]
Whatever the response of others, Phinehas is portrayed as
the strong person who broke ranks with the passivity of the
crowd and provided the shocking example of God's jealous
anger.

He speared Zimri, and pierced Cozbi through the 'belly'
(אֶל־קֳבָתָהּ , *'el-qŏbātāh*)[40] with a spear. Because the spear went
through the both of them it is thought that they were engaged
in sexual intercourse. This target of Phinehas' spear may be a
play on words with קבה (*qubāh*) and also may be significant
because of a relationship between the use of קֵבָה (*qēbāh*) in
Deuteronomy 18:3:

> Now this shall be the priests' due from the people, from those
> who offer a sacrifice, either an ox or a sheep, of which they shall
> give to the priest the shoulder and the two cheeks and the stomach
> (וְהַקֵּבָה, *wĕhaqēbāh*).

---

[38]The Hebrew text (אֶל־קֳבָתָהּ) says 'through *her* body' but for some reason the
NASB does not translate the feminine subject here.

[39]Milgrom, *Numbers*, 214. Moses lacked initiative at other crucial times as well.
Cf. Exodus 14:15; Numbers 14:5; 16:4.

[40]The sexual nature of the offense of Zimri and Cozbi has led Jewish tradition
and commentators to suggest that the translation of אֶל־קֳבָתָהּ should be 'through the
genitals.' Milgrom, *Numbers*, 215. I see no compelling reason in the text to read
into it such a specific meaning.

Milgrom sees a connection here between Phinehas' act and the priestly right to the inner parts of the sacrificial animal.[41]

Many Rabbis, like many of us today, were uncomfortable with Phinehas taking the law into his own hands. It is important to note, however, that Phinehas 'did not act on his own initiative but followed God's command.'[42] God had commanded the killing of the leaders of the apostasy of Israel, and Zimri clearly fit this description. Furthermore, he acted in accordance with his role as the leader of the Tabernacle guards.

Who knows what the result of Phinehas' act would have been if God did not evaluate it for Moses? God himself tells us that Phinehas' violent act was not done in sudden uncontrolled passion. It was motivated by righteous jealousy that mirrored God's jealousy for his own honor.

Verses 10-11: Phinehas' Jealousy

> Then the LORD spoke to Moses, saying, 'Phinehas the son of Eleazar, the son of Aaron the priest, has turned away My wrath from the sons of Israel in that he was jealous[43] (בְּקַנְאוֹ, *běqaně'ô*) with My jealousy among them, so that I did not destroy the sons of Israel in My jealousy.' (Num. 25:10-11)

בְּקַנְאוֹ (*běqaně'ô*) means to express קנא (*qna*) on behalf of, or on account of someone.[44] The emotion that was the catalyst for Phinehas' action was the same jealous anger that God had in response to the apostasy of the nation and of Zimri. Phinehas

---

[41]Ibid.

[42]Ibid., 477.

[43]Milgrom joins the common aversion to 'jealousy' as a translation of קנא (*qna*) here, and prefers the amorphous 'in his becoming impassioned with My passion.' Milgrom *Numbers*, 216. Using 'zeal' or 'passion' here informs us about the degree of Phinehas' and God's passion, but nothing about the exclusive, relational and covenant aspects of that passion, which is clearly present in this passage, and that the translation 'jealousy' clearly does.

[44]This jealousy is similar to Joshua's jealousy on Moses' behalf in Numbers 11:29 when Moses asks him, 'are you jealous on my account?' Levine, *Numbers 21-36*, 289.

acted on behalf of God because he shared in and expressed God's attitude, perspectives and desires. He saw the breach of God's exclusive relational expectations brought about by the nation's adultery. This public harlotry brought Phinehas to his feet in an indignant fury that mirrored God's response. Levine rightly compares Phinehas' reaction on behalf of God to Elijah's when he represents God in taking on the prophets of Baal in 1 Kings 19 and 20.[45] Phinehas' jealousy represents 'that fundamental attitude of Yahweh which defends his own honor, and the actions he takes to defend it.'[46] Phinehas' reaction is not only because of the vile nature of Zimri's sin, but more fundamentally, he reacted with jealousy because the sin represents spiritual adultery before the holy God of the covenant. The personal, relational nature of the offense, and the godly response of Phinehas should not be lost in the dramatic details of the killing. If the action of Phinehas is understood in ethical rather than relational categories, the intended theocentric essence of the narrative is lost. Phinehas understood and shared God's relational jealousy in the face of infidelity. He understood that 'Israel's faith is based on a relationship between God and his people, Yahweh has an absolute claim on Israel's loyalty.'[47]

Although the plague was stopped, lives were spared, and Phinehas received great blessing from God, the pragmatic benefits of his action did not motivate Phinehas. He had no

---

[45]Levine, *Numbers 21-36*, 289. Levine goes on to compare this act of Phinehas with God's 'zeal' on behalf of Israel in Zechariah 1:14-15. In his use of the vague 'zeal,' he fails, in both of these instances, to distinguish between Phinehas' jealousy for God's exclusive relational devotion and God's general zeal for Israel's well being.

[46]Ashley, *Numbers*, 522. As noted in the previous chapter, God's honor and name are fundamentally related to one another and to God's character. Targum Neofiti explains Numbers 25:13 by stating that being jealous for God is to be jealous for his name. It says that Phinehas' unending priesthood was 'in return for his having been *jealous for the Name of his God*, and for having made atonement for the children of Israel.'

[47]Philip J. Budd, *Numbers*, ed. David A. Hubbard and Glenn W. Barker et. al., WBC, vol. 5 (Waco, Tex.: Word, 1984), 280.

way of knowing what the result of his swift action would be. In fact, the only practical outcome he could be confident of was that his killing of Cozbi would start a war. The jealous action of Phinehas had drastic consequences from a practical standpoint. This killing of a Midianite princess certainly meant war. 'There can hardly be a more heinous crime than the open and deliberate murder of a princess by one of the highest officials of another nation.'[48] And war indeed followed this act (Numbers 31). Pragmatism or peace at all costs did not drive Phinehas, jealousy for the honor of his God did. He acted on behalf of God, to defend his honor and exclusive right to be worshiped, no matter the cost.

Phinehas' own character so reflected God's that he responded emotionally and behaviorally as God's representative before the nation. His righteous perspective motivated him to take drastic measures on behalf of God, and God's wrath was appeased. Phinehas' jealous anger 'was so real and deeply felt that it adequately expressed Yahweh's own jealousy, rendering unnecessary any further recriminations on Yahweh's part.'[49] His radical response resulted in appeasing God's wrath and saving lives. Godly human jealousy had an immediate result that was brutal, but in the long run was the most beneficial action for the good of God's people and for the glory of God.

Verses 12-13: Atonement

> Therefore say, Behold, I give him My covenant of peace; and it shall be for him and his descendants after him, a covenant of a perpetual priesthood, because he was jealous for his God and made atonement for the sons of Israel. (Num. 25:12-13)

The Bible unequivocally teaches that atonement is required for sin.[50] Because Phinehas 'had interpreted the mind of God

---

[48]Milgrom, *Numbers*, 214.

[49]Eryl W. Davies, *Numbers*, NCB, ed. Ronald E. Clements (Grand Rapids: Eerdmans, 1995), 289.

precisely,'[51] and acted in his jealous anger, he was able to turn God's wrath away, and made atonement (וַיְכַפֵּר, *wayĕkapēr*) for the sins of the people. 'Because Phinehas executed the sinner, expressing so clearly and visibly God's own anger through his deed, that anger was turned away.'[52]

While the atonement Phinehas secured for the people 'assuaged YHWH's wrath,'[53] it is not the actual killing, but the godly jealousy that motivated it, that God considers meritorious. Because Phinehas shared God's perspective on the sin, God's holy wrath was appeased, and the sin was atoned for. Phinehas' act 'was a spontaneous expression of feeling. But that feeling was so in accordance with the mind of God, that God acknowledged it by receiving what he did as an atonement.'[54] The outward behavior was a manifestation of the character and priorities of Phinehas. Killing Zimri and Cozbi was necessary to demonstrate Phinehas' jealousy for God's honor, and thereby make atonement, '[b]ut the moral element in the transaction—the mind of Phinehas—his zeal for God—his sympathy in God's judgment on sin, this was the atonement, this its essence.'[55]

Verses 12-13: Covenant and Priesthood

> Therefore say, Behold, I give him My covenant of peace; and it shall be for him and his descendants after him, a covenant of a perpetual priesthood, because he was jealous for his God and made atonement for the sons of Israel. (Num. 25:12-13)

---

[50]Exodus 29:36; 30:10; 32:30; Leviticus 4:20, 26, 35; 5:6, 10, 13; 6:30; 7:7; 9:7; 10:17; 12:8; 14:19, 31; 15:15, 30; 16:6, 11, 27; 19:22; Numbers 6:11; 8:12, 21; 15:25; 16:44-50; 28:22; 29:5, 11; 2 Samuel 24:15-24; 2 Chronicles 29:24; Nehemiah 10:33; Ezekiel 45:17; Daniel 9:24; Romans 3:24-25; Ephesians 1:7; 1 John 1:9; 4:9.

[51]Harrison, *Numbers*, 339.

[52]Wenham, *Numbers*, 188.

[53]Levine, *Numbers 21-36*, 290.

[54]J. Campbell McLeod, *The Nature of the Atonement* (Grand Rapids: Eerdmans, 1856, reprint, 1996), 108.

[55]Levine, *Numbers 21-36*, 303.

Because he was motivated by a godly jealousy, Phinehas supplied a deadly cure for a fatal disease. The covenant of everlasting priesthood Phinehas received is a covenant of peace and wholeness. Phinehas and his progeny benefited from this covenant, but so did the people of Israel, for it is the priest that mediates between them and God. Of Phinehas' reward for his action Philo says, 'in recompense for this, for the cutting out of folly, the soul obtains a twofold portion as its reward, peace and priesthood, virtues as near of kin as sisters.'[56]

In Phinehas' jealousy, atonement making, and perpetual priesthood, he stands as a type of Christ. Like Jesus, he represented God's jealous hatred of sin and the judgment it brings. However, the primary difference between Phinehas and Christ is that Jesus represented the guilty sinner as well. '[W]hereas it was Phinehas' spear that pierced the sinners that made atonement for Israel, it was the nails and spear that pierced Jesus that made atonement for the sins of the whole world.'[57]

Conclusions and Implications of Phinehas' Jealousy
In the jealousy of Phinehas we have a clear example of a man who so shared God's perspective that he felt and acted on God's behalf in an accurate and godly way. The godly jealousy expressed by Phinehas is the purest kind, for it is intensely and ultimately concerned about the goal for which God is most intensely and ultimately concerned—his own glory. God's jealous love will tolerate no rival. This is a primary theme of Numbers 25, Numbers itself, and the entire Bible. The story of Phinehas is one of the key examples of godly human jealousy as well as God's jealousy for the faithfulness of his people and ultimately his own glory.

In what ways is Phinehas still an example for Christians in contemporary society who no longer live in the theocracy of

---

[56]*Leg. All. iii*, 242
[57]Wenham, *Numbers*, 189.

Israel? How is he a model of jealous action on behalf of God's honor for believers today? Several aspects of Phinehas' jealous act are important to reiterate in answering this question.

There are several factors to consider regarding Phinehas' jealous act that put limitations on using him as an example today. The first is that Phinehas' brutal killing of the offenders was not an outburst of uncontrolled rage, but an expression of God's explicit instructions in the law and in the situation at Baal-peor. Phinehas cannot be used to defend random acts of violence in the name of godly jealousy. His actions fit within the clear commands of God, not only in the Old Testament law, but also in the specific situation in which he found himself. God had commanded that the leaders of the apostasy be killed and Phinehas was acting within that command. His action also reflects an awareness of the inviolable exclusive relational parameters of the covenant expressed in the Decalogue. So, while we can look to Phinehas as an example of jealous rage on God's behalf that is righteous, we must realize that his jealousy did not lead him to in any way violate God's laws. He acted within God's revealed expectations for a godly man in his situation.

What also puts Phinehas' act in perspective is that he acted not only within the parameters of God's law and commands, but he also acted in accordance with his role as priest and head of the Tabernacle guards. He did not take on the responsibility of something that was outside of the sphere of his Levitical responsibility that God had given him. This should give one pause before leaping into a situation with jealous anger. Phinehas' role as priest and Tabernacle guard, should prompt the question: 'Is this an issue God has clearly called me to rectify?' Before acting in the name of Phinehas, one needs to ask whether the situation fits within one's calling, office, vocation, and role.

While there are aspects that may be unique to Phinehas that should give us pause in seeing him as an example, there are also aspects of his godly jealousy that serve as motivating and convicting examples for believers today. It is important to remember that Phinehas' primary motive in the killing was theological. The theological basis for his actions should not be lost in the ethical violation of Zimri. The honor of God and his exclusive relational demands were the primary issues for Phinehas. Intermarrying with Moabite women involved sexual immorality, but the central issue was that it was leading the people into apostasy and into playing the harlot with foreign gods. It was not primarily the social, ethical, or sexual implications of the sin that drove Phinehas. Rather, as his jealousy shows, it was God's honor that was foundational for his feelings and actions. Zimri's sin was indicative of the spiritual adultery that had overtaken the nation. This was a personal, relational offense against the holy God of the convent. Pragmatic consequences were not the primary issue for Phinehas. Negatively, his actions started a war, positively they stopped a plague and Phinehas and his progeny were greatly blessed. However, it is obvious that God's name was the primary issue for Phinehas. No matter the cost or benefit, Phinehas acted on God's behalf. Bold intervention to protect the honor of God's name should never be quelled by the negative practical ramifications, or primarily motivated by a likely positive outcome. The glory of God and the honor of his name should always take precedence over the temporal, immediate consequences. What is best for the individual, or even the community, is not to be the believer's first priority; God's honor is.

However, this does not mean that God will not bless the faithful actions of a godly man. God responds to the actions of a righteous man (James 5:16). Phinehas atoned for the sin of the people and he was greatly honored and rewarded by God. Phinehas' example shows us that when men act on behalf of God with his honor as their highest goal, he will bless and forgive.

When we look at the other events of Phinehas' life, we see that his behavior at Baal-peor was not an aberration for him. He also led the army against the Midianites, challenged the two and a half tribes that built an altar, and went to war against the Benjamites. His jealous act at Baal-peor was indicative of his character. His radical behavior flowed out of a godly character and perspective and that enabled him to have the courage necessary to boldly act on God's behalf. It was his internal jealous disposition, not primarily his actions that God commends. His internal condition was the catalyst for his outward behavior and this internal condition was the key element in the atonement he accomplished. Just as sinful behavior originates in the heart (Matt. 15:19), so does righteous, godly behavior. The essence of his actions was a character and heart that shared in God's jealous desire that his people love only him and thereby honor his name.

Another significant aspect of Phinehas' jealousy that stands as a powerful example today was that his jealousy made him willing to act as a lone example for the rest of the community. Majority rule does not determine truth, and godly jealousy emboldens godly people even if they are in the minority.

The last point to be made about Phinehas is that his godly jealousy foreshadowed the jealousy of Jesus. As we shall see in the following chapter, Jesus' jealousy for God's honor was a primary aspect in his life and ministry. The priesthood and atonement of Phinehas point us to the jealousy of Jesus.

The next great leader of God's people who exhibited godly jealousy also foreshadowed Christ in many ways. We now turn out attention to the godly jealousy of King David.

David

David stands as another leader of God's people who was intensely jealous for God's honor. As a young boy, before he was even King, David was described as a 'man after God's own heart' (1 Sam. 13:14; Acts 13:22). This devotion to God is recounted by the psalmist.

Remember, O Lord, on David's behalf, all his affliction; how he swore to the Lord and vowed to the Mighty One of Jacob, 'Surely

I will not enter my house, nor lie on my bed; I will not give sleep to
my eyes or slumber to my eyelids, until I find a place for the LORD,
a dwelling place for the Mighty One of Jacob.' (Ps. 132:1-5)

This relentless pursuit of God's honor made David's will and
motives so linked with God's that when a challenge to God's
honor arose, David reacted with jealous indignation. His
worship was marked by an acute realization that God alone is
worthy of worship. Godly jealousy was a central driving force
in his life.[58]

Goliath
When God was mocked, David took it personally. His jealousy
for God's honor must have stood behind his bravery and
indignation as a young shepherd boy, as he stood before the
giant from Gath and asked, 'What will be done for the man
who kills this Philistine and takes away the reproach from
Israel? For who is this uncircumcised Philistine, that he should
taunt the armies of the living God?' (1 Sam. 17:26). The
giant taunted and challenged the armies of Israel. 'Again the
Philistine said, "*I defy the ranks of Israel* this day; give me a
man that we may fight together" ' (1 Sam. 17:10). Rather than
focusing on his own abilities and personal safety, God's honor
was David's primary concern. His reference to 'the living
God' of Israel is not only a statement of the living nature of
Yahweh, it is also an assessment of Dagon, the Philistine god,
as dead.[59] This reality had been vividly demonstrated when
the idol of Dagon ended up prostrate, armless, and headless,
before the Ark of the Covenant in 1 Samuel 5. David would
not allow Yahweh to be slandered by one who worshiped
idols. This theocentric response is in striking contrast to the
response of the soldiers who were focused on their immediate,

---

[58]This is in no way to suggest that there were not times that David failed in his
respect for God's honor, as well as Uriah's! (2 Sam. 11:1-17).

[59]Ralph W. Klein, *I Samuel*, WBC, ed. John D. Watts, vol. 10 (Waco, Tex.: Word,
1983), 178.

personal condition and abilities rather than on the honor of God's name and his power. Boogaart points out this contrast, and the following differences between the men of Israel and David.[60] The self-focused soldiers call Goliath 'this man' who 'comes out to defy Israel' (v. 25). David calls Goliath 'this uncircumcised Philistine' who came to 'defy the armies of the living God' (v. 26). David's refusal to call Goliath by name, instead calling him an 'uncircumcised Philistine,' not only shows his disdain for the giant, but makes a theological and religious distinction between Goliath and the Israelites.[61] This is not merely a political battle; it is fundamentally a 'theological struggle.'[62] The theological nature of the battle is heightened when Goliath curses David 'by his gods' (v. 43). David recognized the relationship between Goliath's defiance of Israel, and the disgrace it brought on God's people and therefore God himself.

While the men referred to the one who took on the giant as merely 'the man who kills him' (v. 25), David showed his concern for the disgraceful effect of the defiance, in referring to him as 'the man who kills this Philistine and removes this disgrace from Israel' (v. 25). The other men 'see an insuperable, fearsome giant who is reproaching Israel; David saw merely an uncircumcised Philistine who had the audacity to reproach the armies of the living God.'[63] The difference in perspectives determined their respective behavior. David's theocentric perspective, as opposed to the circumstantial perspective of the other men, is the main point of the narrative as a whole. We are intended to recognize 'the marvelous overruling of all the circumstances by God himself.'[64] The men were most

---

[60]T. A. Boogaart, 'History and Drama in the Story of David and Goliath,' *Reformed Review* 38 (1985): 208-09.

[61]Klein, *I Samuel*, 179.

[62]Ibid.

[63]Boogaart, 'History and Drama in the Story of David and Goliath,' 208.

[64]C.F. Keil and F. Delitzsch, *Commentary on the Old Testament*, vol. 2, *Biblical Commentary on the Books of Samuel*, trans. James Martin (Eerdmans, 1956), 176.

concerned about their immediate situation and they were
fearful and passive. David was jealous for God's honor and
courageously rose like Phinehas to meet the challenge to that
honor. His confidence in God, and bold indignant response to
the humiliation of God's representatives, is striking, especially
for one so young. 'Your servant has killed both the lion and the
bear; and this uncircumcised Philistine will be like one of them,
since he has defied the armies of the living God' (1 Sam. 17:36).
This was no naïve youthful bravado; his jealous concern on
behalf of Yahweh enabled him to see the situation radically
differently than his fellow Israelites. 'David's courage rested,
therefore, upon his confident belief that the living God would
not let His people be defied by the heathen with impunity.'[65]
His resolve and theocentric perspective did not dwindle when
the boy came face-to-face with the cursing angry giant.

> Then David said to the Philistine, 'You come to me with a sword,
> a spear, and a javelin, but *I come to you in the name of the* LORD
> *of hosts*, the God of the armies of Israel, whom you have taunted.
> This day *the* LORD *will deliver* you up into my hands, and I will
> strike you down and remove your head from you. And I will give
> the dead bodies of the army of the Philistines this day to the birds
> of the sky and the wild beasts of the earth, that *all the earth may
> know that there is a God in Israel*, and that all this assembly
> may know that the LORD does not deliver by sword or by spear;
> for *the battle is the* LORD'*s* and He will give you into our hands.'
> (1 Sam. 17:45-47)

David's own reputation was not his ultimate goal in this battle.
Nor was the success of the army of Israel. He was not seeking
rewards or acclaim. He fought 'quite simply because he finds
it scandalous that an uncircumcised man, a worshiper of dead
gods (cf. ch 5) should insult the people of God and therefore
the living God himself.'[66] David's ultimate goal was 'that all

---

[65]Ibid., 182.
[66]Hans Wilhelm Hertzberg, *1 & 2 Samuel*, trans. J. S. Bowden, OTL, ed. G. Ernst
Wright et.al., vol. 9 (Philadelphia: Westminster, 1964), 151.

the earth may know that there is a God in Israel' (v. 46). The honor and glory of God before the nations drove David to meet the challenge before him.

The circumstances of David's victory, against all earthly odds, insured that God received the glory for the favorable outcome. David was a sorry sight in comparison to this great warrior. The text reminds us that the battle was won without even the use of a sword (v. 50). As we saw in chapters 2 and 3, God insured that his power was displayed through frail earthen vessels so there would be no doubt about the source of victory, and therefore no doubt about who should receive the glory (2 Cor. 4:7). This was a battle 'in which God's honor was at stake, and in this circumstance David's exposure to danger permitted God's honour to be more clearly acknowledged than if David had more obviously been a match for the Philistine.'[67]

David's godly jealousy on behalf of God was not only contrasted with the ambivalence among the armies of God, it was also sandwiched between the ungodly personal jealousy of Eliab, that precedes David's heroics (v. 28), and Saul's ungodly jealousy that follows (1 Sam. 18:6-16).

David's Jealousy on Saul's Behalf

Of all the impressive accomplishments David achieved, perhaps his most impressive was when he refrained from acting. In the midst of fierce persecution by Saul, David had the opportunity to kill him twice, and he refused (1 Samuel 24 and 25). Both times, the reason David did not kill Saul was because he was God's anointed leader of Israel.

♦ 1 Samuel 24:6: So he said to his men, 'Far be it from me because of the LORD that I should do this thing to my lord, *the LORD's anointed*, to stretch out my hand against him, since he is the LORD's anointed.'

---

[67]Joyce G. Baldwin, *1 & 2 Samuel*, TOTC, ed. D. J. Wiseman, vol. 9 (Downers Grove, Ill.: InterVarsity, 1988), 145.

♦ 1 Samuel 26:9,11: But David said to Abishai, 'Do not destroy him, for who can stretch out his hand against *the* Lᴏʀᴅ*'s anointed* and be without guilt?... The Lᴏʀᴅ forbid that I should stretch out my hand against *the* Lᴏʀᴅ*'s anointed.*'

Again, David took God's side and cared more about the honor of Yahweh's anointed representative than his own temporal well being. Phinehas' and David's jealousy drove them to act in violent and bold ways. Here, David's jealousy for Saul's, and ultimately God's honor, caused him to stay his hand from killing Saul.

This jealousy on Saul's behalf had a drastic consequence in the life of the young Amalekite who claimed to have killed Saul. 'Then David said to him, "How is it you were not afraid to stretch out your hand to destroy *the* Lᴏʀᴅ*'s anointed* ?" And David called one of the young men and said, "Go, cut him down." So he struck him and he died' (2 Sam. 1:14-15). Even after Saul was dead, David was concerned about his honor as God's anointed. The young man, hoping for a reward, was swiftly killed for his insolence against God's representative.

David's jealous devotion to Yahweh alone was grounded in the exclusive demands of the Mosaic Covenant. This exclusive devotion was evident when David praised God after the Ark was brought to Jerusalem. 'For great is the Lᴏʀᴅ, and greatly to be praised; *He also is to be feared above all gods.* For *all the gods of the peoples are idols*, but the Lᴏʀᴅ made the heavens' (1 Chron. 16:25).

The Davidic Covenant

We see this same jealousy in David's response to the covenant God established with him. After David fought the wars necessary to establish Israel in the Land, he proposed building a temple for the ark of God. God would not allow this because David was a man of war. Nathan brought wonderful news to David in the midst of this denial (2 Sam. 7:8-16). He promised David that one of his offspring would be established as King in the land, that his name would be great. This son would build a house for God's name and the throne of his kingdom would last forever. After David was blessed with this amazing covenant, he entered the sanctuary, and expressed his heart of devotion and gratitude (2 Sam. 7:18-29). This expression gives us insight into David's jealousy for God's exclusive right to ultimate worship and devotion as the only true God.

> For this reason You are great, O Lord GOD; for *there is none like You, and there is no God besides You*, according to all that we have heard with our ears. And what one nation on the earth is like Your people Israel, whom God went to redeem for Himself as a people and to make a name for Himself, and to do a great thing for You and awesome things for Your land, before *Your people whom You have redeemed for Yourself from Egypt, from nations and their gods?* For You have established for Yourself Your people Israel as Your own people forever, and *You, O LORD, have become their God.* (2 Sam. 7:22-24; Cf. 1 Chron. 17:20-22)

As we saw in chapter 2, God's jealousy for the faithfulness of his people is grounded in the exclusive demands of the first and second commandments. David's worshipful response to the covenant God established with him reflects an awareness of the same exclusive demands of the Mosaic covenant. David's jealous affirmation in his response to the covenant was that God is unique in his perfections, with no rival, and that he alone is Israel's God.

David's dying prayer was a request that perfect devotion to Yahweh would remain in his son and Israel forever.

> O LORD, the God of Abraham, Isaac and Israel, our fathers, preserve this forever in the intentions of the heart of Your people, and direct their heart to You; and give to my son Solomon a perfect heart to keep Your commandments, Your testimonies and Your statutes, and to do *them* all, and to build the temple, for which I have made provision. (1 Chron. 29:18-19)

David's Jealousy: The Standard of the King of Israel
When kings of Israel were assessed in the Old Testament, the
standard they were measured against was David. And it was
David's jealousy for God's exclusive right to be worshipped
that was often the basis of the comparison. Whether or not
the king in question stamped out idolatry was the greatest
concern.

♦ 1 Kings 15:11-15: Asa did what was right in the sight of the
   LORD, like David his father. He also put away the male cult
   prostitutes from the land and removed all the idols which
   his fathers had made. He also removed Maacah his mother
   from *being* queen mother, because she had made a horrid
   image as an Asherah; and Asa cut down her horrid image
   and burned *it* at the brook Kidron. But the high places were
   not taken away; *nevertheless the heart of Asa was wholly
   devoted t*o the LORD all *his days*. He brought into the house
   of the LORD the dedicated things of his father and his own
   dedicated things: silver and gold and utensils.

♦ 2 Chronicles 34:1-7: Josiah *was* eight years old when he
   became king, and he reigned thirty-one years in Jerusalem.
   He did right in the sight of the LORD, and walked in the ways
   of his father David and did not turn aside to the right or to
   the left. For in the eighth year of his reign while he was still
   a youth, he began to seek the God of his father David; and
   in the twelfth year he began to purge Judah and Jerusalem
   of the high places, the Asherim, the carved images and the
   molten images. They tore down the altars of the Baals in his
   presence, and the incense altars that were high above them
   he chopped down; also the Asherim, the carved images
   and the molten images he broke in pieces and ground to
   powder[68] and scattered *it* on the graves of those who had
   sacrificed to them. Then he burned the bones of the priests
   on their altars and purged Judah and Jerusalem. In the cities

---

[68]In Josiah's grinding the images to powder, we see a similar response to that of
Moses, who did the same with the golden calf in Exodus 32:20.

of Manasseh, Ephraim, Simeon, even as far as Naphtali, in their surrounding ruins, he also tore down the altars and beat the Asherim and the carved images into powder, and chopped down all the incense altars throughout the land of Israel. Then he returned to Jerusalem.

These faithful kings were compared to David in their jealous response to idolatry in the land.

David's Jealous Psalms

In the psalms attributed to David, we get great insight into the jealous heart of the person who ran to meet Goliath.[69] The following psalms express a jealous desire that God alone be worshiped and any rival to him abolished. They take God's position and on behalf of him demand exclusive devotion.

- Psalm 4:2: O sons of men, how long will my honor become a reproach? *How long* will you *love what is worthless and seek false gods*?
- Psalm 9:17: The wicked will return to Sheol, *even* all the *nations who forget God.*
- Psalm 16:4a: The sorrows of those who run after other gods will be multiplied.
- Psalm 24:3-4: Who may ascend into the hill of the LORD? And who may stand in His holy place? He who has clean hands and a pure heart, *who has not lifted up his soul to an idol* and has not sworn deceitfully.
- Psalm 31:6: *I hate those who regard vain idols*, but I trust in the LORD.
- Psalm 35:10a: *All my bones will say, 'LORD, who is like You?'*

---

[69]Many modern interpreters have emphasized the corporate dimension of the psalms. However, VanGemeren rightly observes that 'Old Testament scholars have been guilty of emphasizing Israel's collective experiences as a worshiping community to the virtual exclusion of the individual use.' VanGemeren, *Psalms*, 7.

♦ Psalm 71:19b: *O God, who is like You?*

♦ Psalm 86:8: *There is no one like You among the gods*,
O Lord, nor are there any works like Yours. All nations
whom You have made shall come and worship before You,
O Lord, and *they shall glorify Your name*. For You are great
and do wondrous deeds; *You alone are God.*

♦ Psalm 138:1: I will give You thanks with all my heart; *I will
sing praises to You before the gods.*

As we saw in chapter 2, God's jealousy for his own glory is
often expressed when he acts 'for the sake of his name.' His
name is a window into his character and is another way of
expressing the sum total of who God is. In addition to this,
God's name and glory are used as almost interchangeable
terms. As David pleaded with God for kindness and revival,
he did so with God's glory, through his name, as the ultimate
goal. David was aligned with God's concern for his own glory,
and so he asked him to answer his prayer 'for the sake of his
name.'

♦ Psalm 109:21: But You, O GOD, the Lord, *deal kindly with
me for Your name's sake*; because Your lovingkindness is
good, deliver me;

♦ Psalm 143:11: *For the sake of Your name, O LORD*, revive
me. In Your righteousness bring my soul out of trouble.

God's glory, exclusively exalted through the praise of his
name, was David's jealous driving motivation, and this was
what made him a man after God's own heart. 'Let them praise
the name of the LORD, for *His name alone is exalted*; His glory
is above earth and heaven' (Ps. 148:13).

Psalm 69:9

In Psalm 69:9 David expressed his jealousy for God's honor
when he said, 'For zeal (קִנְאַת, *qin'at*) for Your house has
consumed me, and the reproaches of those who reproach You
have fallen on me.' This same expression, of being consumed

by one's קָנָא (*qna*), is also used in Psalm 119:139: 'My zeal has consumed me, because my adversaries have forgotten Your words.'

Kraus classifies Psalm 69 as a 'prayer song.'[70] This imprecatory Psalm occurs in Book 2 of the Psalms and is considered messianic because it is extensively quoted in the New Testament in reference to Jesus.[71] It is similar in structure and content to Psalms 22 and 102.[72]

We have a difficult time understanding how the vengeful, angry attitude expressed in imprecatory psalms could align with a Christian perspective. How could someone who follows the one who told us to love our enemies, and to turn the other cheek, reconcile David's cursing of his enemies? Is there any place for a godly Christian to say with David: 'Pour out Your indignation on them, and may Your burning anger overtake them. May their camp be desolate; may none dwell in their tents' (Ps. 69:24-25)?

To understand how a godly person could express feelings like this, one must understand the jealousy for God's honor at the root of these emotions. Because godly individuals take God's side and speak from his perspective, when sin and idolatry reign, they react with jealous, angry indignation on God's behalf. When God's name is disparaged by the success of evil, the proper reaction is jealous outrage. VanGemeren explains it well:

> The psalmists wrote under the inspiration of God regarding the nature of evil. They were *intoxicated with God's character and name* (9:16-20; 83:16-17) and were *concerned with the manifestation of God's righteousness and holiness on earth.* Since evil contrasts in every way with God's nature and plan, the psalmists prayed for divine retribution, by which God's order

---

[70]Hans-Joachim Kraus, *Psalms 60-150*, 1978, trans. Hilton C. Oswald (Minneapolis: Augsburg, 1989), 60.

[71]Matthew 27:34; John 2:17; 15:25; 19:29; Acts 1:20; Romans 11:29, 15:3.

[72]Marvin E. Tate, *Psalms 51-100*, WBC, ed. David A. Hubbard, vol. 20 (Waco, Tex.: Word, 1990), 194-95.

would be re-established (109:6-21) and God's people would be reassured of his love (109:21, 26).[73]

While David expressed his honest hatred for God's (and his) enemies, and asks for their downfall in Psalm 69, he ended his prayer like most imprecatory and lament psalms end, with hopeful confident praise to the God who can and will save his persecuted followers.

> But I am afflicted and in pain; may Your salvation, O God, set me *securely* on high. I will praise the name of God with song and magnify Him with thanksgiving. And it will please the LORD better than an ox *or* a young bull with horns and hoofs. The humble have seen *it and* are glad; you who seek God, let your heart revive. For the LORD hears the needy and does not despise His *who are* prisoners. Let heaven and earth praise Him, the seas and everything that moves in them. (Ps. 69:29-34)

There are two sections to Psalm 69, a lament (vv. 1-28), and a hymn of praise (vv. 29-36). The structure of the hymn is as follows:[74]

A. Prayer Out of Personal Need (vv. 1-4)
    B. Affirmation of God's Knowledge (v. 5)
        C. Disgrace for the Sake of God (vv. 6-12)
        C¹. Deliverance for the Sake of God's Servant (vv. 13-18)
    B¹. Affirmation of God's Knowledge (vv. 19-21)
A¹. Prayer for God's Judgment on the Wicked (vv. 22-28)

The title of the psalm says that it is 'of David.' Determining just what this means and the authorship of certain Psalms can be difficult.[75] Many commentators assume Psalm 69 to be post-

---

[73]Willem A. VanGemeren, *Psalms*, EBC, ed. Frank E. Gaebelein, vol. 5 (Grand Rapids: Zondervan, 1991), 831. (Author has added the Italics)

[74]This is the structure provided by VanGemeren, *Psalms*, 831.

[75]For an excellent discussion of determining authorship of the Psalms and interpreting their superscriptions, see VanGemeren, *Psalms*, 18-20, 33-37.

exilic. I agree with the traditional interpretation that assumes David is the author of Psalm 69 because (1) the superscript attributes it to him and (2) Paul says that David is the author when he quotes verse 22 in Romans 11:9: '*And David says,* "LET THEIR TABLE BECOME A SNARE AND A TRAP, AND A STUMBLING BLOCK AND A RETRIBUTION TO THEM." ' Calvin and Kidner also assume Davidic authorship.[76] To agree with Paul, and the title of the Psalm, brings us into 'the almost head-on clash between modern opinion and the testimony of the text itself—for the titles are part of the text, appearing in the Hebrew Bible as verse 1, or as part of it, wherever they occur.'[77] It seems best then to allow the text to represent the context the title ascribes to them rather than 'the un-wisdom of dismissing part of our data unheard.'[78]

Psalm 69 does not specify the historical context of the suffering and persecution that David was enduring. However, it does parallel the situation he found himself in as he was on the run and facing the unfair charges of Saul. If David is the author, we gain rich insight into David's psyche and worship linked to real life experience. 'If we are intended to share the heart-searchings of a man as exceptional and as sorely tried as David, we shall be the poorer if we insist on treating his works as anonymous and divorced from his eventful life.'[79]

David metaphorically describes his weary and desperate condition before his enemies: 'Save me, O God, for the waters have threatened my life. I have sunk in deep mire, and there is no foothold; I have come into deep waters, and a flood overflows me' (vv. 1-2). In the midst of his suffering, the weariness was intensified as he waited for the vindication of God who had yet to come to his rescue: 'I am weary with my crying; my throat is parched; my eyes fail while I wait for my God' (v. 3).

---

[76]John Calvin, *Commentary on the Book of Psalms*, trans. James Anderson (Grand Rapids: Baker, 1979), 54; Derek Kidner, *Psalms 1-72*, TOTC, ed. D. J. Wiseman, vol. 19 (Downers Grove, Ill.: InterVarsity, 1973), 16-17, 245.

[77]Kidner, *Psalms*, 17.

[78]Ibid.

[79]Ibid.

In his desperate condition, David felt helpless before his numerous enemies who hated him without due cause: 'Those who hate me without a cause are more than the hairs of my head; those who would destroy me are powerful, being wrongfully my enemies; what I did not steal, I then have to restore' (v. 4). David had a similar complaint in Psalm 38:19: 'But my enemies are vigorous *and* strong, and many are those *who hate me wrongfully.*'

Jesus experienced this same situation of being persecuted without warrant. 'But *they have done this* to fulfill the word that is written in their Law, "*THEY HATED ME WITHOUT A CAUSE*" ' (John 15:25). Jesus also told his disciples that this kind of unjust hatred will come to them from the world as well because 'all these things they will do to you for My name's sake, because they do not know the One who sent Me' (John 15:21). This kind of total identification between God and the believer is central to understanding the attitude behind an imprecatory psalm like Psalm 69. David's cause is God's cause. Because of this, to persecute him is to persecute God. God anointed David king and gave him the success that stoked Saul's evil jealousy. And now as David ran for his life, he expressed a godly hatred for all that opposed God's plan and will.

Although David identified himself with God's causes, he was not self-righteous, and never blurred the difference between God and himself. He recognized that he was innocent of the charges of his enemies, but he was not under the pretension that he had no sin in his life. He made this clear in verse 5: 'O God, it is You who knows my folly, and my wrongs are not hidden from You.' David's acknowledgment of his sin was not an admission that the persecution he was suffering was somehow justified by or caused by his sin. On the contrary, his devotion to God brought his difficulty. 'He suffers עָלֶיךָ (*'ālāy,* v. 7), in place of Yahweh—for Yahweh. His suffering is not the result of guilt (v. 4) but a result of this devotion and his "enthusiastic dedication" to Yahweh.'[80]

David was not only focused on his immediate condition. The welfare of God's faithful was on his mind as well. He asked that his miserable condition not be a cause of disgrace or shame to others who were likewise devoted to God. 'May those who wait for You not be ashamed through me, O Lord GOD of hosts; may those who seek You not be dishonored through me, O God of Israel.' His primary concern was for God's honor and the welfare of those devoted to him.

Not only was God's honor his main concern; his miserable condition was the result of his great devotion to God. He endured scorn and shame for the sake of the Lord. 'Because for Your sake I have borne reproach; dishonor has covered my face' (v. 7). 'The confession comes close to the notion that the petitioner suffers slander "for Yahweh," "in the place of Yahweh." '[81]

The sons of Korah and Jeremiah expressed this same perspective; that their suffering and persecution was done for God's sake.

♦ Psalm 44:22: But *for Your sake* we are killed all day long; we are considered as sheep to be slaughtered.[82]

♦ Jeremiah 15:15: You who know, O LORD, remember me, take notice of me, and take vengeance for me on my persecutors. Do not, in view of Your patience, take me away; know that *for Your sake* I endure reproach.

Godly human jealousy is the result of identifying with God and his causes to the point where you respond emotionally and behaviorally as he would in the face of a challenge to him or his ways. When one is living for God's kingdom, the persecution that comes as a result is endured 'for his sake.' 'What the

---

[80]Kraus, *Psalms*, 62.

[81]Ibid.

[82]Paul comforts his readers by reminding them that those devoted to God will suffer righteously. He quotes Psalm 44:22 to accomplish this: Just as it is written, 'FOR YOUR SAKE WE ARE BEING PUT TO DEATH ALL DAY LONG; WE WERE CONSIDERED AS SHEEP TO BE SLAUGHTERED' (Rom. 8:36).

righteous sufferer endured was a result of his obedience and zeal. If he had not been God's man he would not have reaped the unpopularity he did.'[83]

As we have seen, Jesus demands devotion to himself even if it will bring division and strife within one's own family. 'He who loves father or mother more than Me is not worthy of Me; and he who loves son or daughter more than Me is not worthy of Me' (Matt. 10:37). Indeed, Jesus himself experienced this rejection from his own family. 'For not even His brothers were believing in Him' (John 7:5). David, too, experienced this kind of familial alienation because of his devotion to Yahweh: 'I have become estranged from my brothers and an alien to my mother's sons' (v. 8).

> The Psalmist farther aggravates his complaint by the additional circumstance, that he was cruelly cast off by his own relations and friends; from which we are taught, that when by our devotedness to the cause of religion we cannot avoid exciting the displeasure of our brethren against us, it is our duty simply to follow God, and not to confer with flesh and blood.[84]

This response to being rejected by family was especially difficult in David's culture 'where the bonds of kinship and life in the family unit are fundamental. The picture is one of complete forsakenness.'[85]

David's persecution comes even from drunkards and others on the margin of society. 'Those who sit in the gate talk about me, and I *am* the song of the drunkards' (v. 12). And it also comes as David weeps, fasts, and endures scorn: 'While he prays and fasts on account of his adversity and the prevalent godlessness, people respond with laughter, mocking, and drinking songs (vv. 10-12).'[86] This is reminiscent of the

---

[83]Robert Alden, *Psalms: Songs of Dedication* (Chicago: Moody, 1975), 49.

[84]Calvin, *Psalms*, 54.

[85]J. W. Rogerson and J. W. McKay, *Psalms 51-100*, The Cambridge Bible Commentary, ed. P. R. Ackroyd, A. R. C. Leaney, and J. W. Packer (London: Cambridge University Press, 1977), 95.

mourning and weeping of the congregation in Numbers 25, when Zimri essentially mocked their condition with his sin. Phinehas, too, was consumed with קנא (*qna*) for the house of the Lord. The fasting and weeping of Phinehas and David were not primarily for their personal need, but 'rather for the sake of the house of Yahweh.'[87] A central message of the Bible, that is seldom heard today, is that devotion to God often brings greater immediate, temporal difficulty and pain. Indeed, '[l]oyalty to God leads to the cruelest isolation (v.8).'[88]

Jealousy for God's House

In verse 9, David recognized that a main reason for his persecution was found in his jealousy for God's house. 'For zeal (קנאת, *qin'at*) for Your house has consumed me, and the reproaches of those who reproach You have fallen on me.' Again, David expresses his close identification with God and his causes. His jealous passion for the 'house' of the Lord was based in 'his desire to uphold the honour of God.'[89] David was consumed by 'the zeal for the Divine glory by which true believers are animated.'[90]

Because I am assuming Davidic authorship, I am obviously assuming that 'your house' does not refer to the physical Temple, but rather to the broad 'household of faith.'[91] The house of the Lord represents the community of Yahweh. The things that most concern God consumed David. As Tate observes,

> The meaning of 'your house' can extend beyond the temple to involve the idea of the 'household' of Yahweh—the people of Yahweh. The context of the speaker's zealous action is unfocused,

---

[86]VanGemeren, *Psalms*, 456.

[87]Kraus, *Psalms*, 62.

[88]J. H. Eaton, *Psalms: Introduction and Commentary*, Torch Bible Commentary, ed. John Marsh and Alan Richardson (London: SCM, 1967), 176.

[89]A. A. Anderson, *The Book of Psalms*, NCBC, ed. Ronald E. Clements, vol. 1 (Grand Rapids: Eerdmans, 1972), 502.

[90]Calvin, *Psalms*, 54.

[91]Calvin (54), Anderson (502), and Tate (192) recognize the feasibility of this broader interpretation.

but the context suggests deep concern about the behavior of some in the community whose actions are contrary to those appropriate for the 'house' of God.[92]

God uses this same 'house' metaphor to describe his people in Jeremiah 12:7: 'I have *forsaken My house*, I have abandoned My inheritance; I have given *the beloved of My soul* into the hand of her enemies.'

For David, his 'unswerving devotion to God's house (or "household") has been the cause of his ruin.'[93] This devotion was only intensified when confronted with evildoers in his life. 'What is dear to the heart of the psalmist is the "house" of the Lord (v.9). He was so desirous of pleasing God in the face of ignominy that his "zeal" consumed him, like "a devouring flame."'[94] David 'burned with a holy zeal to maintain the Church and at the same time the glory of God, with which it is inseparably connected.'[95] David's jealousy for God's 'house' is not something incidental to his identity. When it was inflamed by circumstances that challenged God's ways, he was consumed 'to the point of extinction.'[96]

In the midst of his difficulty, David longed for the day when he could fulfill his purpose in life—to praise the name of his God. 'I will praise the *name of God* with song and magnify Him with thanksgiving' (Ps. 69:30).

Foreshadowing of Christ
The life of David has many similarities with one of the other jealous men we will look at in our study—Jesus. Jesus is often referred to in the New Testament as the Son of David.[97] Recognizing the fundamental connection between God and his human representatives such as David is vital to relating to God properly.

---

[92]Tate, *Psalms*, 196.
[93]Anderson, *Psalms*, 502.
[94]VanGemeren, *Psalms*, 457.
[95]Calvin, *Psalms*, 54.
[96]Tate, *Psalms*, 197.
[97]Matthew 1:1, 20; 9:27; 12:23; 15:22; 20:30, 31; 21:9, 15; 22:42; Mark 10:47, 48; 12:35; Luke 3:31; 18:38, 39.

[S]ince the days of David, Yahweh has revealed the fact that trust in him is concomitant with trust in his appointed *vassal* the Davidic king (Pss 2; 72; 89; 132). The Davidic king is his *instrument* of extending his kingdom to all the earth.[98]

The vital connection between David and Jesus in Psalm 69 is evident in the many passages that are quoted in the New Testament to describe events in the life of Christ.[99] And while the suffering of David for God's sake in Psalm 69 'made the psalm especially adaptable to Christ's ministry and passion,'[100] for our study, the most important of these New Testament quotations is where David's jealousy in verse 9 is remembered in the New Testament. This occurs in John 2:17: 'His disciples remembered that it was written, "ZEAL (ζῆλος, *zēlos*) FOR YOUR HOUSE WILL CONSUME ME." ' Jesus' cleansing of the temple brought about this remembrance of David's קנא (*qna*). For the disciples, Jesus' jealous passion for proper temple reverence and access brought to mind David's jealousy for Yahweh's house in the midst of persecution. 'The zeal that Jesus showed when He ran the merchandisers out of the Temple was a zeal, a jealousy, for God's house.'[101] It is not only the suffering of Christ that David foreshadows in Psalm 69. Perhaps even more important is the jealous loyalty to God that led Jesus to submit to the Father's will, and suffer shame and persecution. The messianic interpretation of this Psalm 'is in the form of an application to the life of devotion to God by the Lord Jesus Christ.'[102]

Like Phinehas before him, and Jesus after, David was motivated primarily by an intense jealousy on behalf of God's glory. This jealousy caused them to rise out of the apathy, ambivalence, cowardice, and idolatry of their communities, and boldly meet a challenge to the honor of their God. They

---

[98]VanGemeren, *Psalms*, 17.

[99]Matthew 27:34; John 2:17; 15:25; 19:29; Acts 1:20; Romans 11:29; 15:3.

[100]Tate, *Psalms*, 202.

[101]Alden, *Psalms*, 50.

[102]VanGemeren, *Psalms*, 17.

are also comparable to the next jealous man we will look at—
Elijah. David is indeed

> comparable to Elijah and other men of God in the OT who with
> radicality and severity—to the dismay of entire generations—
> made their appearance and to many seemed to be subverters.
> Enthusiasts do not arise on their own initiative. They think of
> themselves as called and ordained for their service, which
> excludes all purely personal interests. An intolerable burden rests
> upon them.[103]

Conclusions and Implications of David's Jealousy

As with Phinehas, there are limitations to the extent that David's
jealousy serves as an example to contemporary Christians.
One needs to consider David's role as King within a theocracy
before applying his example too quickly. His context, namely
a theocracy that was often at war, also determined how he
expressed his godly jealousy. These roles and contexts must be
considered when the expression of his godly jealousy is used
as an example. The internal emotional response to a challenge
to God's honor should remain consistent in each believer, but
the proper outward expression of it today will be very different
than it was for David. The Christian should feel jealous anger
when God or his people are mocked, but because his situation
and office is distinctly different than David's, picking up
stones is no longer the godly manifestation of this jealousy.
Like Phinehas, David never took the law into his own hands.
Rather, he acted within God's clear commands for his situation
as well as the office and calling God had given him.

So what *can* we take as an example from David's angry
cries for retribution as we find in Psalm 69? We have discussed
the nature and basis for imprecatory Psalms, like Psalm 69,
and saw that the angry appeal to God for vengeance is based in
deep identification with God and his purposes. To share God's
perspective will bring godly feelings of hatred toward evil

---

[103]Kraus, *Psalms*, 62.

and anything that opposes God. However we must realize that the appeals for vengeance are made to God, the one to whom vengeance belongs.

While David's context and role may serve to limit the degree he remains an example for the Christian, there are several ways that David's jealous example is thoroughly applicable today. One of these is his thoroughly theocentric motives. As we read the key jealousy passages from his life it is obvious that God and his honor was the goal of his life. This is at the core of what made him 'a man after God's own heart.' Reputation and rewards were not his ultimate goal in the battles he fought. He was not seeking rewards or acclaim. Even the success of the armies was not the final objective. He fought, refrained from killing Saul, and suffered persecution, all for the sake of the honor of the name of Yahweh. David's ultimate goal was 'that all the earth may know that there is a God in Israel' (1 Sam. 17:46). The honor and glory of God before the nations drove David to meet the challenge before him. Jealous aversion to any rival to God made David the standard by which all kings after him were compared.

Another important aspect of David's jealousy that should be incorporated into our understanding of how this emotion functions is found in his refusal to kill Saul. His jealousy for God's anointed representative led him to risk his own life and allow for continued persecution for himself. At times, jealous respect for God's honor will cause a believer to refuse to defend himself or improve his circumstances.

David also showed us that when one is God's representative, this role might incur suffering and persecution, even from within one's own family. His jealousy 'consumed' him inwardly, as wicked men apparently thwarted God's ways, and outwardly as they brought reproach on him. A central aspect of this suffering shows that at times one may become a lone voice for righteousness. Like Phinehas, David was alone in his jealousy before Goliath, and he became a righteous, persecuted minority as he was on the run from Saul. An important message of the Bible, that is seldom heard today, is that devotion to God often brings greater immediate, temporal difficulty, pain, and alienation.

David's role as a righteous, persecuted sufferer, as we saw in Psalm 69, is one of the key ways he foreshadows the Messiah. Like Phinehas, David stands as one who points us to Jesus in his godly jealousy for God's honor. This is also true of another jealous leader of God's people – the prophet Elijah.

Elijah

Elijah is another major figure in the Bible who expressed godly jealousy on behalf of God's honor. This is what motivated him to risk his life and take on Ahab and the 450 prophets of Baal. As he fled for his life from Jezebel, after killing the prophets of Baal on Mount Carmel, in his despondence he revealed the emotion that was behind his bravery in confronting the prophets. He cried to God,

> I have been very jealous (קַנֹּא קִנֵּאתִי *qannö' qinnë°'tî*) for the LORD, the God of hosts; for the people of Israel have forsaken thy covenant, thrown down thy altars, and slain thy prophets with the sword; and I, even I only, am left; and they seek my life, to take it away. (1 Kings 19:10, RSV)

God then assured Elijah that he was not alone in his jealousy for God's honor. He tells him to go and anoint Hazael, Jehu, and Elisha as his successors who will carry on his jealousy for the honor of God and the fidelity of his people. God also lets Elijah know that he has reserved 7000 in Israel who have stood with him and not succumbed to playing the harlot for Baal.

Elijah the man

Who is this jealous prophet of God from Tishbe? Perhaps his name tells us something about his character. אֵלִיָּהוּ (*'ëliyyä°hû*, Elijah) is a name that expresses jealousy for God's honor. It literally means, 'my God is Yahweh' or 'Yah is God.'

For a man of Elijah's stature, he appears for the first time rather suddenly, prophetically warning King Ahab about an impending drought (1 Kings 17:1). After his announcement, Elijah followed God's command and retreated to a hiding-place by the brook Cherith, beyond Jordan. For the two years of famine, God miraculously fed him by ravens and then the widow of Zarephath. During this time, Elijah brought the widow's son back to life (1 Kings 17:2-24). After these two years Elijah met Obadiah who was sent by Ahab to find land to graze his cattle. He told Obadiah he wanted to meet with the King. This confrontation initiated the distinctive event in Elijah's life.

The Confrontation with Ahab
This story of Elijah's confrontation with the prophets of Baal spoke powerfully to an exilic audience that was surrounded by temptations of syncretism.

After developing a reputation as a difficult man, Elijah had been able to elude Ahab's pursuit. When he finally decided to have a showdown with Ahab, he promised Obadiah that he would present himself to Ahab. He makes this promise by saying, 'As the LORD of hosts lives, before whom I stand, I will surely show myself to him today' (1 Kings 18:15). This is the first time יְהוָה צְבָאוֹת (*yhwh('ädönäy) cübä'ôt*, "Lord of hosts") is used in Kings and it is significant as Elijah begins the confrontation with Baal. This name for God was particularly associated with the covenant God of Israel. All that Israel had come to learn of the character of the God she served was expressed in that title.

> LORD *of Hosts* expressed therefore the character and demands of Yahweh the God of Israel, and embodied the emotional force of the loyalty which Israel felt to her own history, tradition and forefathers.[104]

---

[104]J. Robinson, *The First Book of Kings*, CBC (London: CUP, 1972), 206.

On meeting Elijah, Ahab insinuated that the prophet was the cause of the drought that had overtaken the land by calling him 'you troubler of Israel.' Elijah's brash reply gave the real cause of the famine. 'I have not troubled Israel, but you and your father's house *have,* because you have forsaken the commandments of the LORD and you have followed the Baals' (1 Kings 18:18). What had incurred God's wrath was the idolatry of Ahab and the kings that preceded him. The text is not specific about which Baal was the source of the apostasy. It could have been Melqart, Baal Shamem, the local Baal of Carmel, or the Canaanite god Baal Hadad. This lack of specificity is important.

> Indeed the narrative's refusal to be precise is itself testimony to the worthlessness of all other gods. They are lumped together and dismissed. To specify precisely which Baal failed at Carmel would dilute the sweeping condemnation of them all.[105]

Elijah then offers a challenge to Baal. He asks for the people of Israel,[106] and 450 prophets of Baal, and 400 prophets of Asherah,[107] to meet on Mount Carmel. It was important for the people of Israel to be present at the showdown because 'it is their exclusive loyalty to Yahweh that is at stake.'[108]

The Confrontation with the People

When the gathering comes together, Elijah had a stern rebuke and challenge for the people of Israel.

> Elijah came near to all the people and said, 'How long *will* you hesitate between two opinions? If the LORD is God, follow Him; but if Baal, follow him.' But the people did not answer him a word. (1 Kings 18:21)

---

[105]Richard D. Nelson, *First and Second Kings*, Interpretation, ed. Patrick D. Miller (Atlanta: John Knox, 1987), 116.

[106]The text says 'all Israel' was summoned to Mount Carmel (vv. 19, 21). This most likely means key representatives, or an official assembly of the nation. Robinson (208) and Wiseman (168) hold this view as well.

[107]For an unknown reason the prophets of Asherah are not mentioned in the rest of the narrative.

[108]Nelson, *First and Second Kings*, 116.

Elijah accuses the people of wavering between two opinions. The expression, פֹּסְחִים עַל־שְׁתֵּי הַסְּעִפִּים (*pösHîm `al-šTê hassü`iPPîm*) literally means 'to bestride two branches.' It can also mean 'to limp,' inferring here that the Israelites are 'walking unsteadily and uncertainly because one leg walked for Baal and the other for Yahweh.'[109]

The silence of the people is like Ahab's passivity in the events of the challenge. He makes no decisions, and does not seem to take a stand of any kind. The silence of the people, and Ahab's ambivalence 'is a searing condemnation of any reader who seeks to hide from God's demand for commitment behind the screen of non-involvement, apathy, or the daily struggle to find grass for the horses.'[110] The passive infidelity of the people and Ahab is as bad as active rebellion. The result is the same. In this narrative, 'only Elijah and the prophets of Baal have any conviction.'[111]

The Confrontation with the Prophets of Baal
The point of the contest with the prophets of Baal was to determine the identity of the true God, by allowing him to show his acceptance of one of the sacrifices by starting the fire to consume it himself.

> Then Elijah said to the people, 'I alone am left a prophet of the LORD, but Baal's prophets are 450 men. Now let them give us two oxen; and let them choose one ox for themselves and cut it up, and place it on the wood, but put no fire *under it;* and I will prepare the other ox and lay it on the wood, and I will not put a fire *under it.* Then you call on the name of your god, and I will call on the name of the LORD, and the God who answers by fire, He is God.' And all the people said, 'That is a good idea.' (1 Kings 18:22-24)

Elijah was not primarily out to prove that Ahab was the troubler of Israel rather than himself, 'but to put before the eyes of the

---

[109]Robinson, *The First Book of Kings*, 209.
[110]Ibid., 121.
[111]Paul R. House, *1, 2 Kings*, NAC, ed. Ray E. Clendenen, vol. 8 (New York: Broadman and Holman, 1995), 219.

whole nation a convincing practical proof of the sole deity of
Jehovah and of the nothingness of the Baals...to give a death
blow to idolatry in Israel.'[112]

The Mocking of the Prophets
The prophets of Baal went to great lengths to invoke a response
from their god:

> Then they took the ox which was given them and they prepared
> it and called on the name of Baal from morning until noon
> saying, 'O Baal, answer us.' But there was no voice and no one
> answered. And they leaped about the altar which they made.
> (1 Kings 18:26)

They danced or limped around the altar. The same verb Elijah
used to describe the wavering of the people in verse 21 (פסח
PsH) is used here to describe the gyrations of the prophets.
Elijah mocks the prophets by describing their way of relating
to their god, so that it was obvious that they treat him as if he
were a mere human.

> It came about at noon, that Elijah mocked them and said, 'Call
> out with a loud voice, for he is a god; either he is occupied or
> gone aside, or is on a journey, or perhaps he is asleep and needs
> to be awakened.' (1 Kings 18:27)

Elijah suggests that perhaps Baal is asleep. It was absurd for
Israelites to imagine that Yahweh would ever be susceptible
to that limitation. 'He will not allow your foot to slip; He who
keeps you will not slumber. Behold, He who keeps Israel will
neither slumber nor sleep' (Ps. 121:3-4).

While we do not know for sure, 'the common suggestion that
"he has gone aside" refers to Baal's being preoccupied with a

---

[112]C. F. Keil, *The Books of the Kings*, trans. James Martin, Commentary on the
Old Testament in Ten Volumes, ed. C. F. Keil and F. Delitzsch (Grand Rapids:
Eerdmans, reprint 1982), 245.

bowel movement certainly captures Elijah's insulting tone!'[113] His scathing ridicule makes a joke out of the prophets and their god. James Montgomery suggests that Elijah's mocking of the Baal prophets in this way 'is the raciest comment ever made on Pagan mythology.'[114]

Elijah's mocking points out major deficiencies in the prophet's conception of their god. In contrast to the perfections of Yahweh, Baal was treated as if he is limited like a mere human. Their rituals betrayed a conception of Baal that lacked omniscience, omnipresence, and omnipotence.

Mockery is not usually considered a godly activity. However, idolatry and wickedness by the creature deserve to be derisively mocked by a holy Creator. When men forget the Creator-creature distinction, and they rise up in their *hubris* to challenge Almighty God in some way, God derides this attitude as absurd folly.

♦ Exodus 10:2: and that you may tell in the hearing of your son, and of your grandson, *how I made a mockery of the Egyptians* and how I performed My signs among them, that you may know that I am the LORD.

♦ Psalm 2:4: He who sits in the heavens laughs, the Lord scoffs at them.

♦ Psalm 59:8: But You, O LORD, laugh at them; You scoff at all the nations.

♦ Proverbs 1:26: I will also laugh at your calamity; I will mock when your dread comes.

God scoffs at the vain attempts of prideful men to challenge him in any way. Idolatry also deserves to be jealously mocked by godly men on God's behalf. Because Elijah saw the efforts of the Baal prophets from the perspective of a man who was miraculously fed by Yahweh for two years, and was enabled by God to raise a boy back to life, he recognized the absolute

---

[113]Nelson, *First and Second Kings*, 117.

[114]James A. Montgomery and Henry Snyder Gehman, *The Book of Kings*, ICC (Edinburgh: T & T Clark, 1960), 302.

power of Yahweh and the absurd emptiness of their endeavors. Elijah's mocking brings to mind other prophets, derisively pointing out the foolishness of idolatry.

♦ Isaiah 44:14-17: Surely he cuts cedars for himself, and takes a cypress or an oak and raises *it* for himself among the trees of the forest. He plants a fir, and the rain makes it grow. Then it becomes *something* for a man to burn, so he takes one of them and warms himself; he also makes a fire to bake bread. He also makes a god and worships it; he makes it a graven image and falls down before it. Half of it he burns in the fire; over *this* half he eats meat as he roasts a roast and is satisfied. He also warms himself and says, 'Aha! I am warm, I have seen the fire.' But the rest of it he makes into a god, his graven image. He falls down before it and worships; he also prays to it and says, 'Deliver me, for you are my god.'

♦ Jeremiah 10:3-6: For the customs of the peoples are delusion; because it is wood cut from the forest, the work of the hands of a craftsman with a cutting tool. They decorate *it* with silver and with gold; they fasten it with nails and with hammers so that it will not totter. *Like a scarecrow in a cucumber field are they, and they cannot speak; they must be carried, because they cannot walk*! Do not fear them, for they can do no harm, nor can they do any good.' There is none like You, O LORD; You are great, and great is Your name in might.

♦ Jeremiah 10:14-15: Every man is stupid, devoid of know-ledge; every goldsmith is put to shame by his idols; for his molten images are deceitful, and there is no breath in them. *They are worthless, a work of mockery*; in the time of their punishment they will perish.

♦ Habakkuk 2:18-20: What profit is the idol when its maker has carved it, *or* an image, a teacher of falsehood? For *its* maker trusts in his *own* handiwork when he fashions speechless idols. *Woe to him who says to a piece of wood,*

'Awake!' To a mute stone, 'Arise!' And that is *your* teacher? Behold, it is overlaid with gold and silver, And there is no breath at all inside it. But the LORD is in His holy temple. Let all the earth be silent before Him.

♦ Revelation 9:20: The rest of mankind, who were not killed by these plagues, did not repent of the works of their hands, so as not to worship demons, and the idols of gold and of silver and of brass and of stone and of wood, *which can neither see nor hear nor walk.*

Elijah's mocking only intensified the efforts of the prophets; thereby further validating Elijah's assessment of the impotence of Baal.

So they cried with a loud voice and cut themselves according to their custom with swords and lances until the blood gushed out on them. When midday was past, they raved until the time of the offering of the *evening* sacrifice; but there was no voice, no one answered, and no one paid attention. (1 Kings 18:28-29)

Twice, the narrative emphatically states that there was no response at all from Baal.

♦ 1 Kings 18:26b: But there was no voice and no one answered.

♦ 1 Kings 18:29b: But there was no voice, no one answered, and no one paid attention.

The silence of Baal proves that the silence of Ahab and the people of Israel in their unwillingness to choose to follow Yahweh is foolish unfaithfulness. "What seems at first to be a battle between two competing gods turns out instead to be a contest between God and an empty delusion."[115]

Elijah's Offering
Elijah rebuilt an altar using twelve stones to represent the tribes of Israel.

---

[115]Nelson, *First and Second Kings*, 121.

Then Elijah said to all the people, 'Come near to me.' So all the people came near to him. And he repaired the altar of the LORD which had been torn down. Elijah took twelve stones according to the number of the tribes of the sons of Jacob, to whom the word of the LORD had come, saying, 'Israel shall be your name.' So with the stones he built an altar in the name of the LORD, and he made a trench around the altar, large enough to hold two measures of seed. (1 Kings 18:30-32)

The altar was rebuilt in sight of the people. The changing of Jacob's name by the word of the Lord was recalled, and it was done 'in the name of the LORD.' This object lesson served to remind the people regarding the covenant that made them God's people, and demanded absolute loyalty to Yahweh. Perhaps he uses 'sons of Jacob' rather than 'sons of Israel' as a rebuke for Israel's apostasy.[116]

Elijah then had the people soak the altar in water three times. By doing this he went to great lengths to demonstrate the miraculous nature of God's acceptance of it.

The main purpose of this sacrifice was to demonstrate the power of the living God, and the impotency of the non-existent Baal. In demonstrating this, the objective was to restore undivided loyalty in the hearts of God's people. Elijah's simple prayer before his sacrifice reveals this goal. 'Answer me, O LORD, answer me, that this people may know that You, O LORD, are God, and *that* You have turned their heart back again' (1 Kings 18:37).

'Then the fire of the LORD fell and consumed the burnt offering and the wood and the stones and the dust, and licked up the water that was in the trench' (1 Kings 18:38). The fire from heaven consumed not only the sacrifice, but even the stones and soil around it. We saw in chapter 2 that God often expresses his anger and power through fire.[117] Fire 'is the

---

[116]Donald J. Wiseman, *1 and 2 Kings*, TOTC, ed. Donald J. Wiseman, vol. 9 (Downers Grove, Ill.: InterVarsity, 1993), 170.

[117]For example: Genesis 19:24; Exodus 9:23; Numbers 11:1; 16:35; 1 Kings 18:23; 2 Kings 1:10; Matthew 13:12; Mark 9:43; Acts 2:19; Revelation 14:6.

weapon of Yahweh the divine warrior.'[118] With this awesome and sudden display of divine power, there was no doubt that God responded to Elijah's simple prayer.

The Response of the People
The previously silent, non-committal people were struck with a fear of the Lord, and responded with sudden assurance of Yahweh's sole identity as God. When all the people saw the fire from heaven consume the sacrifice and the altar with it, they fell on their faces; and they said, 'The LORD, He is God; the LORD, He is God.' (1 Kings 18:39)

Elijah's objective was accomplished as the people expressed their recaptured devotion to Yahweh. They finally were compelled to agree with Elijah and 'accept the incompatibility of divided loyalties.'[119] The emphatic response of the people, 'The LORD, He is God; the LORD, He is God,'[120] reflects a central affirmation of God's people when they are at their best. We find this jealous affirmation throughout the Old Testament.

♦ Deuteronomy 4:35: To you it was shown that you might know that the LORD, He is God; there is no other besides Him.

♦ Deuteronomy 4:39: Know therefore today, and take it to your heart, that the LORD, He is God in heaven above and on the earth below; there is no other.

♦ Deuteronomy 7:9: Know therefore that the LORD your God, He is God, the faithful God, who keeps His covenant and His loving-kindness to a thousandth generation with those who love Him and keep His commandments.

♦ 1 Kings 8:60: so that all the peoples of the earth may know that the LORD is God; there is no one else.

♦ Psalm 95:7: For He is our God, and we are the people of His pasture and the sheep of His hand.

---

[118]Nelson, *First and Second Kings*, 118.

[119]Ibid., 121.

[120]הָאֱלֹהִים הוּא יְהוָה *yhwh('ädönäy) hû'hä'élöhîm* conveys the same meaning as Elijah's name.

♦ Psalm 100:3: Know that the L<small>ORD</small> Himself is God; it is He who has made us, and not we ourselves; *we are* His people and the sheep of His pasture.

♦ Psalm 105:7: He is the L<small>ORD</small> our God; His judgments are in all the earth.

The Killing of the Prophets

The contest with the prophets of Baal ended in a bloody killing, as did the jealous action of Phinehas and David.

> Then Elijah said to them, 'Seize the prophets of Baal; do not let one of them escape.' So they seized them; and Elijah brought them down to the brook Kishon, and slew them there. (1 Kings 18:40)

The representatives of the apostasy were slaughtered to purge the land from their influence. Like Phinehas and David, Elijah's jealousy led him to kill the leaders of the apostasy. It is important that we realize that all of these men acted in accordance with God's clear commands. In killing the prophets of Baal, Elijah acted 'in accordance with Deuteronomistic principles.'[121] The severe treatment of anyone who leads the people into idolatry is clearly proscribed in the law:

> If you hear in one of your cities, which the L<small>ORD</small> your God is giving you to live in, *anyone* saying *that* some worthless men have gone out from among you and have seduced the inhabitants of their city, saying, 'Let us go and serve other gods' (whom you have not known), then you shall investigate and search out and inquire thoroughly. If it is true *and* the matter established that this abomination has been done among you, you shall surely strike the inhabitants of that city with the edge of the sword, utterly destroying it and all that is in it and its cattle with the edge of the sword. (Deut. 13:12-15)

The prophets of Baal suffered the 'necessary retribution, ordered by Elijah as the "new Moses" on behalf of God, against false

---

[121]Nelson, *First and Second Kings*, 118.

prophets as decreed in Deuteronomy (13:5, 13-18; 17:2-5) following the action of Moses and Phinehas (Num. 25:1-13).'[122] However, the example of these jealous men should never be used to excuse violence today. 'Christians view idolatry as no less sinful, but see total judgment as reserved for the final Day.'[123]

After the killing of the prophets the drought is coming to an end and so Ahab celebrated. Elijah, on the other hand, found solitude on the top of Mount Carmel. 'So Ahab went up to eat and drink. But Elijah went up to the top of Carmel; and he crouched down on the earth and put his face between his knees' (1 Kings 18:42). I agree with Keil who interprets this action of Elijah to mean that he assumed an 'attitude of deep absorption in God.'[124] He is showing the emotional and spiritual effects of an intense confrontation with evil. It is also likely that it was here that he prays for God to send rain.

> Elijah was a man with a nature like ours, and he prayed earnestly that it would not rain, and it did not rain on the earth for three years and six months. Then he prayed again, and the sky poured rain and the earth produced its fruit. (James 5:17-18)

The drought ends in a way similar to how the plague in Numbers 25 ended when Phinehas made atonement for the people. 'The Mount Carmel contest, as Elijah's prayer pointed out (vv. 36-37), forced the people to choose Yahweh over Baal and to turn their backs on the apostasy that occasioned the drought.'[125]

The contest with the prophets of Baal powerfully captures the central themes of Kings and also of salvation history as a whole.

> Yahweh is truly and exclusively God. God punishes apostasy, in this case by drought; but God also rewards fidelity, as evidenced by the rainstorm that follows the people's return to faith.[126]

---

[122]Wiseman, *Kings*, 171.
[123]Ibid., 170.
[124]Keil, *Kings*, 251.
[125]Nelson, *First and Second Kings*, 119.
[126]Ibid.

These themes are intended to motivate devotion to Yahweh as the only true God. Idolatry is portrayed as the farcical nonsense it is. Religious pluralism and syncretism are denounced in no uncertain terms. 'The point of the narrative is not just that Yahweh is the God of Israel, but that Yahweh is God, period.'[127]

The Persecution of Jezebel

Jezebel reacted to Elijah's victory, not by bowing her knee to Yahweh and proclaiming that he alone is God, but by becoming further entrenched in her apostasy. She vows by her gods that Elijah will suffer the same demise as her prophets. 'Then Jezebel sent a messenger to Elijah, saying, "So may the gods do to me and even more, if I do not make your life as the life of one of them by tomorrow about this time" ' (1 Kings 19:2). This vow made by her gods shows us that Jezebel was a primary catalyst in the apostasy of Baal worship.

Elijah responded to Jezebel's threat by running away—discouraged and disillusioned. All of his jealous action, and God's miraculous power seemed to have only offered temporary victory.

> And he was afraid (or he saw) and arose and ran for his life and came to Beersheba, which belongs to Judah, and left his servant there. But he himself went a day's journey into the wilderness, and came and sat down under a juniper tree; and he requested for himself that he might die, and said, 'It is enough; now, O LORD, take my life, for I am not better than my fathers.' (1 Kings 19:3-4)

In verse 3, the LXX, Mss, G, Syr, and Vg have וַיִּרָא (*wayya°r'*) 'and he was afraid,' while the MT reading is וַיַּרְא (*wayyar'*) 'and he saw.' Most modern commentators follow the reading of the LXX and believe that the MT reading is an ideological attempt to reconcile the bold and confident Elijah of Mount Carmel with the fearful Elijah of 19:3.[128] Of course if one does

---

[127]Ibid., 120.
[128]Eg. Rice (157), Jones (329), House (222), Montgomery (312), DeVries (232).

not see this narrative as a literary unit, there is no difficulty explaining the discrepancy.[129] While the manuscript evidence is debatable, I agree with Keil who suggests that the 'and he was afraid' reading is based on 'erroneous conjecture.'[130] Wiseman also believes that the 'he saw' reading is an equally valid reading,[131] and it certainly fits the narrative and character of Elijah better. It is difficult to imagine that this incredibly jealous, courageous, faithful, theocentric prophet suddenly becomes so fearful of Jezebel's vain threat after being so bold and confident in God's power. It does not seem that fear of preserving his own life is his main concern, for he asks God to take his life in verse 4 and could have fled to the protection of Judah rather than flee to the wilderness to pour out his heart to his God.[132] It is more likely that the exhausted, discouraged prophet is consumed by his jealousy for God's honor like David in Psalm 69, and went into the desert 'to commit his soul or his life to the Lord his God in the solitude of the desert, and see what He would determine concerning him.'[133] Like David in Psalm 69, Elijah is a righteous sufferer who is being been persecuted for his jealousy for God's honor, and is consumed by the frustration of the persistence of evildoers. The people had forsaken the Lord in spite of his miraculous revelation. It is not only Ahab and Jezebel that failed to respond with loyalty to Yahweh, but apparently the response of the people on Mount Carmel was short-lived as well.

> He said, 'I have been very zealous for the LORD, the God of hosts; for the sons of Israel have forsaken Your covenant, torn down Your altars and killed Your prophets with the sword. And *I alone am left*; and they seek my life, to take it away.' (1 Kings 19:10)

---

[129]DeVries believes that Chapters 18 and 19 are independent narratives. Simon J. DeVries, *1 Kings*, WBC, ed. John Watts, vol. 12 (Waco: Word, 1985), 235.

[130]Keil, *Kings*, 253.

[131]Wiseman, *Kings*, 172.

[132]Keil, *Kings*, 253.

[133]Ibid.

God does not contradict Elijah's assessment of the overall failure of the people to maintain their commitment to the Lord. Elijah was assured that there was a faithful remnant preserved by the Lord, but it does seem that the people had not stayed true to their commitment on Carmel.

> One can well imagine what thoughts he must have had about the resistance of the human heart to God and the fickleness of the people who on Mt. Carmel had confessed 'The Lord he is God; the Lord, he is God.'[134]

Elijah's reaction in chapter 19 should be seen as expressing weariness and frustration at being greatly jealous for God's honor without seeing lasting results in the nation. Godly men often feel frustrated and isolated in carrying out their prophetic role among a stiff-necked people. We can hardly think of one great leader of God's people who has not experienced this kind of frustrating and lonely despondence in the midst of a corrupt people who refuse to respond to God's revelation of himself. When he asks God to take his life because he was no better than his fathers, he was in effect saying, 'I have worked and endured enough, and deserve no longer life than my fathers.'[135]

After God miraculously took care of his physical needs, Elijah continues his journey until he arrives at a place packed with theological significance.

> So he arose and ate and drank, and went in the strength of that food forty days and forty nights to Horeb, the mountain of God. Then he came there to a cave and lodged there. (1 Kings 19:8-9a)

Elijah's flight to Horeb (Sinai) is fraught with symbolism, and in many ways is similar to Moses' encounter with God at Sinai. That it took him forty days to arrive recalls the forty days Moses spent on Sinai meeting with God and receiving the covenant

---

[134]Gene Rice, *A Commentary on the Book of 1 Kings*, ITC, ed. Fredrick Carlson Holmgren (Grand Rapids: Eerdmans, 1990), 159.

[135]Keil, *Kings*, 254.

commands that Elijah had just jealously defended. He fled to the place where God established the nation and covenant that now seemed at the brink of its demise. It is here that Yahweh met with Moses and revealed his jealous character as 'the God whose name is jealous' (Exod. 34:14). Elijah's going into a cave is similar to Moses' encounter with Yahweh when Moses needed assurance of his continued presence (Exod. 33:21).[136] It was in a cave at Sinai that God gave that assurance by proclaiming his name and giving a glimpse of his glory to Moses. Elijah's flight seems more than just an emotional or psychological break; it is more likely a theological quest for divine assurance and direction in the thick of a spiritual battle.

Elijah's Jealousy
God twice asked Elijah why he had come to Horeb. Both times his answer was the same. His exceeding jealousy on behalf of God seemed to have come to naught, his life was in danger, and he feels alone in his jealousy.

> Behold, the word of the LORD *came* to him, and He said to him, 'What are you doing here, Elijah?' He said, 'I have been very zealous (קַנֹּא קִנֵּאתִי, *qannö' qinnë°'tî*)[137] for the LORD, the God of hosts; for the sons of Israel have forsaken Your covenant, torn down Your altars and killed Your prophets with the sword. And I alone am left; and they seek my life, to take it away.' (1 Kings 19:9b-10)

---

[136]Robinson, *1 Kings*, 219.

[137]Older versions translated קִנֵּאתִי קַנֹּא (*qannö' qinnë°'tî*) as 'very jealous' (KJV, ASV, RSV, WEB, RWB, Darby), while more recent translations opt for the more general 'very zealous' (NIV, NAS, NASB, NRS, NKJV). Jones (331) and Rice (158) also translate קִנֵּאתִי קַנֹּא (*qannö' qinnë°'tî*) 'very jealous.' DeVries opts for 'furiously zealous,' Devries, *Kings*, 233, and Gray prefers 'very fanatic,' Gray, *Kings*, 406. I see no reason to use the more vague 'zeal' or 'fanatic,' when jealous conveys the situation much more accurately. The conditions for jealousy are clearly present. There is a lover (Yahweh), a beloved (Israel), a rival (Baal), infidelity with that rival (Baal worship), and a strong emotional display against that infidelity (the challenge on Mt. Carmel). Other key concepts indicating the jealousy motif are present as well: idolatry, sexual imagery (v. 18), covenant themes, and divine anger.

Elijah's answer gives us significant insight into the emotional
motivation and 'state of his inner being.'[138] The driving
emotion that drove Elijah's courageous actions on Carmel was
jealousy on God's behalf. Elijah described his inner disposition
in his confrontation with the prophets of Baal as being צְבָאוֹת
קַנֹּא קִנֵּאתִי לַיהוָה אֱלֹהֵי (*qannö' qinnë°'tî lyhwh(la'dönäy) 'élöhê
cübä'ôt,* 'very jealous for the LORD, the God of hosts') and
his despondence was because he believed that he was alone in
being 'enthusiastically and exclusively devoted' to Yahweh.[139]
The main issue for Elijah was the honor of Yahweh expressed
through the covenant fidelity of his people. We have pointed
out the similarities between Elijah's experience at Horeb
and Moses' at Sinai. It has been suggested that the use of קִנֹּא
(*qannō'*) here is a deliberate attempt to bring to mind the
jealous God of Sinai in Exodus 20:5 and Deuteronomy 4:24.[140]
Elijah acted on behalf of God, to bring about loyalty to the
demands of the first and second commandments. The covenant
between Yahweh and his people required exclusive fidelity, and
godly men react with God's jealousy whenever that covenant is
violated. Elijah was God's jealous representative on Carmel.

> [T]he particular covenantal relationship of people and Yahweh
> was the essence of the faith of which Elijah was the protagonist
> against the broad universalism which Jezebel sought to promote
> in the name of Baal.[141]

Elijah sought to inspire this covenant faithfulness on Carmel.
And the threat of Jezebel, the apathy of Ahab, and the continued
apostasy of the people, led Elijah to consider 'his efforts there
to have been in vain and the forces of Baal to have been
victorious.'[142]

---

[138]Rice, *Kings*, 158.

[139]Wiseman *Kings*, 173.

[140]R. A. Carlson, 'Élie À l'Horeb,' *Vetus Testamentum* 19 (1969): 432.

[141]John Gray, *1 & 2 Kings*, ed. Peter Ackroyd, et al., OTL (Philadelphia:
Westminster, 1964), 410.

[142]Rice, *Kings*, 158.

I seriously doubt that the discouragement and depression that Elijah was experiencing when he fled from Jezebel was the result of excessive *hubris* as Hubbard suggests.[143] Rather, this jealousy 'recalls to mind the zeal of Phinehas which put an end to the whoredom of the sons of Israel with the daughters of Moab.'[144] Elijah's jealousy was godly and sincere, and expressed on behalf of Yahweh.

> But whereas Phinehas received the promise of an everlasting priesthood for his zeal, Elijah had seen so little fruit from his zeal against the worshippers of Baal, that they actually sought his life.[145]

The Jealous Remnant

To encourage Elijah, God gives him a sense of his presence and assures him that he is not alone in his jealousy. Elisha and Jehu will take the baton from Elijah and continue his jealous efforts for the honor of Yahweh among his people.

> The LORD said to him, 'Go, return on your way to the wilderness of Damascus, and when you have arrived, you shall anoint Hazael king over Aram; and Jehu the son of Nimshi you shall anoint king over Israel; and Elisha the son of Shaphat of Abel-meholah you shall anoint as prophet in your place. It shall come about, the one who escapes from the sword of Hazael, Jehu shall put to death, and the one who escapes from the sword of Jehu, Elisha shall put to death. Yet I will leave 7,000 in Israel, all the knees that have not bowed to Baal and every mouth that has not kissed him.' (1 Kings 19:15-18)

Elisha took Elijah's mantle and carried on his jealous ministry against apostasy. Jehu was indeed jealous for God's honor. When he went to wipe out Ahab's entire family, he asked

---

[143]R. L. Hubbard, *First and Second Kings*, EBC, ed. Frank E. Gabelein. (Grand Rapids: Zondervan, 1991), 234. 'His God-given successes had fostered an inordinate pride (cf. vv. 4, 10, 14) that had made him take his own importance too seriously.'

[144]Keil, *Kings*, 256.

[145]Ibid., 257.

Jehonadab to come to witness his jealousy for God. 'He said, "Come with me and see my zeal for the LORD (בְּקִנְאָתִי לַיהוָה *Büqin'ä tî lyhwh(la'dönäy)*)" ' (2 Kings 10:16). In response to Joram, he expressed his intolerance for idolatry. 'When Joram saw Jehu, he said, "Is it peace, Jehu?" And he answered, "What peace, so long as the harlotries of your mother Jezebel and her witchcrafts are so many?" ' For his jealousy, Jehu received a great blessing from the Lord.

> The LORD said to Jehu, 'Because you have done well in executing what is right in My eyes, *and* have done to the house of Ahab according to all that *was* in My heart, your sons of the fourth generation shall sit on the throne of Israel.' (2 Kings 10:30)

However, Jehu also stands as an example of jealousy that begins as a godly emotion but is then taken to an extreme and expressed in ungodly ways. His brutality in slaughtering idolaters of the land incurred God's judgment:

> And the LORD said to him, 'Name him Jezreel; for yet a little while, and I will punish the house of Jehu for the bloodshed of Jezreel, and I will put an end to the kingdom of the house of Israel.' (Hosea 1:4)

In addition to Elisha and Jehu, God assures Elijah that he is far from alone in his godly jealousy because the Lord has preserved a faithful remnant who had remained faithful to their divine husband. There were 'seven thousand others who are loyal and who share the responsibility for God's cause.'[146] Although the faithful remnant is outnumbered by the masses of adulterers,[147] it is obvious that God is certain that they will be able to maintain enough of a presence so that their significance will be felt, and his purposes will prevail.

---

[146]Rice, *Kings*, 163.

[147]Wiseman believes that 7000 may by symbolic of a perfect and significant number. Wiseman, *Kings*, 174.

The physical or sexual imagery so often employed in jealous expression is used in describing the pure state of the 7000. They are those who have not bowed their knees to or kissed Baal with their mouths. Bowing to and kissing Baal may be metaphorical, but probably has literal meaning as well. 'Worshipers kissed images of the gods to show their devotion.'[148] Hosea sheds light on this practice of kissing the idol that is the object of veneration.

And now they sin more and more, and make for themselves molten images, idols skillfully made from their silver, all of them the work of craftsmen. They say of them, 'Let the men who sacrifice *kiss the calves!*' (Hosea 13:2)

The episode at Carmel reveals God's intense desire that his people hold no rival to him in their lives. It also shows us a godly man who saw idolatry from God's perspective, and shouldered his jealous cause, and fought against that perversion. '[T]he Elijah episode can be seen as a call to a commitment which burns all bridges to other loyalties.'[149]

After this defining event in Elijah's life, he continued to speak the hard words of a true prophet of God. Six years after the events at Carmel and Horeb, Elijah told Ahab and Jezebel that they would die violent deaths (1 Kings 21:19-24; 22:38). He continued this role as prophet of doom four years later by warning Ahab's son Ahaziah of his impending death (2 Kings 1:1-16).

Elijah passed on his prophetic role to Elisha. As they journeyed together, at the edge of Elijah's homeland of Gilead, which he had left to serve as God's representative, Elijah left the earth in a most dramatic fashion:

As they were going along and talking, behold, *there appeared* a chariot of fire and horses of fire which separated the two

---

[148]Robinson, *1 Kings*, 222.
[149]Nelson, *First and Second Kings*, 128.

of them. And Elijah went up by a whirlwind to heaven.
(2 Kings 2:11)

Elijah's jealous confrontation with the prophets of Baal made
a profound impression on the psyche of the nation of Israel.
He became such a significant figure that at the close of the Old
Testament, it is Elijah that the people are told to look for, in
the restoration of God's people. The coming of the Day of the
Lord was to be preceded by the coming of the prophet from
Tishbe:

> Behold, I am going to send you Elijah the prophet before the
> coming of the great and terrible day of the LORD. He will restore
> the hearts of the fathers to *their* children and the hearts of the
> children to their fathers, so that I will not come and smite the land
> with a curse. (Mal. 4:5-6)

Elijah in the New Testament

Elijah is mentioned in the New Testament more than any
other Old Testament prophet. Elijah was a type of another
jealous prophet—John the Baptist. Like Elijah, he appeared
on the scene as suddenly and boldly (1 Kings 17:1; Luke 3:2),
and was considered the 'Elijah' who was to precede the
coming of the Messiah. John is also like Elijah in his jealous
rebukes and warnings (Matt. 14:3-5; Mark 6:18; Luke 3:19).
John's outward appearance was even like Elijah's in his wild
wilderness apparel (2 Kings 1:8; Matt. 3:4). The priests asked
John why he was baptizing if he was not either the Christ or
Elijah (John 1:25).

It is no wonder that many assumed that John the Baptist was
a second coming of Elijah. 'They asked him, "What then? Are
you Elijah?" And he said, "I am not." "Are you the Prophet?"
And he answered, "No." ' (John 1:21).

This comparison was intended within God's plan of bringing salvation through the Messiah. The coming of Elijah
prophesied in Malachi 4:5 was fulfilled in the ministry of John
the Baptist. The angel of the Lord told Zechariah that his son

would fulfill the role of Elijah in his jealous pursuit of devotion to God and his commands among God's people.

> And he will turn many of the sons of Israel back to the Lord their God. It is he who will go *as a forerunner* before Him in the spirit and power of Elijah, TO TURN THE HEARTS OF THE FATHERS BACK TO THE CHILDREN, and the disobedient to the attitude of the righteous, so as to make ready a people prepared for the Lord. (Luke 1:16-17)

Jesus affirmed that John fulfilled this role: 'For all the prophets and the Law prophesied until John. And if you are willing to accept *it,* John himself is Elijah who was to come' (Matt. 11:13-14). The forerunner who prepared the way for the Messiah, was like his predecessor, and like the One he prepared the way for, in his intense jealousy for God's glory and honor.

While John the Baptist was the 'Elijah' that prepared the way for the Messiah, the messianic ideal was often associated with Elijah. When Jesus' public ministry began to take off, some wondered if he was Elijah:

> Now Herod the tetrarch heard of all that was happening; and he was greatly perplexed, because it was said by some that John had risen from the dead, and by some that Elijah had appeared, and by others that one of the prophets of old had risen again. (Luke 9:7-8)

When Jesus asked his disciples who people were saying he was, they replied, 'Some *say* John the Baptist; and others, Elijah; but still others, Jeremiah, or one of the prophets (Matt. 16:14).

And even at his crucifixion it was assumed that Jesus was calling on Elijah in his time of need. 'When some of the bystanders heard it, they *began* saying, "Behold, He is calling for Elijah" ' (Mark 15:35).

When Paul wanted to remind the Roman Christians about God's faithfulness to his promises, he refers to Elijah's inter-action with Yahweh at Horeb:

God has not rejected His people whom He foreknew. Or do you not know what the Scripture says in *the passage about* Elijah, how he pleads with God against Israel? 'Lord, THEY HAVE KILLED YOUR PROPHETS, THEY HAVE TORN DOWN YOUR ALTARS, AND I ALONE AM LEFT, AND THEY ARE SEEKING MY LIFE.' But what is the divine response to him? 'I HAVE KEPT for Myself SEVEN THOUSAND MEN WHO HAVE NOT BOWED THE KNEE TO BAAL.' In the same way then, there has also come to be at the present time a remnant according to *God's* gracious choice. But if it is by grace, it is no longer on the basis of works, otherwise grace is no longer grace. (Rom. 11:2-6)

James uses Elijah's prayer at Carmel as an example of righteous, faithful prayer.

Elijah was a man with a nature like ours, and he prayed earnestly that it would not rain, and it did not rain on the earth for three years and six months. Then he prayed again, and the sky poured rain and the earth produced its fruit. (James 5:17-18)

The last time we see Elijah in the Bible he is standing with Moses and Jesus in glorious splendor at the Transfiguration:

And behold, two men were talking with Him; and they were Moses and Elijah, who, appearing in glory, were speaking of His departure which He was about to accomplish at Jerusalem. (Luke 9:30-31)

That Elijah appears with Moses and the Messiah does not appear to have surprised the disciples (Luke 9:33). In their minds he stood in the line of great godly men who jealously sought to see God glorified and his honor protected.

Conclusions and Implications of Elijah's Jealousy
Elijah's courageous and faithful jealousy for God's honor stands as a powerful example for anyone who claims to be a follower of Yahweh. However, before considering his example

for believers today, it is important to consider the ways the manifestation of his jealousy may be unique to Elijah.

Like Phinehas and David, Elijah's role and context allowed for a bloody and violent expression of his godly jealousy. Within his calling as a prophet and according to the Old Testament law, Elijah manifested his jealousy as God prescribed. According to the law, the representatives of the apostasy were slaughtered to purge the land from their influence (Deut. 13:12-15). Elijah's example should never be used to excuse violence if it is not done within the clear commandments of God, within the context at hand. The great commission, which views the gospel as the answer to idolatry, and Jesus' teaching to 'love your enemies' (Luke 6:27) gives the Christian a different focus in combating false gods. Add to this the future reality of the final judgment, and the Christian finds rest in anticipating the day when Jesus will silence the foolishness of any rival to the one true God. In assessing the example of Phinehas, David, and Elijah, 'Christians view idolatry as no less sinful, but see total judgment as reserved for the final day.'[150]

Like Phinehas and David, Elijah also teaches us that the man who expresses godly jealousy may have to stand alone against the majority and the powerful. The apathy of the people and Ahab resulted in Elijah needing to have the courage to be the lone representative of Yahweh at Carmel. However, there is encouragement to be found in Elijah's story as well. His feelings of alienation and loneliness were not true in light of the bigger picture, because God maintained a faithful remnant of others who had jealousy for God's honor as well.

It is also important to consider that Elijah's focus was the exclusive devotion to God *among the people of God.* Although like David, Elijah no doubt cared that 'all the world would know that there is a God in Israel,' fidelity among the covenant people was his main objective. This could help the Christian narrow his efforts as his jealousy motivates him to action.

---

[150]Wiseman, *Kings*, 170.

Expressions of jealousy for God's honor should begin among those who claim to be part of the bride of Christ.

Perhaps the most important application for the contemporary Christian of Elijah's confrontation with the Baal prophets is the absolute rejection of religious pluralism that it portrays. It appears that the challenge before Israel was similar to the current challenge to Christians, that is, there is more than one way to God. Israel was not being tempted to reject Yahweh outright, just to allow for other gods in her religious experience. The example of Elijah shows that this idea is contrary to the fundamental expectations of the covenant and amounts to idolatrous foolishness. There is no place for religious pluralism and syncretism among God's people. Elijah shows us "not just that Yahweh is the God of Israel, but that Yahweh is God period."[151]

Finally, like Phinehas and David, Elijah has strong messianic elements to his person and work. In his life as the righteous, lone, persecuted sufferer who boldly preached the exclusive claims of God, he points us to Christ.

---

[151]Ibid., 120

Chapter 6

Godly Human Jealousy in the New Testament

While the Old Testament has more vivid examples of godly human jealousy on behalf of God, the New Testament has numerous examples of individuals who shared in God's jealous defense of his honor.[1] John the Baptist jealously spoke against unrighteousness and came to turn the sons of Israel away from idolatry and 'back to the Lord their God' (Luke 1:16b). When the Apostles were ordered not to preach the gospel, they fearlessly demonstrated their jealous loyalty to God at the risk of their own lives: 'But Peter and John answered and said to them, "Whether it is right in the sight of God to give heed to you rather than to God, you be the judge; for we cannot stop speaking about what we have seen and heard" ' (Acts 4:19-20); 'But Peter and the apostles answered, "*We must obey God rather than men*" ' (Acts 5:28).

Stephen showed this same jealous loyalty in his last sermon to the Sanhedrin (Acts 7:2-53). As he retold the history of Israel, he implicated the Pharisees in the idolatry and rebellion of their fathers who worshiped other gods (Acts 7:39-43, 51-53).[2]

---

[1]I found sixty-six passages in the New Testament where persons expressed jealousy on behalf of God for his honor. They are (italicised passages have the ζῆλος (*zēlos*) word group in them): Matthew 4:10; 6:24; 16:23; 21:12-13; 22:21, 37-40; 24:15-20; Mark 8:33; 11:15-18; 12:17, 29-31; 13:14; Luke 1:16-17; 4:5-8; 9:62; 16:13; 19:45-46; John *2:13-17*; 3:29-30; 12:27-28; 17:1-5; Acts 4:18-20; 5:28-30; 7:39-43; 10:25-26; 13:8-12; 14:14-15; 17:16, 29-30; 19:26-27; Romans 1:21-25; 7:1-4; 11:2-6; 12:10-11; 1 Corinthians 3:3-9; 4:18-21; 6:18-20; 7:23, 32-35; 8:4-5; 10:6-8; 10:14, 18-21; 2 Corinthians 6:14-18; 7:11; *11:1-4*; Galatians 1:6; 5:11-12; Philippians 2:20-21; 3:2-3; 1 Thessalonians 1:9-10; Hebrews 3:3-6; James 4:4; 1 Peter 2:9; 4:3; 2 Peter 2:1, 22; 1 John 5:21; Jude 1:10; Revelation 9:20-21; 15:3-4; 17:5; 19:1, 9-10; 21:8; 22:8-9. The men who express godly jealousy in these passages are: *Jesus*, John the Baptist, Peter, John, Stephen, *Paul*, Barnabas, James, Jude, those who had been victorious over the Beast and the image, a righteous multitude, and an angel.

[2]Stephen's indignant rebuke of the Pharisees is a fine example of godly jealousy because it shows that although a man can be angry and righteously jealous, he can

The author of Hebrews is jealously concerned that God's Anointed, Jesus, receives more glory and honor than Moses: 'For He has been counted worthy of more glory than Moses, by just so much as the builder of the house had more honor than the house' (Heb. 3:3).

James calls worldly Christians adulteresses, and exhorts them to be exclusively devoted to their true husband: 'You adulteresses, do you not know that friendship with the world is hostility toward God? Therefore whoever wishes to be a friend of the world makes himself an enemy of God' (James 4:4).

Peter also expresses jealousy on behalf of God's honor.[3] He chooses to obey God rather than seek the approval of men (Acts 4:18-20; 5:28-30), and in his Epistles he stresses that Christians are the exclusive possession of God:

♦ 1 Peter 2:9: But you are A CHOSEN RACE, A royal PRIEST-HOOD, A HOLY NATION, *A PEOPLE FOR God's OWN POSSESSION.*

♦ 2 Peter 2:1b: There will also be false teachers among you, who will secretly introduce destructive heresies, *even denying the Master who bought them,* bringing swift destruction upon themselves.

Peter also denounces 'abominable idolatries' (1 Pet. 4:3), and indignantly describes apostate teachers as dogs returning to their own vomit and pigs wallowing in the mire (2 Pet. 2:22).

In his epistles John expresses godly jealousy as well, as he pleads: 'Little children, guard yourselves from idols' (1 John 5:21)[4]

Jude denounces, with the same kind of angry degrading imagery as Peter, the licentious false teachers who were leading his audience away from the true gospel: 'But these men revile the things which they do not understand; and the

---

also ask God to forgive those with whom he is angry—even when they are stoning him.

[3]Peter expresses godly jealousy on God's behalf in the following seven passages: Acts 4:18-20; 5:28-30; 10:25-26; 1 Peter 2:9; 4:3; 2 Peter 2:1, 22.

[4]John's jealousy on God's behalf can be seen in the following passages: Acts 4:18; 1 John 5:21; Revelation 9:20-21; 21:8.

things which they know by instinct, *like unreasoning animals,* by these things they are destroyed' (Jude 1:10).

In Revelation, when entire, exclusive loyalty and devotion to God is established forever, and false worship is annihilated, we hear the triumphant jealous declarations of those who have overcome the idolatry of the world:

> Who will not fear, O Lord, and glorify Your name? For *You alone are holy*; For ALL THE NATIONS WILL COME AND WORSHIP BEFORE YOU, FOR YOUR RIGHTEOUS ACTS HAVE BEEN REVEALED. (Rev. 15:4)[5]

In Revelation, we also can see godly jealousy expressed on God's behalf by an angel when he rejects John's attempt to worship him.[6]

♦ 19:10: Then I fell at his feet to worship him. But he said to me, '*Do not do that*; I am a fellow servant of yours and your brethren who hold the testimony of Jesus; *worship God.* For the testimony of Jesus is the spirit of prophecy.'

♦ 22:8-9: I, John, am the one who heard and saw these things. And when I heard and saw, I fell down to worship at the feet of the angel who showed me these things. But he said to me, '*Do not do that*. I am a fellow servant of yours and of your brethren the prophets and of those who heed the words of this book. *Worship God.*'

Of all the men in the New Testament who express jealousy on God's behalf, Jesus and Paul stand out as the clearest examples of this emotion. Forty-six of the sixty-six passages in this category are expressed by one of these two individuals, and they are the only ones who actually have ζῆλος (*zēlos*) used to describe them where the jealousy is godly and on behalf of

---

[5]Passages in Revelation where godly human jealousy on God's behalf can be seen are: Revelation 9:20-21; 15:3-4; 17:5; 19:1; 21:8.

[6]This reaction of the angel is reminiscent of the reaction of Paul and Barnabas when the people of Lystra tried to worship them (Acts 14:12-15).

God (John 2:17 and 2 Cor. 11:2). Therefore, they will be the main focus of our study in this chapter, and the two passages where the ζῆλ- root is used will serve as our key texts. We now turn our focus to Jesus and his jealousy on behalf of God's honor and glory.

Jesus' Godly Jealousy

Like John the Baptist (Matt. 14:3; Mark 6:18; Luke 3:19), Jesus expresses jealousy on behalf of others, as he demands faithfulness in marriage and honor to one's parents (Mark 10:11-12; Matt. 19:4-9; Mark 7:9-13). However the vast majority of examples of Jesus' jealousy are on behalf of God.

Jesus' jealousy on behalf of God's honor is found often throughout the Gospels.[7] Because of the two natures in his one Person it is difficult to categorize Jesus' actions and words as either human or divine. Whenever the incarnate Christ acts, he always does so as God. However, he is truly intended to be our human example (1 Pet. 2:21). When Jesus seeks glory for himself, or receives worship as the divine Son of God, we are not intended to follow his example. But when he is led by the Spirit (Luke 4:1), washes his disciples' feet, or serves self-sacrificially (Phil. 2:5-8), we are expected to follow in his steps. He is not only intended to be an example to us in his humility (John 13:15), but also in his jealous desire that his Father be honored, glorified, and obeyed.

Jesus is an example to us when he represents and defends the honor and purposes of God the Father (Luke 22:42). We see Jesus do this in his response to Satan when tempted by him with worldly power and wealth in exchange for worship: 'Then Jesus said to him, "Go, Satan! For it is written, 'YOU SHALL WORSHIP THE LORD YOUR GOD, AND SERVE HIM ONLY' " ' (Matt. 4:10).[8] Jesus' jealous response clearly

---

[7] I found twenty passages where Jesus expresses godly jealousy on God's behalf. Matthew 4:10; 6:24; 14:3-5; 16:23; 19:4-9; 21:12-13; 22:21, 37-40; 24:15-20; Mark 6:18; 7:9-13; 8:33; 10:11; 11:15-18; 12:17, 29-31; 13:14; Luke 3:19-20; 4:5-8; 9:62; 16:13; 19:45-46; John 2:13-17; 12:27-28; 17:1-5.

[8] Cf., Luke 4:8.

asserts the exclusive right of God alone to be worshiped, and left no room for a Messianic Kingdom without a cross. Jesus vehemently demanded absolute commitment to the Father's will whenever the necessity of his death was questioned. After he predicted his death and Peter rebuked him for suggesting such an idea, Jesus calls Peter 'Satan' for suggesting the same 'kingdom without a cross' idea that Satan did at Christ's temptation (Matt. 4:10): 'But turning around and seeing His disciples, He rebuked Peter and said, "Get behind Me, Satan; for you are not setting your mind on God's interests, but man's"' (Mark 8:33; cf. Matt. 16:23).

God's objectives, rather than worldly interests, must rule in the believer's life. Jesus submitted his own will to his Father's (Matt. 26:39) and demanded the same from others. His teaching left no room for compromise in one's devotion to God, and this had non-negotiable ramifications for one's attitude toward money as well: 'No one can serve two masters; for either he will hate the one and love the other, or he will be devoted to one and despise the other. You cannot serve God and wealth' (Matt. 6:24; cf. Luke 16:13).

When asked about paying taxes to Caesar, Jesus taught that those bearing the image of their Creator belong entirely to him. 'And Jesus said to them, "Render to Caesar the things that are Caesar's, and to God the things that are God's." And they were amazed at Him' (Mark 12:17; cf., Matt. 22:21).

Jesus taught that love and devotion to God must encompass every aspect of one's being. His central affirmation of how life in the Kingdom of God was to be lived expresses this absolute demand of the covenant:

And He said to him, 'YOU SHALL LOVE THE LORD YOUR GOD WITH ALL YOUR HEART, AND WITH ALL YOUR SOUL, AND WITH ALL YOUR MIND. This is the great and foremost commandment. The second is like it, YOU SHALL LOVE YOUR NEIGHBOR AS YOURSELF. On these two commandments depend the whole Law and the Prophets.' (Matt. 22:37-40; cf. Mark 12:29)

This summary of the law and prophets expresses the exhaustive devotion that should typify a member of God's Kingdom. Faithfulness to God and his Kingdom demands non-compromising devotion that allows for no competition or distraction. 'But Jesus said to him, "No one, after putting his hand to the plow and looking back, is fit for the kingdom of God" ' (Luke 9:62).

The Temple Cleansing
The most important passage where Jesus expresses godly jealousy is in John's account when Jesus cleanses the temple. Here the internal motivation for Jesus' action is given through the remembrance of Psalm 69:9 by his disciples.

> The Passover of the Jews was near, and Jesus went up to Jerusalem. And He found in the temple those who were selling oxen and sheep and doves, and the money changers seated *at their tables*. And He made a scourge of cords, and drove *them* all out of the temple, with the sheep and the oxen; and He poured out the coins of the money changers and overturned their tables; and to those who were selling the doves He said, 'Take these things away; stop making My Father's house a place of business.' His disciples remembered that it was written, 'ZEAL (ζῆλος, *zēlos*) FOR YOUR HOUSE WILL CONSUME ME.' (John 2:13-17; cf. Matt. 21:12-13; Mark 11:15-18; Luke 19:45)

The jealous attitude of Jesus stands behind his wrath as he overturns tables in the temple and drives out the moneychangers with a whip. His disciples recognized this attitude as similar to that of David. For it is his words from Psalm 69 they recall after Jesus cleanses the temple, 'His disciples remembered that it was written, "Zeal (ζῆλος, *zēlos*) for your house will consume me." '[9]

---

[9]There is no English translation that I know of that translates ζῆλος (*zēlos*) here as 'jealousy.' However, the context, in which Jesus is restoring unhindered worship of God by cleansing the Temple of the idolatries of materialism and commercialism, warrants 'jealousy' as a preferable translation.

The Synoptic Comparison

All four Gospels have an account of Jesus cleansing the Temple (Matt. 21:12-13; Mark 11:15-17; Luke 19:45-46; John 2:13-17). The accounts differ in certain details. However, the primary differences between John and the Synoptics is the chronological placement in Jesus' ministry and the disciples' remembrance in verse 17. In John, the Temple cleansing is the first major public event of Jesus' ministry, but in the Synoptics it is the last. Most commentators believe this is because John moved it to the beginning for theological emphasis. A few commentators think the Synoptic authors moved it. A third option is that Jesus cleansed the Temple twice.[10] That there were two cleansings seems to fit most naturally with the structure and intent of the Synoptic writers as well as of John.

The meaning of the cleansing in both John and the Synoptics seems to have generally the same theological significance. They both are 'a protest like the prophets of old against the profanation of God's house and a sign that the messianic purification of the Temple was at hand.'[11]

The Offense

Jesus found money changing and selling going on in the Temple during Passover in Jerusalem. What was it that so incensed Jesus, that he violently purged the Temple of the commerce that had become commonplace?

Part of the offence may have been connected to the inhibiting effect the trade had on the only worship space available to Gentile proselytes. Although the word used is the general word for the Temple (ἱερῷ, *hierō*), undoubtedly

---

[10]The following commentators hold this view: Donald A. Carson, *The Gospel According to John* (Grand Rapids: InterVarsity, 1991), 178; Leon Morris, *The Gospel According to John*, NICNT, ed. Ned B. Stonehouse, et al, (Grand Rapids: Eerdmans, 1995), 188-91; W. Hendriksen, *Exposition of the Gospel According to John* (Grand Rapids: Baker, 1953), 120; R. V. G. Tasker, *The Gospel According to St. John*, TNTC (Grand Rapids: Eerdmans, 1960), 61.

[11]Raymond E. Brown, *The Gospel According to John*, The Anchor Bible, ed. William F. Albright and David N. Freedman (New York: Doubleday, 1966), 121.

the selling was going on in the outer courts, most likely the court of the Gentiles.[12] This was the only place the Gentiles could enter the Temple and offer prayer.[13] For this reason the Temple cleaning would have been especially meaningful to the Gentiles. The significance of the cleansing to the Gentiles is possibly indicated in John 12:20-21:

> Now there were some Greeks among those who were going up to worship at the feast; these then came to Philip, who was from Bethsaida of Galilee, and *began to* ask him, saying, 'Sir, we wish to see Jesus.'

This passage occurs immediately after the Triumphal Entry, which is where the second cleansing takes place in the Synoptics. The desire of the Gentiles to meet with Jesus in Jerusalem at this time may be indicative of the powerful message Jesus sent to them when he jealously demanded that they have meaningful access to the Temple.[14]

The changing of currency by the moneychangers was not necessarily an evil activity. It enabled those traveling from outside Jerusalem to buy an animal to sacrifice. However there is good evidence that this had become a corrupt business. It appears that the moneychangers 'had a monopoly and often charged exorbitant rates.'[15] In the Synoptic Gospels, the Temple cleansing seems to emphasize the underhanded business practices of the sellers, for they record Jesus' words when he quotes Jeremiah 7:11, and calls them 'a den of robbers' (Matt. 21:13; Mark 11:17; Luke 19:45).

> In the Temple of God with the approval of the priests, behold the altar of Mammon, with all the sweltering of a dirty cattle market and the haggling of a dirtier money one![16]

---

[12]Morris, *John*, 192.

[13]Archibald M. Hunter, *The Work and Words of Jesus* (Philadelphia: Westminster, 1950), 141.

[14]I first heard this idea in a lecture by J. Julius Scott in a class titled 'Jewish Backgrounds of the New Testament' at Wheaton College in 1992.

[15]Morris, *John*, 192 n. 66.

[16]Hunter, *Work and Words of Jesus*, 141.

While the business going on in the Temple was undoubtedly shady, the emphasis in John is not so much on the unscrupulous business practices but on the very existence of a market in the Temple at all. Jesus' angry statement to those he was driving out of the Temple provides the main reason he found their selling so repugnant. 'And to those who were selling the doves He said, "Take these things away; stop making My Father's house[17] a place of business" '[18] (John 2:16). Jesus accuses the moneychangers of trivializing the sacred worship space by turning it into a market place.

Convenience had overtaken reverence and Jesus would not stand for it. Worship of God should not be interfered with for the sake of business. 'Instead of brokenness and contrition, holy adoration and prolonged petition, there is noisy commerce.'[19] Jesus was reacting to the profanation of pure worship to God. The presence of animals in the Temple precinct, which was probably an innovation of Caiaphas,[20] as well as the hawking of goods, trivialized the sacred area and angered Jesus.

Ridderbos accurately describes the nature of the offense in the Temple and why Jesus reacted the way he did:

> Jesus' fury and severity were not directed against the merchants' or money changers' profits but by the very fact of business being conducted in the precincts of the sanctuary. For to him it was intolerable that the place of access to God's holy dwelling and to communion with God himself was made into a place of trade in animals and money, a business for which in the nature of the case the temple was not intended.[21]

---

[17]Morris points out that Jesus' use of 'my Father's house' is a powerful indicator of his awareness of his unique relationship with the Father and is tantamount to claiming his own deity, Morris, *John*, 193 n. 73.

[18]The NAB and NRS miss the play on words between οἶκον τοῦ πατρός (*oikon tou patros*, 'house of my Father') and οἶκον ἐμπορίου (*oikon emporiou*, 'house of business').

[19]Carson, *John*, 179.

[20]Brown, *John*, 121.

[21]Herman N. Ridderbos, *The Gospel According to John: A Theological Commentary*, 1987, trans. John Vriend (Grand Rapids: Eerdmans, 1992), 116.

Jesus' Jealous Reaction

Jesus' role as 'the avenger and restorer of the kingdom of God,'[22] which was central to his ministry, motivates him to physically and verbally drive the sellers from the Temple. John's account portrays this act most graphically, as Jesus makes and uses a whip to drive them all from the Temple.[23] While Jesus' use of physical force may come as a shock, coming from the one who said, 'Blessed are the peacemakers,' it is important to remember that 'it was not so much the physical force as the moral power he employed that emptied the courts.'[24] Jesus' violent reaction was not an impetuous thoughtless display of emotion, but a principled righteous act with prophetic basis in the Old Testament. There are several Old Testament passages that stand behind Jesus' actions in cleansing the Temple. In the Synoptics, Jesus' rebuke of the sellers contains language from Jeremiah when he condemned the corrupt ways of the priests.

♦ Matthew 21:13: And He said to them, 'It is written, "MY HOUSE SHALL BE CALLED A HOUSE OF PRAYER"; but you are making it a ROBBERS' DEN.'

♦ Jeremiah 7:11: 'Has this house, which is called by My name, become a den of robbers in your sight? Behold, I, even I, have seen *it,'* declares the LORD.

The Temple was to be a sacred place where God's people offered sacrifice and prayer to Yahweh. The prophets foretold the coming Day of the Lord, when worship at the Temple would be as it was intended.

♦ Isaiah 56:7: Even those I will bring to My holy mountain and make them joyful in My house of prayer. Their burnt offerings and their sacrifices will be acceptable on My altar;

---

[22]John Calvin, *The Gospel According to St John*, 1552, trans. T. H. L. Parker, ed. David W. Torrance and Thomas F. Torrance (Grand Rapids: Eerdmans, 1959), 53.

[23]The πάντας (*pantas*) in verse 15 gives us good reason to assume that Jesus used the whip to drive both the animals *and* people from the Temple.

[24]Morris, *John*, 193.

for My house will be called a house of prayer for all the peoples.'

♦ Zechariah 14:21b: And there shall no longer be a trader (כְּנַעֲנִי, *kĕna'ăni*) in the house of the LORD of hosts on that day.

This Day of the Lord, where the Temple became the holy sanctuary it was intended to be, would be ushered in through the Messiah:

♦ Malachi 3:1: 'Behold, I am going to send My messenger, and he will clear the way before Me. And the Lord, whom you seek, will suddenly come to His temple; and the messenger of the covenant, in whom you delight, behold, He is coming,' says the LORD of hosts.

♦ Malachi 3:3: He will sit as a smelter and purifier of silver, and He will purify the sons of Levi and refine them like gold and silver, so that they may present to the LORD offerings in righteousness.

This prophecy of Malachi 'said to Israel that her King would announce Himself, not by a miracle of power, but by an act of holiness.'[25] This act of holiness was Jesus' cleansing of the Temple, which was motivated by jealous and righteous indignation. It was not primarily a political, economic, or even ethical statement Jesus was making; it was a profoundly theological one. 'Jesus is seen as taking action to bring about the eschatological order wherein God will be glorified in his house and in the worship of his people.'[26] Relationship with, and worship of, God as he intended was the main issue Jesus addressed in the Temple that day. His purpose was to 'restore the worship of God to its integrity, which had been corrupted by the wickedness of men and in this way to renew

---

[25]F. Godet, *Commentary on the Gospel of John*, 1864, trans. Timothy Dwight (New York: Funk & Wagnalls, 1886), 361.

[26]George R. Beasley-Murray, *John*, WBC, ed. Ralph P. Martin, vol. 36 (Waco, Tex.: Word, 1987), 39.

and defend the holiness of the Temple.'[27] Respect for God's 'concern for pure worship, a right relationship with God at the place supremely designated to serve as the focal point of the relationship between God and man,'[28] drove Jesus to upset the status quo.

The Disciple's Remembrance

> His disciples remembered that it was written, 'ZEAL (ζῆλος, *zēlos*) FOR YOUR HOUSE WILL CONSUME ME' (John 2:17).

We have seen that Jesus' actions in cleansing the Temple were grounded in Old Testament prophetic tradition. After the event, another Old Testament passage came to the minds of the disciples. It was the anguish-filled cry of David in Psalm 69:9 that the disciples thought of after Jesus' angry display:

> Because for Your sake I have borne reproach; dishonor has covered my face. I have become estranged from my brothers and an alien to my mother's sons. For zeal (קִנְאַת, *qinat*) for Your house has consumed me, and the reproaches of those who reproach You have fallen on me. (Ps. 69:7-9)

We have already dealt with Psalm 69 when we looked at David's jealousy on behalf of God.[29] This cry of David is that of the righteous sufferer on behalf of God. This Messianic Psalm is quoted often in the New Testament in reference to Jesus,[30] and is used here to show the consuming jealousy of Jesus, as well as the fatal effects this jealousy will have for him.

David recognized that a main reason for his persecution was found in his jealousy for God's house. David expressed

---

[27]Calvin, *John*, 52.

[28]Ibid., 180.

[29]Because Psalm 69 has been examined in depth already in chapter 5, we will not spend much time on it here. I refer the reader to the discussion on David in the last chapter for the Old Testament background of the disciple's remembrance of David's quote.

[30]Cf. Matthew 27:34; John 2:17; 15:25; 19:29; Acts 1:20; Romans 11:29; 15:3.

his close identification with God and his causes. His jealous passion for the 'house' of the Lord was based in 'his desire to uphold the honour of God.'[31] David was consumed by 'the zeal for the Divine glory by which true believers are animated.'[32]

Jesus' cleansing of the temple brought about this remembrance of David's קנא (*qna*, 'jealousy'). For the disciples, Jesus' jealous passion for proper temple reverence and access brought to mind David's jealousy for Yahweh's house in the midst of persecution. 'The zeal that Jesus showed when He ran the merchandisers out of the Temple was a zeal, a jealousy, for God's house.'[33] It is not only the suffering of Christ that David foreshadows in Psalm 69. Perhaps even more important is the jealous loyalty to the Father that led Jesus to submit to his will, and suffer shame and persecution. The messianic interpretation of this Psalm 'is in the form of an application to the life of devotion to God by the Lord Jesus Christ.'[34]

The remembrance of Psalm 69 in reference to Jesus' cleansing of the Temple shows that the actions of Jesus are part of God's Messianic fulfillment foretold in the Old Testament.[35] David's words in Psalm 69 represent the 'theocratic righteous person, suffering for the cause of God. The highest realization of this ideal is the Messiah.'[36] John is concerned that his readers recognize that Jesus' actions have immediate meaning and application, as well as deeper eternal implications. 'John detects in the experiences of David a prophetic paradigm that anticipates what must take place in the life of "great David's greater Son." '[37] To highlight the prophetic sense of David's words, John changes the verb for 'consume' from the aorist

[31]Anderson, *Psalms*, 502.

[32]Calvin, *Psalms*, 54.

[33]Robert Alden, *Psalms: Songs of Dedication* (Chicago: Moody, 1975), 50.

[34]VanGemeren, *Psalms*, 17.

[35]Morris, *John*, 194.

[36]Godet, *John*, 364.

[37]Carson, *John*, 180.

tense of the Septuagint (κατέφαγέν, *katephagen*) to the future (καταφάγεται, *kataphagetai*).[38]

The actions of Jesus in the Temple cleansing have precedent not only in the life of David, for they are similar to the jealous indignation of both God and godly men throughout Scripture.

> Jesus' zealous reaction to the temple merchants (2:17) closely mirrors God's anger at Sinai when the people played the harlot and worshipped around the golden calf (cf. Exod. 32:10; Deut. 9:14). It also is not very different from Paul's view of the wrath of God against ungodliness in Rom. 1:18-32. In this text the disciples are said to have viewed the action as righteous indignation and indeed as the fulfillment of Scripture. (2:17; cf. Ps. 69:9)[39]

While the prophetic demand and the opportunity for the deeper lesson about his death and resurrection (vv. 18-22) motivated Jesus to cleanse the Temple, the genuine, deeply felt, jealous anger of Jesus should not be minimized. While not impetuous, Jesus' jealousy was real and visceral. These feelings led Jesus to act in such a way that, like David, he incurred the reproaches of those who do not share in his ardent passion for God's glory.

> He was so anxious to defend God's glory that he willingly accepted on his own head all the reproaches that the wicked cast at God; and that he burned with such zeal that this one feeling swallowed up all others.[40]

David felt consumed by his jealousy for God's house, and this brought increased suffering in his life. 'He tells us that he himself felt like this; but there can be no doubt that in his own person he was describing what properly pertained to the Messiah.'[41]

---

[38]The LXX more accurately translates the *qal* perfect אֲכָלָתְנִי (*akalateni*) of the Masoretic Text.

[39]Gerald L. Borchert, *John 1-11*, NAC, ed. David S. Dockery, vol. 25A (New York: Broadman & Holman, 1996), 165.

[40]Calvin, *John*, 53.

[41]Ibid.

The text does not tell us when Jesus' disciples remembered David's words in connection to the Temple cleansing. Some commentators believe that the remembrance was at the time of the cleansing, and therefore believe that the emphasis is on 'the consuming force of His zeal.'[42] Others think they did not make the Davidic connection until after his resurrection (cf. verse 22), and therefore believe that Jesus' being consumed is no longer 'a simple reference to the burning intensity of the zeal,'[43] but a sober realization that 'the dangerous consequences of Jesus' action: his zeal for the house of God "will cost him his life."'[44] Whenever the remembrance of the disciples took place, we are able to learn from Jesus' godly jealousy the deeper eternal consequences of his actions in salvation history.

The Jewish Response

Following the cleansing, the Jews challenged Jesus to give a miraculous sign to prove he had the authority to do what he did. His answer points us to a deeper reality and message of the cleansing of the Temple. Jesus answered them, 'Destroy this temple, and in three days I will raise it up' (John 2:19). He used their challenges to give a cryptic teaching on the deeper meaning of his actions in the Temple. 'His own body, first destroyed and then raised from the dead, is to be the true Temple.'[45]

Although the Jews and the disciples did not see that Jesus was referring to himself, he was bringing out a central theme of his ministry. His jealous actions in cleansing the Temple demonstrated his deep desire to preserve God's honor and pure worship, but it also pointed to a vital teaching concerning himself, that 'in Jesus the eternal purposes of God find their fulfillment.'[46] He was the fulfillment of the intent of the Temple;

---

[42]Godet, *John*, 364.

[43]Brown, *John*, 124.

[44]Schnackenburg, *The Gospel According to St John*, trans. Smyth Kevin, Herder's Theological Commentary on the New Testament, ed. J. Ford and Smyth Kevin, vol. 1 (New York: Herder and Herder, 1968), 347.

[45]C. K. Barrett, *The Gospel According to St John* (London: S.P.C.K., 1962), 163.

[46]Barrett, *John*, 163.

pure and perfect communion with God through Jesus' ultimate atonement and intercession. Jesus' intent was not to repudiate temple worship, but to remove any barriers to true worship. 'Jesus had come to open up the way to the true worship of God, and this motif lies at the heart of the narrative and dialogue.'[47] Jesus achieved this access to God temporarily in clearing the Temple precinct of the market, and eternally by his death and resurrection.

Conclusions and Implications of Jesus' Jealousy

Jesus' example of jealousy for God's honor is one of the most important examples he left for us. He is certainly intended to be an example in his jealous desire that his Father be honored, glorified, and obeyed. However, like the other jealous leaders we have studied, there are aspects of the expression of Jesus' jealousy that put limits on the direct application of his jealous behavior. As with Phinehas, David, and Elijah, we must consider Jesus' specific role and offices before applying his example to our lives. Because he was the Son of God and the Messiah, cleansing his Temple clearly fit within his identity and calling. Jesus acted within his intended function as Messiah and Son of God, and before cleansing a temple in our situation we must first ask if it is a responsibility God has given to us.

Another qualification of Jesus' jealous behavior is that he had a greater teaching purpose behind the cleansing of the Temple. The cleansing was not an end in itself; it provided the opportunity to teach that he was the true Temple. However, while the opportunity for the deeper lesson about his death and resurrection (vv. 18-22) motivated Jesus to cleanse the Temple, the genuine, deeply felt, jealous anger of Jesus should not be ignored. He really was jealous, and reacted with strong emotional response to the perversion of Temple worship. These feelings led Jesus to act in such a way that, like David, he incurred the reproaches of those who did not share his ardent passion for God's glory.

---

[47]Beasley-Murray, *John*, 40.

Two other considerations are important as we follow Jesus' example in the Temple cleansing. First, Jesus was jealous for God's honor while also tenderly and compassionately caring for people and reaching out to sinners and the outcasts of society. He showed love, compassion and patience as well as jealous anger. Second, like the other men we have studied, Jesus' jealous wrath was focused on God's people and their Temple worship, not Roman society or other areas. Jealousy for God's honor must begin with God's people. Reform should begin within the Church. Jesus was primarily concerned that God be honored and worshiped appropriately. His focus was not merely ethical, sociological, or economic, it was profoundly theological. He demanded pure worship and absolute devotion to God and he perfectly demonstrated this in his own life.

Jesus' jealousy in the Temple shows us the connection between godly jealousy and godly anger that we saw in the Old Testament. These negatively perceived emotions have a place in the life of godly Christians. The angry jealousy of Jesus in the Temple stands in stark contrast to the benign, effeminate idea of Jesus that dominates so many contemporary conceptions of him. He reacted in his jealousy on God's behalf, with swift and angry action, as did the godly men previously considered. Following in the footsteps of Phinehas, David, and Elijah, as well as those of Jesus, is Paul.

Paul's Godly Jealousy

Paul was intensely jealous for God's honor. Before and after his conversion, strong emotion was a distinctive characteristic of this great godly leader. He persecuted the Church with the same kind of intense zeal with which he later propagated the gospel (Phil. 3:6). Apathy and lack of conviction was not a problem for Paul. His passion for the truth of the gospel dominated his life and resulted in tremendous boldness and courage to preach that message, regardless of the persecution that resulted. When the gospel was compromised, he would respond with hard words.[48] His life exemplified intense religious zeal.[49] One of the ways this is evident is in his frequent use of the ζηλ- root in his writings. A form of this word group occurs thirty nine times in the New Testament.[50] Of these occurrences, Paul uses twenty-four of them.[51] Thirteen of these use the word in a positive sense,[52] and eight negatively.[53] The remaining three uses do not clearly indicate whether it is being used positively or negatively.[54] Paul is the subject of this zeal/jealousy four

---

[48]To be sure, Paul balanced this hard passion with the tender heart of a pastor. Paul is jealous for God's glory and the fidelity of his people but he also has a deep love and affection for people. For example, when he tells the Romans: 'I have great sorrow and unceasing grief in my heart. For I could wish that I myself were accursed, *separated* from Christ for the sake of my brethren, my kinsmen according to the flesh' (Rom. 9:2-3). And he tells the Thessalonians that he was 'gentle among them' and he cared for them 'as a nursing *mother* tenderly cares for her own children.' But he could also have the same furious jealousy of Jesus when he cleansed the temple. When someone compromised the gospel and thereby injured the flock he would respond with jealous anger (1 Cor. 4:21; Gal. 5:12; Phil. 3:2).

[49]In the following passages we can see examples of Paul's religious zeal: Acts 9:20-29; 13:16-52; 14:1-28; 15:26, 30-36, 41; 16:10, 13, 17, 31-32; 17:2-3, 16-17, 22-31; 18:4-6, 19, 23; 19:8-10, 21; 20:7, 18-27, 31, 33-34; 21:13; 24:14-25; 26:1-29; 28:23-28, 30-31; Romans 1:1, 9-15; 9:1-3; 10:1; 11:13, 14; 15:15-32; 1 Corinthians 1:17, 23; 2:1-7, 13; 3:1-2, 5-7; 4:1-21; 9:12, 15-23, 27; 10:33; 11:1; 13:1; 15:1-32; 2 Corinthians 1:12, 17-19, 24; 2:12-17; 3:6, 12; 4:1, 2, 5, 8-15; 5:11, 13, 14, 18, 20; 6:3-10; 7:2; 10:3, 14-16; 11:7, 12, 19, 22-33; 12:10, 14-19, 21; 13:6-9; Galatians 1:10, 15-16; 2:2; 3:1; 4:11, 19; 5:11; Ephesians 6:17, 20; Philippians 1:17, 18, 20, 22-25, 27; 2:16, 17; 3:4-17; 4:11, 12, 17; Colossians 1:24, 28, 29; 2:1; 1 Thessalonians 1:5, 6; 2:2-6, 8-11; 2 Thessalonians 3:7-9; 1 Timothy 4:10; 2 Timothy 1:3, 7, 11-13; 2:9-10; 3:10-11. I was pointed to most of these references by Orville J. Nave's entry for 'Zeal, religious,' in *Nave's Topical Bible*, 1896, available at *http://bible.crosswalk. com/Concordances/NavesTopicalBible/ntb.cgi?number=T52506*, internet.

[50]Luke 6:15; John 2:17; Acts 1:13; 5:17; 7:9; 13:45; 17:5; 21:20; 22:3; Romans 10:2, 19; 11:11, 14; 13:13; 1 Corinthians 3:3; 10:22; 12:31; 13:4; 14:1, 12, 39; 2 Corinthians 7:7, 11; 9:2; 11:2; 12:20; Galatians 1:14; 4:17, 18; 5:20; Philippians 3:6; Titus 2:14; Hebrews 10:27; James 3:14, 16; 1 Peter 3:13; Revelation 3:19.

[51]Acts 22:3; Romans 10:2, 19; 11:11, 14; 13:13; 1 Corinthians 3:3; 10:22; 12:31; 13:4; 14:1, 12, 39; 2 Corinthians 7:7, 11; 9:2; 11:2; 12:20; Galatians 1:14; 4:17, 18; 5:20; Philippians 3:6; Titus 2:14.

[52]Romans 10:19; 11:11, 14; 1 Corinthians 10:22; 12:31; 14:1, 12, 39; 2 Corinthians 7:7, 11; 9:2; 11:2; Titus 2:14.

[53]Romans 10:2; 13:13; 1 Corinthians 3:3; 13:4; 2 Corinthians 12:20; Galatians 4:17; 5:20; Philippians 3:6.

[54]Acts 22:3; Galatians 1:14; 4:18.

times, twice neutrally (Acts 22:3; Gal. 1:14), once positively (2 Cor. 11:2), and once negatively (Phil. 3:6).

For Paul, the key attribute of the life of a Pharisee was zeal for God. And although this zeal was often without knowledge or misguided, one gets the sense that Paul saw great value in this kind of intensity of desire.

♦ Acts 22:3: I am a Jew, born in Tarsus of Cilicia, but brought up in this city, educated under Gamaliel, strictly according to the law of our fathers, *being zealous for God* just as you all are today.

♦ Romans 10:2: For I testify about them that they have a *zeal for God*, but not in accordance with knowledge.

♦ Philippians 3:6: *as to zeal, a persecutor of the church*; as to the righteousness which is in the Law, found blameless.

♦ Galatians 1:14: and I was advancing in Judaism beyond many of my contemporaries among my countrymen, being *more extremely zealous for my ancestral traditions.*

He often exhorted and commended zealous passion in the lives of God's people:

♦ Romans 12:10-11: *Be* devoted to one another in brotherly love; give preference to one another in honor; not lagging behind in diligence (NIV = *never lacking in zeal*), fervent in spirit, serving the Lord;

♦ 1 Corinthians 12:31: But *earnestly desire* (ζηλοῦτε, *zēloute*) the greater gifts. And I show you a still more excellent way.

♦ 1 Corinthians 14:1: Pursue love, yet *desire earnestly* (ζηλοῦτε, *zēloute*) spiritual *gifts,* but especially that you may prophesy.

♦ 1 Corinthians 14:12: So also you, since you are *zealous of spiritual gifts,* seek to abound for the edification of the church.

♦ 1 Corinthians 14:39: Therefore..., *desire earnestly* (ζηλοῦτε, *zēloute*) to prophesy, and do not forbid to speak in tongues.

♦ 2 Corinthians 7:7: and not only by his coming, but also by the comfort with which he was comforted in you, as he reported to us your longing, your mourning, *your zeal for me*; so that I rejoiced even more.

♦ 2 Corinthians 7:11: For behold what earnestness this very thing, this godly sorrow, has produced in you: what vindication of yourselves, what indignation, what fear, what longing, *what zeal*, what avenging of wrong! In everything you demonstrated yourselves to be innocent in the matter.

♦ 2 Corinthians 9:2: for I know your readiness, of which I boast about you to the Macedonians, *namely,* that Achaia has been prepared since last year, and *your zeal has stirred up most of them.*

♦ Galatians 4:18: But it is good always to be *eagerly sought* (ζηλοῦσθαι, *zēlousthai*) in a commendable manner, and not only when I am present with you.

♦ Titus 2:14: who gave Himself for us to redeem us from every lawless deed, and to purify for Himself a people for His own possession, *zealous for good deeds.*

Zeal is the more general emotion of which jealousy is a sub-category. Jealousy is always a zealous emotion, but zeal is not always expressed as jealousy.[55] Because Paul put such high importance on zeal, it is not surprising that he is a major example of jealousy as well.

Paul expresses godly jealousy more times than any other person in the New Testament.[56] He expresses the jealous desire for the Corinthians to remain faithful to him as their spiritual father.

---

[55]To state our definition again: Jealousy is the ardent desire to maintain exclusive relational faithfulness from a person in the face of a challenge to that faithfulness.

[56]Of the seventy-six New Testament passages where persons express godly jealousy, Paul expresses twenty-eight of them. These are found in: Acts 13:8-12; 14:14-15; 17:16, 29-30; 19:26-27; Romans 1:21-25; 7:1-4; 11:2-6; 12:10-11; 1 Corinthians 3:3-9; 4:18-21; 6:18-20; 7:1-4, 23, 32-35; 8:4-5; 10:6-8, 14,

♦ 2 Corinthians 11:2: For *I am jealous for you with a godly jealousy*; for I betrothed you to one husband, so that to Christ I might present you *as* a pure virgin.

♦ 2 Corinthians: 12:14: Here for this third time I am ready to come to you, and I will not be a burden to you; for *I do not seek what is yours, but you*; for children are not responsible to save up for *their* parents, but parents for *their* children.

Although not married himself, he also expressed jealousy on behalf of those who are married for faithfulness in the marriage relationship (Rom. 7:2-3; 1 Cor. 7:1-4).[57]

However, the vast majority of the examples of Paul's jealousy are when he is jealous on behalf of God. This jealousy is seen in his strong rebuke of Elymas the magician: 'You who are full of all deceit and fraud, you son of the devil, you enemy of all righteousness, will you not cease to make crooked the straight ways of the Lord?' (Acts 13:10)

When the people at Lystra began worshipping Paul and Barnabas because of their healing power, they reacted with horror, and made sure the people understood that only the true God should receive worship:

> But when the apostles Barnabas and Paul heard of it, they tore their robes and rushed out into the crowd, crying out and saying, 'Men, why are you doing these things? We are also men of the same nature as you, and preach the gospel to you that you should turn from these vain things to a living God, WHO MADE THE HEAVEN AND THE EARTH AND THE SEA AND ALL THAT IS IN THEM. (Acts 14:14-15)

Like all of the jealous prophets of the Old Testament, Paul denounced idolatry of every kind:

18-21; 2 Corinthians 6:14-18; 7:11; 11:1-4; 12:14; Galatians 1:6; 5:11-12; Philippians 2:20-21; 3:2-3; 1 Thessalonians 1:9-10.

[57]We have seen that John the Baptist (Matt. 14:3; Mark 16:8; Luke 3:19) and Jesus (Matt. 19:4-9; Mark 7:9) expressed this same kind of jealousy.

♦ Acts 17:16: Now while Paul was waiting for them at Athens, *his spirit was being provoked within him (NIV = was greatly distressed) as he was observing the city full of idols.*

♦ Acts 17:29: Being then the children of God, we ought not to think that the Divine Nature is like gold or silver or stone, an image formed by the art and thought of man.

♦ Acts 19:26: You see and hear that not only in Ephesus, but in almost all of Asia, this Paul has persuaded and turned away a considerable number of people, saying that *gods made with hands are no gods at all.*

♦ Romans 1:21-23: For even though they knew God, they *did not honor Him as God* or give thanks, but they became futile in their speculations, and their foolish heart was darkened. Professing to be wise, they became fools, and *exchanged the glory of the incorruptible God for an image in the form of corruptible man and of birds and four-footed animals and crawling creatures.*

♦ 1 Corinthians 8:4-6: Therefore concerning the eating of things sacrificed to idols, we know *that there is no such thing as an idol in the world, and that there is no God but one.* For even if there are so-called gods whether in heaven or on earth, as indeed there are many gods and many lords, yet for us there is *but one God*, the Father, from whom are all things and we *exist* for Him; and *one Lord*, Jesus Christ, by whom are all things, and we *exist* through Him.

♦ 1 Corinthians 10:6-8: Now these things happened as examples for us, so that we would not crave evil things as they also craved. Do not be idolaters, as some of them were; as it is written, 'THE PEOPLE SAT DOWN TO EAT AND DRINK, AND STOOD UP TO PLAY.' Nor let us act immorally, as some of them did, and twenty-three thousand fell in one day.[58]

---

[58]Here Paul is referring to the idolatry of the golden calf (Exodus 32) and Baal-peor (Numbers 25), and is echoing the jealousy of Moses and Phinehas in those events.

- 1 Corinthians 10:14: Therefore, my beloved, *flee from idolatry.*

- 1 Corinthians 10:20-21: *No,* but *I say* that *the things which the Gentiles sacrifice, they sacrifice to demons and not to God*; and I do not want you to become sharers in demons. You cannot drink the cup of the Lord and the cup of demons; you cannot partake of the table of the Lord and the table of demons.

- 2 Corinthians 6:16: Or *what agreement has the temple of God with idols*? For we are the temple of the living God; just as God said, 'I WILL DWELL IN THEM AND WALK AMONG THEM; AND I WILL BE THEIR GOD, AND THEY SHALL BE MY PEOPLE.'

- 1 Thessalonians 1:9: For they themselves report about us what kind of a reception we had with you, and how *you turned to God from idols to serve a living and true God.*

Paul's disdain for idols grew out of a solid understanding of the marriage motif that stood behind the covenant that God had with his people (Rom. 7:1-4). God's people are no longer their own, they are now God's exclusive possession.

- 1 Corinthians 3:9: For we are God's fellow workers; you are God's field, God's building.

- 1 Corinthians 6:19-20: Or do you not know that your body is a temple of the Holy Spirit who is in you, whom you have from God, and that *you are not your own*? *For you have been bought with a price*: therefore glorify God in your body.

- 1 Corinthians 7:23: *You were bought with a price*; do not become slaves of men.

Based upon this exclusive relationship that allows for no rival, Paul's entire ministry to believers could be summed up by his words to the Corinthians. He ministered to 'promote what is appropriate and *to secure undistracted devotion to the Lord*' (1 Cor. 7:35). Paul recognized that any failure to be devoted to the true gospel, without compromise, was tantamount to spiritual adultery (Rom. 7:1-4) and desertion of a spouse. 'I am amazed that you are so quickly deserting Him who called you by the grace of Christ, for a different gospel' (Gal. 1:6).

It is just this sort of desertion that Paul is concerned about in our key text within this study of Paul. We will now examine 2 Corinthians 11:1-4, which is one of the clearest presentations of godly human jealousy in the New Testament.

2 Corinthians 11:1-4

> I wish that you would bear with me in a little foolishness; but indeed you are bearing with me. *For I am jealous for you with a godly jealousy*; for I betrothed you to one husband, so that to Christ I might *present you as a pure virgin*. But I am afraid that, as the serpent deceived Eve by his craftiness, your minds will be led astray from the simplicity *and purity of devotion to Christ*. For if one comes and preaches *another Jesus* whom we have not preached, or you receive a different spirit which you have not received, or a different gospel which you have not accepted, you bear *this* beautifully.

Paul recognized that the Corinthians were flirting with a different gospel and a different spirit than the true one. Their devotion and loyalty to the true Christ was in peril. Their failure to spurn the false teachers in Corinth was adding up to idolatry. Paul knew that to follow after another gospel was to be unfaithful to the one to whom they had been betrothed. The same jealousy that we saw in Phinehas, David, Elijah, and Jesus, also motivated Paul.

Paul's Foolishness

What prompted Paul's statement of his jealousy to the Corin-thians? Paul was concerned that the Corinthians were gullible enough to fall prey to the false teaching of a different gospel. The false teachers in Corinth had challenged his authority, and he feared that the gospel he preached would be lost in favor of one that lacked the essence of the true gospel. His statement of jealousy serves as an excuse for the boasting he is about to engage in. This is especially awkward for him, for he has just criticized self-commendation and boasting in 10:12-18. Because of this, he feels compelled to preface his boasting with his godly and unselfish reasons for it. Paul was concerned that his audience realized that he was about to boast of his apostolic credentials for a very different motive than the 'super apostles' bragged of their own status. His boasting was not based in self-centered aggrandizement, but on a fatherly concern for the spiritual well being of his spiritual children in Corinth. To justify his boasting, Paul prefaced it with three reasons, all introduced by γὰρ (*gar*): (1) his divine jealousy for the Corinthians' doctrinal purity and consequent spiritual chastity (vv. 2-3); (2) their gullible propensity to be seduced by the false gospel of Paul's critics (v. 4); and (3) his legitimate claim to apostolic authority (v. 5). Because Paul's human leadership had become intertwined with divine authority and the true gospel, it became imperative for Paul to establish his human leadership. Although he had an aversion to the kind of self-promotion his challengers espoused, Paul's 'folly' (ἀφροσύνης, *aphrosunēs*) is 'regrettable but necessary' in light of the situation at Corinth.[59]

Paul's goal in his boasting, and in his ministry among the believers as a whole, was to bring about a 'sincere and pure devotion to Christ' (v. 3). His use of ἁπλότητος (*haplotētos*) employs a distinctly Jewish sense here, and means 'sincerity,' 'single hearted devotion,' or 'wholeness.'[60] 'Pure' (ἁγνότητος, *hagnotētos*) can refer to a bride who has not been sexually violated, or who has not 'played the harlot.' Paul uses this imagery of devotion and chastity to speak of the 'wholeness

---

[59]C. K. Barrett, *A Commentary on the Second Epistle to the Corinthians*, Harper's New Testament Commentaries, ed. Henry Chadwick (New York: Harper & Row, 1973), 271.

[60]Victor P. Furnish, *2 Corinthians*, AB, ed. Foxwell A. Albright and David N. Freedman, vol. 32A (Garden City, N.J.: Doubleday, 1984), 487.

and purity which is toward Christ' that he jealously wanted for his flock in Corinth.[61]

> Prompting Paul's jealousy for Corinthian fidelity was his fear, based on disturbing evidence (v. 4), that their minds and affections might be corrupted so that they would lose their single-minded faithfulness to Christ.[62]

The Marriage Covenant

This jealousy Paul experienced was grounded in the marriage metaphor used to describe God's relationship with his people. As we saw in chapter 4, the Church as God's wife is a theme prevalent in the Old Testament (esp. Isa 54:5-6; 62:5; Jer. 3:1; Ezek. 16:8; Hosea 2:19-20) and which only intensifies and is more clearly defined in the New (Eph. 5:23-32; Rev. 19:7-9; 21:2, 9).

The marriage process of Paul's day involved the betrothal, which established the commitment, and the nuptial, which consummated the marriage.[63] The betrothal made the marriage legally binding even though the wife remained a virgin until the nuptial. Often a year would separate the two ceremonies and the betrothal could only be broken by death or divorce. If fidelity to the marriage was broken for any other reason, it was considered adultery, and deserving of the capital punishment of an adulterer (Lev. 20:10). The sober responsibility of preserving the bride's chastity fell on the shoulders of her father (Gen. 29:23; Deut. 22:13-21).[64] Paul's use of the marriage metaphor shows 'the closeness of intimacy and inviolability of the union of the Christian with his Saviour.'[65] It also strongly emphasizes the Lordship of Christ over the Church.[66]

---

[61]Furnish, *2 Corinthians*, 487.

[62]Murray J. Harris, *2 Corinthians*, EBC, ed. Frank E. Gabelein (Grand Rapids: Zondervan, 1976), 385.

[63]R. A. Batey, 'Paul's Bride Image: A Symbol of Realistic Eschatology,' *Interpretation* 17 (1963), 176-82.

[64]Furnish, *2 Corinthians*, 499.

[65]Richard P. Hanson, *The Second Epistle to the Corinthians*, Torch Bible Commentaries, ed. John Marsh, vol. 47 (London: SCM, 1954), 79.

Paul saw himself as this responsible father in the lives of the Corinthian believers. Because his ministry was responsible for their conversions 'Paul sees himself as the agent of God through whom his converts were *betrothed* to Christ.'[67] 'I betrothed you to one husband, so that to Christ I might present you *as* a pure virgin' (v. 2b).[68]

Martin sees the father imagery as possible, but prefers the idea of an 'escort.'[69] This would be similar to John the Baptist's conception of his role as the friend of the bridegroom:

He who has the bride is the bridegroom; but the friend of the bridegroom, who stands and hears him, rejoices greatly because of the bridegroom's voice. So this joy of mine has been made full. (John 3:29)

Chrysostom emphasized the role of friend of the bridegroom in this passage as well. In speaking of Paul he said, 'the apostle is the Bridegroom's friend; he too is jealous, not for himself, but for the Bridegroom. Hear his voice when he is jealous.'[70]

However, the father idea is one that Paul uses elsewhere, and it was a role that he felt keenly in his relationship with the church in Corinth:

♦ 2 Corinthians 12:14: Here for this third time I am ready to come to you, and I will not be a burden to you; for I do not seek what is yours, but you; for children are not responsible to save up for *their* parents, but parents for *their* children.

---

[66]R. A. Batey, *New Testament Nuptial Imagery* (Leiden: Brill, 1971), 68.

[67]Colin G. Kruse, *The Second Epistle of Paul to the Corinthians: An Introduction and Commentary*, TNTC, ed. Leon Morris, vol. 8 (Grand Rapids: Eerdmans, 1987), 183.

[68]The betrothal (ἡρμοσάμην, *hērmosamēn*), is expressed in the middle, rather than active voice, to indicate 'Paul's sense of personal involvement in the matter.' Furnish, *2 Corinthians*, 486.

[69]Ralph P. Martin, *2 Corinthians*, WBC, ed. David A. Hubbard, vol. 40 (Waco, Tex.: Word, 1986), 333.

[70]John Chrysostom, *Nicene and Post Nicene Fathers, Series I, Vol. IX, Homilies on First Corinthians*, available from *http://www.ccel.org/fathers2/NPFN1-09/npfn1-09*; Internet.

♦ 1 Corinthians 4:15: For if you were to have countless tutors in Christ, yet *you would* not *have* many fathers, for in Christ Jesus *I became your father* through the gospel.

The fatherly image perfectly fits the situation Paul is describing in this passage. Paul has put himself in the place of the bride's father (cf. 1 Cor. 4:15; 2 Cor. 12:14), and is fearful she will lose her virginity if she follows the false teaching of his opponents. Her spiritual chastity depends on unswerving commitment to the true gospel.

That Paul's jealousy arose from the feelings of a responsible and loving father gives us a beautiful example of intense jealousy, combined with a tender familial concern. This compassion tempered and informed his angry indignation and jealousy. In addition to his ability for hard rebuke, the Corinthians knew he also had deep love for his people: 'Apart from *such* external things, there is the daily pressure on me *of* concern for all the churches' (2 Cor. 11:28). Paul's boasting did not come from pride or spite, but from fatherly love for the good of his children. 'Paul's God-filled heart yearns to protect them and keep them for the ultimate human experience, *viz.* union with Christ alone.'[71]

His love for them would not allow for passive indifference to their interest in the different gospel that was being offered. His jealousy is based in 'loving anxious concern, for the spiritual welfare of those who are his children in Christ which moves him so strongly.'[72]

Paul's desire was to be able to 'present' (παραστῆσαι, *parastēsai*) the Corinthian believers to Christ without their devotion lacking in any way. The betrothal obviously refers to the conversion of the Corinthians, and the nuptial at the return of Christ.[73]

---

[71]Raymond Ortlund, *Whoredom: God's Unfaithful Wife in Biblical Theology*, (Grand Rapids: Eerdmans, 1996), 149.

[72]Philip E. Hughes, *Paul's Second Epistle to the Corinthians*, NICNT, ed. F. F. Bruce (Grand Rapids: Eerdmans, 1962), 372.

[73]Barrett, *2 Corinthians*, 272.

Paul guards the church of Corinth with affectionate jealousy—not self-regarding but divine—lest anything should rob her of her chastity between betrothal and the day of presentation.[74]

This eschatological idea of being presented to Christ at his return is found elsewhere in Paul's writings:

♦ Romans 14:10: But you, why do you judge your brother? Or you again, why do you regard your brother with contempt? For we will all stand before (παραστησόμεθα, *parastēsometha*) the judgment seat of God.

♦ 1 Corinthians 8:8: But food will not commend us (παραστήσει, *parastēsei*) to God; we are neither the worse if we do not eat, nor the better if we do eat.

♦ 2 Corinthians 4:14: knowing that He who raised the Lord Jesus will raise us also with Jesus and will present (παραστήσει, *parastēsei*) us with you.

♦ Ephesians 5:27: that He might present (παραστήσῃ, *parastēsē*) to Himself the church in all her glory, having no spot or wrinkle or any such thing; but that she would be holy and blameless.

♦ Colossians 1:22: yet He has now reconciled you in His fleshly body through death, in order to present (παραστῆσαι, *parastēsai*) you before Him holy and blameless and beyond reproach.

♦ Colossians 1:28: We proclaim Him, admonishing every man and teaching every man with all wisdom, so that we may present (παραστήσωμεν, *parastēsōmen*) every man complete in Christ.

Paul is aware that the intervening time between the betrothal of conversion and the nuptial of the *parousia* presents perilous challenges to fidelity. He wants the Corinthians to remain chaste for Christ until the wedding day of his return.

---

[74]Fredrick F. Bruce, *1 & 2 Corinthians*, NCBC, ed. Matthew Black (Grand Rapids: Eerdmans, 1971), 234.

But for now the temptations continue and costly decisions must
be made by those who claim the betrothal, for the jealous love
of God calls the bride to keep herself chaste for her coming
bridegroom.[75]

The betrothal of conversion brings about an exclusive
relationship between God and his people. Paul emphasizes this
exclusivity of the church's relationship with Christ with the
'one husband' imagery of verse 2. Christ is the bridegroom of
the Church universal (Eph. 5:25-33), of the local church, and
of the individual Christian.[76] The believer is united to Christ as
a wife to a husband (1 Cor. 6:15-17). Therefore, to love or be
devoted to anyone except Christ is to break the marriage vow.

The Christians in Corinth can no longer claim independence
or autonomy. They belong to Christ now (1 Cor. 3:23).

> He is their one Husband and in anticipation of the coming of
> the Bridegroom they are under obligation to preserve unsullied
> their virginity (cf. 1 Jn 3:3); and Paul, their father in the gospel,
> jealously desires to present them as a pure and faithful bride to
> Christ on that great day.[77]

To break this marriage vow through a relationship with anyone
except the true groom is viewed by Paul as losing one's spiritual
virginity. The believer has been exclusively 'joined' to Christ:

> Therefore, my brethren, you also were made to die to the Law
> through the body of Christ, so that you might be joined (γενέσθαι,
> *genesthai*) to another, to Him who was raised from the dead, in
> order that we might bear fruit for God. (Rom. 7:4)

Until the return of her groom, she is to preserve her 'virgin
status.'[78] Paul desires to protect the purity of the Bride of Christ

---

[75]Ortlund, *Whoredom*, 152.
[76]Hanson, *2 Corinthians*, 79.
[77]Hughes, *2 Corinthians*, 374.
[78]Barrett, *2 Corinthians*, 272.

in Corinth. A pure bride is a symbol of pure doctrine,[79] and this pure doctrine is the essence of maintaining pure devotion to Christ.

Paul's assumption that the Corinthians have pure virginal status before God is an amazing testimony to the power of the gospel. 'Sinners reunited with the Saviour by a new covenant find their lost virginity re-created and the marriage for ever secured.'[80] Those who had previously been fornicators, idolaters, adulterers, effeminate, homosexuals, thieves, covetous, drunkards, revilers, and swindlers (1 Cor. 6:9-11) now stand as pure brides before God. The gospel's power to justify and sanctify the believer (1 Cor. 6:11) is what Paul jealousy seeks to preserve in the lives of the Corinthians.

Paul was fearful that the Corinthians would be led astray by the false teaching of his opponents. He recognized that this false teaching has the same source as any challenge to God's truth from the beginning of human history.

> But I am afraid that, as the serpent deceived Eve by his craftiness, your minds (νοήματα, *noēmata*) will be led astray from the simplicity and purity *of devotion* to Christ. (2 Cor. 11:3)

Paul identified the origin of the false gospel as Satan, who is the ultimate source of all distortion of truth (John 8:44). Believers are 'led astray' into moral ruin by Satan.[81] Like Eve, the Corinthians were in danger of being deceived by Satanic distortions.[82] 'Then the LORD God said to the woman, "What is this you have done?" And the woman said, "The serpent deceived me, and I ate"' (Gen. 3:13). Paul realized that the 'super

---

[79]Martin, *2 Corinthians*, 333.

[80]Ortlund, *Whoredom*, 152.

[81]This verb can be used to specifically describe the seduction of a woman. Furnish, *2 Corinthians*, 487.

[82]Although Eve did not betray her husband in succumbing to Satan's seduction, it is still an apt comparison. This points us to an important assumption of Paul. 'Christ is both God, the second Adam and the husband of the people of God. All lines converge on him.' Ortlund, *Whoredom*, 150 n. 30.

apostles' were Satan's agents (v. 15), who could accomplish in Corinth what the serpent did in the Garden (1 Tim. 2:14). The key danger was not primarily moral corruption, but intellectual deception (see v. 4) leading to spiritual apostasy.[83]

Satan's primary target in drawing believers away from devotion to Christ is their minds. Moral degradation was not Paul's primary concern, the origin of all depravity was. He recognized that every act of adultery, physical and spiritual, is born in the mind. If the Corinthians followed in the way of Eve, their compromise would begin in their thoughts and end up in disobedience to God's demands. Idolatry of the mind is an important concept in 2 Corinthians. Paul is the only writer of the New Testament to use νοήματα (*noēmata*, 'minds'). He uses the word six times, and five of them are in 2 Corinthians.[84]

♦ 2:11: so that no advantage would be taken of us by Satan, for we are not ignorant of his schemes (νοήματα, *noēmata*).

♦ 3:14: But *their minds* (νοήματα, *noēmata*) *were hardened*; for until this very day at the reading of the old covenant the same veil remains unlifted, because it is removed in Christ.

♦ 4:4: in whose case the god of this world has *blinded the minds* (νοήματα, *noēmata*) *of the unbelieving* so that they might not see the light of the gospel of the glory of Christ, who is the image of God.

♦ 10:5: *We are* destroying speculations and every lofty thing raised up against the knowledge of God, and *we are taking every thought* (νόημα, *noēma*) *captive* to the obedience of Christ.

♦ 11:3: But I am afraid that, as the serpent deceived Eve by his craftiness, *your minds* (νοήματα, *noēmata*) *will be led astray* from the simplicity and purity of *devotion* to Christ.

---

[83]Harris, *2 Corinthians*.
[84]2 Corinthians 2:11; 3:14; 4:4; 10:5; 11:3. The other is found in Philippians 4:7.

Unfaithfulness and immorality are primarily issues of the mind. This is especially important for those of us in our contemporary culture to remember. As A. W. Tozer wisely said:

> What comes into our minds when we think about God is the most important thing about us.... Let us beware lest we in our pride accept the erroneous notion that idolatry consists only in kneeling before visible objects of adoration, and that civilized peoples are therefore free from it. The essence of idolatry is the entertainment of thoughts about God that are unworthy of him. It begins in the mind and may be present where no overt act of worship has taken place.[85]

'For even though they knew God, they did not honor Him as God or give thanks, but they became futile in their speculations, and their foolish heart was darkened' (Rom. 1:21). When a person or church is led astray from worship of the true God, this idolatry begins and is sustained in the mind.

The False Teaching in Corinth

Paul thoroughly denounces the teaching of his opponents as representing an entirely different Jesus, spirit, and gospel.

> For if one comes and preaches another Jesus whom we have not preached, or you receive a different spirit which you have not received, or a different gospel which you have not accepted, you bear *this* beautifully. (2 Cor. 11:4)

The precise nature of the false teaching Paul was combating in Corinth is unclear. There is much debate among commentators as to the specific christological error Paul was addressing, and several ideas about the nature of the false teaching have been proposed. One is that Jesus was merely human, and not the risen, reigning Lord. Another is the opposite, Docetic view, that Jesus only appeared to be human. Others think it is the

---

[85]Aiden W. Tozer, *The Knowledge of the Holy* (New York: Harper & Row, 1961), 9, 11-12.

legalism of the Judaizers, similar to the problem in Galatia (Gal. 1:6-9).[86]

What we can be sure of is that the 'another Jesus' of verse 4 is so different from Christ that he represents 'a rival spouse.'[87] Among the many theories, it seems that the 'Jesus' that Paul's critics were espousing was a Christ of triumph only, one that that 'left no room for the experience of weakness or suffering.'[88] This 'Jesus' parallels the ministry approach of the 'super apostles' themselves. Whatever the christological error that was being taught in Corinth, we know that it was 'at odds with Paul's, whether it was gnosticizing, docetic, ebionite or nationalistic.'[89] The point is that any Jesus that does not align with the teaching of the apostles is an adulterous suitor.

The different πνεῦμα (*pneuma*) to which Paul refers is probably not the Holy Spirit as a person.[90] It is unlikely the church at Corinth had developed a pneumatology at odds with Paul's at this point in the first century. It is more likely that the spirit he referred to was their attitude in life and ministry. This πνεῦμα was one that lacked the 'earthen vessels' mentality that Paul espoused (2 Cor. 4:7). The 'spirit' of the false teachers in Corinth seemed to have no place for frailty. 'Their attitude to living before the congregation betrays a spirit in contradiction of Paul's strength-as-weakness teaching and practice.'[91]

Paul referred to the 'gospel' of his opponents as 'another gospel.' It is not just a variation, or insufficient gospel, but an altogether different one. He uses this same terminology in Galatians to describe the teaching of the Judaizers: 'I am amazed that you are so quickly deserting Him who called you by the grace of Christ, for *a different gospel*' (Gal. 1:6). Teaching a different gospel resulted in the false teachers being anathematized: 'As we

---

[86]Barrett, *2 Corinthians*, 276; Hanson, *2 Corinthians*, 81; F. F. Bruce, *1 & 2 Corinthians*, 235.

[87]Martin, *2 Corinthians*, 333.

[88]Kruse, *2 Corinthians*, 184.

[89]Martin, *2 Corinthians*, 336.

[90]Ibid.

[91]Ibid.

have said before, so I say again now, if any man is preaching to you a gospel contrary to what you received, he is to be accursed (ἀνάθεμα, *anathema*)!' (Gal. 1:8).

It is likely that this different gospel is the same as the different Christ and spirit, a gospel that is 'triumphalist' without a theology of the cross.[92] Clearly, the teaching at Corinth challenged the essence of the Christian faith that Paul and the apostolic teaching represented.

It is not clear exactly who Paul's opponents were. What we can be certain of is that they regarded Paul's teaching as wrong and that they had achieved a degree of success in Corinth. This success cause Paul to chide the Corinthians with his sarcastic statement referring to their acceptance of the false teaching: 'You bear this beautifully' (καλῶς ἀνέχεσθε, *kalōs anechesthe*). Jesus employed this same type of sarcastic use of καλῶς (*kalōs*) when he rebuked the Pharisees for holding to their traditions rather than the commandment of God: 'You are experts at setting aside the commandment of God (καλῶς ἀθετεῖτε τὴν ἐντολὴν τοῦ θεου, *kalōs atheteite tēn entolēn tou theou*) in order to keep your tradition (Mark 7:9). Paul was astounded that his flock in Corinth was giving a hearing to this different gospel, especially in light of the incredulity they were expressing toward him.

Paul intends a contrast between the remarkably tolerant way in which his converts will endure the teaching of outsiders who brings a message which is alien from the true gospel, and their critical and truculent attitude towards him.[93]

Paul's Godly Jealousy

Paul's response to the threat of the Corinthians' infidelity is godly jealousy: 'For I am jealous for you with a godly jealousy (ζηλῶ γὰρ ὑμᾶς θεοῦ ζήλῳ, *zēlō gar humas theou zēlō*).' Although Paul is annoyed that the Corinthians had eagerly received the 'super apostles,' and grown critical of him, Paul's

---

[92]Kruse, *2 Corinthians*, 185.
[93]Hanson, *2 Corinthians*, 80.

motivation for establishing his reputation is 'not wounded pride or envy or turf protection but loving jealousy.'[94] His deep love for them brought about a jealousy for their devotion to Christ that mirrored God's. It is not merely a mild interest. He is *consumed* with the jealousy of God, which is 'a term drawn from the character of Yahweh.'[95]

As noted earlier, Paul has an affinity for the ζηλ- word group. Of the twenty-four times Paul uses this root, half of these occur in the epistles to the Corinthians.[96] Six of these are in 2 Corinthians, and all but once it is used positively (12:20). θεοῦ ζήλῳ (*theou zēlō*) in verse 2 is either a genitive of quality, 'divine jealousy,' or more likely, a genitive of origin meaning 'with a jealousy of God himself.'[97] Martin translates it 'a jealousy God inspires.'[98] Because of the marriage and sexual imagery, there is no doubt that 'jealousy rather than zeal is meant, jealousy in the higher sense, as when we are jealous about our own or another person's honour.'[99]

Paul wanted his readers to know that it is not petty selfish human jealousy that is motivating him; it is the very same jealousy that God claims he feels for his people. 'The context requires the full force of the words; it is God's jealousy that lies behind Paul's.'[100] The jealousy of God we discussed in chapters 2 and 3, that is so evident in the Old Testament,

> is no less operative in the Christian church of the New. But now that divine jealousy burns for the perfect union of Christ with his bride. The passage intimates his deity and ultimacy, for it is for Christ that the covenanted people are to be preserved faithful.[101]

---

[94]Ortlund, *Whoredom*, 148.

[95]Martin, *2 Corinthians*, 332.

[96]1 Corinthians 3:3; 10:22; 12:31; 13:4; 14:1, 12, 39; 2 Corinthians 7:7, 11; 9:2; 11:2; 12:20.

[97]Furnish, *2 Corinthians*, 486.

[98]Martin, *2 Corinthians*, 327.

[99]Alfred Plummer, *A Critical and Exegetical Commentary on the Second Epistle of St Paul to the Corinthians*, ICC, ed. J. A. Emerton, *et al*, vol. 47 (Edinburgh: T & T Clark, 1915), 293.

[100]Barrett, *2 Corinthians*, 272.

Paul's godly jealousy for the Corinthians is based in the same deep covenant love that God feels for his people. And 'what God feels is a pure, intense, possessive desire to love the Corinthians and to be loved by the Corinthians within the sanctity of an exclusive covenant of communion.'[102] True love will always respond to covenant infidelity with intense jealousy. 'All love involves jealousy, if its exclusive claim is set aside.'[103] As the Corinthians' devotion to the true Jesus decreased, Paul's jealousy for their devotion increased. 'For those souls are jealous which burn ardently for those they love, and jealousy can in no other way be begotten than out of a vehement affection.'[104]

Although divine love is fully operative in this jealousy, and the well being of the Corinthians is in sight, God's glory is also a motivator for Paul. When Paul desires faithfulness from his flock, 'the honor of God is involved.'[105] The welfare of his people is a driving motivation for Paul, but his jealousy is like God's in that the honor of God's name always remains his ultimate goal.

> His jealousy is directed outwards and as it were protectively over the Corinthians as its object, and, being one with that by which God has for those who are His, it is centred in God and the honour of His supreme Name.[106]

Conclusions and Implications of Paul's Jealousy

Like the other jealous men we have studied, Paul had an important and specific role that God had given him carry out as an apostle. When looking to Paul's example we must always

---

[101]Ortlund, *Whoredom*, 150.

[102]Ibid., 148.

[103]H. L. Goudge, *The Second Epistle to the Corinthians* (London: Methuen, 1927), 101.

[104]John Chrysostom, *Nicene and Post Nicene Fathers, Series I, Vol. XIII, Homilies on First Corinthians*, available from *www.ccel.org/fathers2/NPFN1-12/npfn1-09*; Internet.

[105]Plummer, *2 Corinthians*, 293.

[106]Hughes, *2 Corinthians*, 373.

ask whether his actions or words were a function of his apostolic responsibility. The great responsibility he felt for the churches he started was a result of being their 'father' in the Lord and an apostle. This does not mean that those who are not apostles, or who are not directly responsible for planting a church, should not feel jealousy for the faithfulness of believers whenever infidelity is seen. It does mean that the extent and manner of the expression of that jealousy will depend upon the specific role and relationship to the unfaithful believers one has.

It is also important to point out that the focus of Paul's jealousy was believers. He cared deeply that those who were not Christians would trust Christ, but the main emphasis of his godly jealousy was the Church.

Paul's jealousy must also be considered within the tender pastoral heart that he had for his people. When he rebuked them for their unfaithfulness, it was done so in the context of the holistic loving ministry he had with them. It is safe to say that for Paul the primary focus of shepherding people was in the realm of truth. He realized that the most important way to love his people was to help them know and live the truth. However, Paul balanced this hard passion for truth with the compassionate heart of a father. Paul is jealous for God's glory and the fidelity of his people but he also has a deep love and affection for them (Rom. 9:2-3; 1 Thess. 2:7; 1 Tim. 5:23; Philem. 1:7). He did not express his jealousy with self-righteous detachment, but as a loving father.

Unfaithfulness to God for Paul was to believe in anything apart from the true gospel and the true Christ. Like the Old Testament prophets, Paul understood that any compromise in doctrine was spiritual adultery. Religious pluralism was not an option for Paul.

He not only recognized the idolatrous implications of false belief, he also saw the fundamental connection between God's honor and obedience to him. If a Christian lived as a friend of the world, he was an enemy of God, and this unfaithfulness made Paul very jealous.

Like the rest of the jealous leaders we have studied, Paul was thoroughly theocentric in his jealousy. His love for the people to whom he ministered, and his devotion to their apprehension of the true gospel, was grounded in his ultimate goal in everything he did – the glory of God (Rom. 15:7; 1 Cor. 10:31; 2 Cor. 1:20, 4:15; Phil. 2:11).

Chapter 7

Conclusions and Implications
of Godly Human Jealousy

In our study of godly human jealousy we have seen several vital themes woven throughout Scripture. In this chapter we will draw conclusions and make implications for life and doctrine based upon what we have learned in the previous six chapters. As we established the foundation for godly human jealousy in chapters 2 and 3, we saw that God is intensely jealous for his own glory and honor. Therefore, when human jealousy is most godly, it must have God's glory as its ultimate goal. For those who seek to embody godly jealousy, a theocentric purpose in life and ministry is essential.

In chapter 4 we learned that the primary way God receives glory in human history is through the uncompromising faithfulness of his people. His jealousy is based on the covenant he established with his people. We also saw that the marriage metaphor is the central expression of this relationship. Although God's jealousy is in no way tainted with sin as human jealousy so often is, it is nevertheless a real, and deeply felt emotion he experiences. This genuine experience of emotion in no way detracts from his transcendence, sovereignty, or omniscience. Chapter 3 also showed us that God's jealousy for the devotion of his people means that he has no tolerance for idolatry of any kind. The great contemporary challenge of religious pluralism is recognized as spiritual adultery, and rejected without exception.

In chapters 5 and 6, we saw the theocentric focus and rejection of idolatry that are the foundational responses of godly jealousy in the lives of five great leaders of God's people. In Phinehas, David, Elijah, Jesus, and Paul we saw powerful examples of men who were jealous for God's honor, and consequently jealous for faithfulness among God's people. As we look to these men, we can apply much of their example to the Christian life today. However, we also saw a few limitations that must be considered before too quickly following their examples.

We will now explore the four main conclusions and implications of this study for the church today. The theocentric perspective at the heart of godly jealousy, the legitimacy of this deeply felt godly emotion, the rejection of religious pluralism, and the main application and limitations of the examples of the jealous men we studied, will be explored in greater depth.

Theocentric Perspective

We have seen that God's primary goal in human history, a goal for which he is intensely jealous, is his own glory and honor. This jealousy is foundational for all godly jealousy. God desires the fidelity of his people because he loves them, but ultimately because he is most glorified when they ascribe to him the honor that belongs to him alone. This goal is achieved by God making himself known, so that people will acknowledge, fear, worship, and obey him as the one and only Lord. This goal is evident at every key stage of salvation history. God's covenant love and compassion are no less operational than his jealousy. He is jealous for the devotion of his people because he has the loving heart of a father, but ultimately because he desires to protect the honor of his name.

Human jealousy that is most like God's seeks his glory above all else. When God is truly known, he is worshipped, feared, and obeyed as the only true Lord. The jealous person desires this response from others as well.

Any cause in Scripture is part of the greater purpose of displaying God's glory. God is righteous, and therefore values above all else what is of ultimate value. He loves most what is most worthy of being loved. His own character, being, perfections, are this object. As creator, God alone is worthy of ultimate honor.[1] Specifically because he is God, he is therefore rightly jealous. To concede he is something other than the center of all, and rightly to be worshiped and adored, would debase his very Godhood. He is God who, entirely rightly, does not give his glory to another.[2]

God's jealousy for his glory does not conflict with his love. God is unique in that he alone is able to love perfectly while seeking his own glory. God's perfect justice and love necessitate his own self-exaltation.

The 'seeker sensitive' approach of many churches today runs the risk of having the 'felt needs' of unbelievers be a greater priority than God's glory. A desire to be 'relevant' and attractive can encourage a marketing mentality in the church that lacks jealousy for God's honor. Add to this the heavy influence of psychology in our culture, and a therapeutic, self-centered approach to ministry can also detract from God's glory being the supreme objective when Christians gather. These influences of the church growth movement can lead the church to become a pragmatically oriented self-help group, rather than a God-glorifying community. It can also provide only shallow solutions to man's deepest problems. Man can only glorify God as intended by redemption through Christ and thereby fulfill his reason for being.

If jealousy for God's honor is a predominant emotion, it will have profound implications for the life of the church. Godly jealousy would cause a shift in contemporary thinking from its emphasis on obedience to God because it is what is pragmatically best for the obedient individual. A theocentric perspective cultivates godly jealousy and godly jealousy encourages a greater emphasis on God's character and glory. If this divine jealousy is properly understood, taught and appreciated, the church would preserve the profoundly God-centered perspective it is intended to have.

---

[1]God's exclusive right to be worshiped and honored is often linked to his identity as creator. The following passages show this connection: Nehemiah 9:5-6; Psalms 33:6,9; 89:111; 148:5; Isaiah 42:5; Acts 14:15; 17:24; 1 Corinthians 4:7; Colossians 1:16; Hebrews 11:3; Revelation 4:11.

[2]Carson, *Love of God*, 39.

The Transcendence and Immanence of God

We also saw that God is personal, relational, and has entered into a covenant relationship with his people that he compares to a marriage. God's jealousy is an actual emotion that he experiences when his people are unfaithful to him. Yahweh as the husband of his people is a central metaphor used to describe the relationship he has with his people. God's jealousy brings out both God's unique holiness as well as his personal intimate relation to his people.

> Jealousy expresses the unique character of the covenant relationship between Yahweh and his people, translates perfectly the living and concrete aspect of a personal being and underlines his passionate character.[3]

Theologians concerned with preserving belief in God's eternal, transcendent, sovereign nature may fail to fully appreciate his genuine emotions. They may wrongly dismiss his emotions as anthropopathisms with no real meaning except to describe his outward actions.[4]

At the other end of the spectrum, theologians concerned that we appreciate how significantly God relates to his creation want to maintain actual emotions in God. However, at times they only want to emphasize emotions that fit with contemporary sensibilities and may conceptualize God as so related to his creation that he is no longer truly transcendent, omniscient, or sovereign.[5]

Impassibility and immutability must be defined so that they still allow for God's genuine personal interaction with his

---

[3]Renaud, Je Suis un Dieu Jaloux,153. La jalousie a pour elle d'exprimer le caractère unique des relations d'alliance entre Yahvé et son people, de traduire parfaitement l'aspect vivant et concret d'un être personnel et de souligner son character passionnel.

[4]See chapter 1, note 42 for examples of this.

[5]Examples of this overemphasis can be found in: John Sanders, *The God Who Risks: A Theology of Providence* (Downers Grove, Ill.: InterVarsity, 1998) and Clark Pinnock *et al.*, *The Open View of God: A Biblical Challenge to the Traditional View of God*, (Downers Grove, Ill.: InterVarsity, 1994).

creation.[6] Wayne Grudem's definition of immutability shows an appreciation for the biblical tension between transcendence and immanence when he says that God is 'unchanging in his being, perfections, purposes, and promises,' but he makes an important qualification by adding, 'yet God does act and feel emotions, and he acts and feels differently in response to different situations.' Obviously this definition shows an effort to not err on either side of the transcendence/immanence tension. This approach requires a healthy appreciation of the ultimate incomprehensibility and mystery which is always present when finite beings seek to understand the infinite yet personal God.[7] D. A. Carson is worth quoting at length on this subject when he speaks of God's wrath.

---

[6]For a good summary of the contemporary discussion on the suffering and passibility of God, see Richard Bauckham, ' "Only the Suffering God Can Help': Divine Passibility in Modern Theology,' *Themelios* 9, no. 3 (April, 1984 1985): 6-12. Other helpful treatments of this issue which seek to allow for the Biblical tension between transcendence and immanence are Donald Macleod, *Behold Your God*, revised and expanded edition, (Geanies House, Fearn, Ross-shire: Scotland, Great Britain: Christian Focus, 1995), 31-37). D. A. Carson, *Love of God*, esp. 21-64; Millard J. Erickson, 'God and Change,' *The Southern Baptist Journal of Theology* (1997): 38-51; Hallman, 'The Emotions of God.' Two outstanding treatments of the issue of impassibility are written by Bruce Ware. In his 'An Exposition and Critique of the Process Doctrines of Divine Mutability and Immutability,' *WTJ* 47 (1985): 175-96, Ware summarizes the process theology of Charles Hartshorne and contends, *contra* Hartshorne, that God's personal intimate involvement with the world does not demand a denial of his self-sufficiency, and self-sufficiency does not demand indifference on God's part. In his 'An Evangelical Reformulation of the Doctrine of the Immutability of God,' *JETS* 29, no. 4 (December 1986): 431-46, Ware shows appreciation for contemporary attempts to grapple with God's 'real relatedness to the world.' The main point of this article is that God's relational mutability does not change his essence. Divine emotions like wrath should not be dismissed as anthropopathisms because they do not require the denial of other passages of Scripture. Emotions have potential for good or bad. God is a genuinely emotional being, and we should view our emotions as theomorphic. Cf. Peter D. Anders, 'Divine Impassibility and Our Suffering God: How an Evangelical Theology of the Cross Can and Should Affirm Both,' *Modern Reformation* (July/ August 1997): 24-30. Anders attempts to resolve the issue by making a distinction between the economic and immanent Trinity.

[7]This is an appreciation that Clark Pinnock seems to lack when he says 'Bruce Ware and Wayne Grudem are good examples of theologians who accept the need to reformulate immutability but refuse to surrender timelessness, all-controlling sovereignty and exhaustive omniscience. It remains a mystery how one can say

Wrath, like love, includes emotion as a necessary component. Here again, if impassibility is defined in terms of the complete absence of all 'passions,' not only will you fly in the face of the biblical evidence, but you tumble into fresh errors that touch the very holiness of God. The reason is that in itself, wrath, unlike love, is *not* one of the intrinsic perfections of God. Rather, it is a function of God's holiness against sin. Where there is no sin, there is no wrath – but there will always be love in God. Where God in his holiness confronts his image-bearers in their rebellion, there *must* be wrath, *or God is not the jealous God he claims to be, and his holiness is impugned.* The price of diluting God's wrath is diminishing God's holiness.[8]

Neglecting God's transcendence can begin the downward journey to process or open theism, and to slight his immanence can lead to deism. Both of these approaches result in a theology that falls far short of the God of the Bible.

A biblically accurate understanding of the jealousy of God will insure that this vital transcendence/immanence tension will remain at the heart of our understanding of God. God's jealousy affirms his transcendence in his demand that he not be compared to anything in all of creation. God's jealousy also affirms his personal nature and is an actual emotion that God experiences when his people are unfaithful to him. Yahweh

---

that God acts and feels in response to different situations whilst saying that he causes everything and knows everything.' Clark H. Pinnock, *Most Moved Mover: a Theology of God's Openness* (Grand Rapids: Baker 2001), 77. It indeed remains a mystery, a wonderful mystery. And this should not come as a surprise to us, or as a source of doubt or frustration. Rather, the fact that the eternal, infinite, unchanging, self-sufficient God has chosen to personally enter time/space and human history as the husband of his people should cause us to be humbled and awestruck as Job was when he said at the end of his ordeal, 'Surely I spoke of things I did not understand, things too wonderful for me to know (NIV),' or as Charles Wesley when staggered by the wonder of the death of Christ says 'Tis mystery all! The immortal dies! Who can express His strange design?' Along with the incomprehensibility of God, we must remember that when finite language is used to describe him it may have absolute truth value, but will always be limited analogical language and therefore never yield either univocal or equivocal statements about God. For an excellent treatment of this issue see Michael S. Horton, 'Hellenistic or Hebrew: Open Theism and Reformed Theological Method,' *JETS*, Vol. 45, No. 2, (June, 2002).

[8]Carson, *Love of God*, 67.

deeply cares that his creation knows and recognizes him as the only true God. Yahweh as the husband of his people is a central metaphor used to describe the relationship he has with his people and his jealousy is grounded in this relational depth that he has chosen to bring about. Although God is independent, self-sufficient, eternal, and transcendent, he is also relational, engaged, personal, and immanent. The legitimate emotional response of divine jealousy in no way detracts from God's holiness or transcendence. Rather, it affirms both, and the reality of his eternal yet personal nature makes his jealousy necessary. Donald Bloesch describes the imbalance today in holding these two poles in their biblical tension:

> Any cursory examination of academic theology today will reveal a mounting controversy over the concept of God. The current emphases are not altogether unbiblical, but they are irremediably imbalanced. God is portrayed as vulnerable, as lover, as friend, as empowerer. What is lacking in so many instances is a strong affirmation of the holiness and almightiness of God. God is not simply *with* us and *in* us, but he is also *against* us and *over* us. He is judge as well as savior, master as well as friend, transcendent as well as immanent.[9]

Divine jealousy is a foundational emotion from which divine wrath is expressed. Like wrath, jealousy is a genuine emotional response of God that is demanded by his holiness to any rival to his glory. God's jealousy is never unwarranted or uncontrolled as human jealousy so often is. Rather, for God, 'it is an entirely reasonable and willed response to an offense against his holiness.'[10]

God's transcendence and immanence are both affirmed by God's jealousy.

> Transcendence because it expresses incommensurable divine holiness that puts the divine being beyond all human category,

---

[9]Donald Bloesch, *God the Almighty* (Downers Grove, Ill.: Intervarsity, 1995), 13-14.

[10]Ibid., 67.

immanence because it is the love that wants to insert itself into the heart of history. Thus, is verified the apparently paradoxical affirmation: 'where God appears most human, he reveals himself to be most transcendent.' Far from belittling divinity, divine jealousy that expresses this will of God to commune with man, of Yahweh with his people, makes one aware in this same experience of the selective and purifying demands of his holiness.[11]

The God of the Bible is not the detached, absent god of the deist. 'God is not only the master who commands, he is the Father who loves and passes this love into the reality of the life of human history.'[12] The jealousy of God affirms his loving fatherly care of his creation. 'God does not view the cosmos with detachment, but with intense (jealous/zealous) care.'[13]

Religious Pluralism

A shift away from the distinct teaching of the particularity and exclusivity of Jesus is pervading the church at every level. Even if religious pluralism is not explicitly affirmed, it is often the implicit understanding among many today. Pluralists like John Hick, Paul Knitter, and Sallie McFague have been greatly influenced by Kantian dualism, which confines knowledge of God to the unknowable noumenal realm, as well as a Troeltschian historicism, which rejects a salvation history scheme.[14] Consequently, they do not believe

---

[11]Renaud, Je Suis un Dieu Jaloux, 153. Transcendance parce qu'elle exprime la Sainteté divine incommensurable qui situe l'Être divin audelà de toute catégorie humaine, Immanence parce qu'elle est l'Amour qui veut s'insérer au cœur de l'histoire. Ainsi se vérifie cette affirmation au premier abord si paradoxale: 'Là où Dieu apparaît le plus humain, il se révèle le plus Transcendant.' Loin de rabaisser la divinité, la jalousie divine qui exprime cette volonté de communion de Dieu avec l'homme, de Yahvé avec son peuple, fait prendre conscience, dans cette expérience même des exigences sélectives et purificatrices de sa Sainteté.

[12]Renaud, Dieu Jaloux, 70-71. 'Dieu n'est pas seulement le Maître qui commande, il est le Père qui aime et qui fait passer cet amour dans la réalité de la vie et de l'histoire humaine.'

[13]Bernard Ramm, *Special Revelation and the Word of God* (Grand Rapids: Eerdmans, 1961), 90.

[14]John Hick, *The Myth of God Incarnate* (London: SCM, 1977); Sallie McFague, 'The Christian Paradigm,' in *Christian Theology*, ed. Peter C. Hodgson and Robert

that absolute truth is accessible to humans. They understand theology to be a constructive enterprise and Christianity to be merely one religion among many. God is not found in one particular deposit of sacred writings or in one paradigm for the divine-human relationship. Rather, God is found in the existential experience an individual has with it through whatever means his culture provides. Lesslie Newbigin defines religious pluralism as,

> The belief that differences between religions are not a matter of truth and falsehood, but of different perceptions of the one truth; that to speak of religious belief as true or false is inadmissible. Religious belief is a private matter.[15]

The 'Christian' pluralist finds God when he has an experience with the relative truths of the Christian way. This way is just one of many ways to approach God. Therefore, the contemporary Christian must be open to, and actively 'seek correctives from other religions.'[16] This is because the model Jesus offers is only one historically conditioned symbol among humankind's vast offering of equally valid symbols of the divine-human relationship. Once the relativity of religion is acknowledged, the theologian is no longer bound to the 'idolatry' of a fixed absolute concept of God.

So how should evangelicals respond to the claims of religious pluralism? Often the Christian has rightly sought to refute the pluralist on his own terms. Because pluralism rejects the Bible as the last word on God's nature, and how he is to be worshiped, it is helpful to point out the philosophical, logical, and experiential inconsistencies of claiming that all religions are fundamentally the same.

H. King (Philadelphia: Fortress, 1985), 377-90; Paul Knitter, *No Other Name? A Critical Survey of Christian Attitudes Toward the World Religions* (New York: Orbis, 1986).

[15]Lesslie Newbigin, *The Gospel in a Pluralist Society* (Grand Rapids: Eerdmans, 1992), 14.

[16]McFague, 'Christian Paradigm,' 323.

It is also important to point out that evangelical theological method does not see reason and experience alone as the norm of theological method, but Jesus Christ himself. Jesus is not a 'bygone savior,'[17] but is alive and actively involved in our search for God. He is the starting point and goal of the theological quest. God is not an inanimate object knowable through sense perception alone. God must act if he is to be known, and he revealed himself ultimately in Jesus Christ. The transcendent, eternal incomprehensible God of the universe has broken through the barrier of Kantian dualism and has shown that history is heading somewhere. The radical and central teaching of the historic Christian faith is that God definitively revealed himself in time and space and became a man 2000 years ago.

For those who rely on God's definitive revelation of himself in his word, Scripture is used to reject religious pluralism. Key texts that teach that Jesus is the exclusive way to know and approach God (John 14:6; Acts 4:12; 1 Tim. 2:5; Rom. 10:13-15) are appealed to, in order to affirm the particularity and uniqueness of Christ. However, the Christian theologian would be well served to put his emphasis on the basis for the exclusivity found within the Christian way, which is the very nature of God. God is personal, and this personal God has entered into personal, covenant relationship with his people that he compares to a marriage. This relationship makes the invitation to 'seek correctives from other religions'[18] an invitation to spiritual adultery. And God's response to this adultery is intense and consistent jealousy.

How then should a Christian respond to invitations to partake of religions that fall outside of the bounds of the historic Christian faith of the Bible? The jealousy of God affirms and demonstrates his personal and relational nature that must be denied if pluralism is embraced. His jealousy shows that he is not the impersonal force that we can only call 'the real,'

---

[17]Ibid.
[18]Ibid.

but rather it shows that he is the personal, loving, jealous God of the covenant. Although today's culture often sees tolerance as the highest virtue, '[n]o religion claiming possession of a divine revelation can afford to be tolerant.'[19]

God claims the right to an exclusive relationship with his people. This exclusivity is not merely because of the ethical insufficiency of alternative religions. He alone is to be worshipped because he is a jealous God.

If one takes the marriage metaphor at the heart of the covenant seriously, the encouragement of the pluralist to alter the Christian message by the influence of other religions is an encouragement to harlotry. It is to suggest that a wife can love her husband equally effectively in the bed of another lover. The pluralist notion suggests that believers commit adultery, and then tell their jealous and angry husband that when they were making love to that other lover, they were really making love to him. The bride must stay chaste for her groom. If not, God reacts with angry jealousy.

> The covenant creates a sacred boundary not to be encroached upon. It warrants a lawful sense of entitlement within God which, when violated, generates intense emotional upheaval (Prov. 6:34; 27:4).[20]

It was during one of Israel's darkest times of her history that her harlotry was greatest. When she was in danger of Assyrian assault in the eighth century and the pressures of the world closed in on her, she fled to the arms of other gods. She felt pressured to conform to the world around her by becoming more inclusive and open to other religions. The Church of Jesus Christ at present is feeling this same pressure. The situation in Hosea's day could easily pass for a description of the Church today:

---

[19]Robert Pfeiffer, 'The Polemic Against Idolatry in the Old Testament,' *JBL* 43 (1924): 16.

[20]Ortlund, *Whoredom*, 30.

...[c]lassical Yahwism was losing its compelling power among the people. It was being redefined with fewer sharp edges and more open doors as a broadly inclusive religion, increasingly tolerant of elements of paganism. What one observes in Hosea's historical situation is the admixture of contrary theologies made congenial not by logic of principle but by fashion and feeling.[21]

The religious pluralist invites the people of God to act like the wild animals in heat to which Jeremiah likens the Israelites:

How can you say, 'I am not defiled, I have not gone after the Baals'? Look at your way in the valley! Know what you have done! You are a swift young camel entangling her ways, a wild donkey accustomed to the wilderness, that sniffs the wind in her passion. In *the time of* her heat who can turn her away? All who seek her will not become weary; in her month they will find her. Keep your feet from being unshod and your throat from thirst; but you said, 'It is hopeless! No! For I have loved strangers, and after them I will walk.' (Jer. 2:23-25)

This offensive image is intended to show the disgusting nature of seeking Yahweh in other religions.

When religious devotion is left in the realm of philosophical ideas and ethical concepts, openness to and experimentation with other religions seem obvious and potentially fruitful avenues. But when religious devotion involves an intimate love relationship with a jealous personal God, openness to, and experimentation with other religions are nothing short of playing the harlot.

Although those who hold to the exclusive claims of Christ will be seen as arrogant, bigoted and narrow, those wedded to him have no other choice if they are to heed the words of their Bridegroom when he said, 'For whoever is ashamed of Me and of My words in this adulterous and sinful generation, of him will the Son of Man also be ashamed, when He comes in glory of His Father with the holy angels' (Mark 8:38).

---

[21]Ibid, 48

Jealous Scholarship

Any distortion of the true gospel amounts to idolatry and spiritual adultery. In light of this, the jealousy of God has great implications for evangelical scholarship. The jealous Christian scholar will react with godly jealousy whenever the clear teaching of Scripture is violated. In a proper effort to be irenic, gracious, and fair, it will nevertheless be impossible to remain ambivalent when the deposit of truth entrusted to him is distorted. An example of evangelical scholarship that seems to lack jealousy is in Alister McGrath's response to John Hick's testimony of how he went from believing the gospel to embracing radical pluralism. McGrath begins his response by saying,

> Professor Hick's essay is lucid and articulate, and I found it easy to interact with. *I particularly enjoyed reading the account of his conversion from conservative evangelicalism to liberalism*, not least because my own intellectual pilgrimage was in the opposite direction (italics mine).[22]

How could McGrath *enjoy* the story of a man who descended into apostasy? For a Christian to enjoy reading Hick's pilgrimage is as absurd as someone who had come out of a life of prostitution, saying how much they enjoyed hearing of someone plummeting into that wretched lifestyle. Godly jealousy demands that Christian scholars abhor and denounce false teaching, even if he will be considered divisive, intolerant, and uncharitable.

Leaders of the church, especially theologians, who wish to hold to a faith that even remotely resembles the true faith of Christianity, must hold to the exclusive truth claims of the church throughout the centuries. God, whose name is Jealous, demands that his people remain devoted to the true gospel without compromise.

---

[22]Alister McGrath, 'Response to John Hick,' in *More than One Way?: Four Views on Salvation in a Pluralistic World*, ed. Dennis Okholm and Timothy Phillips, (Grand Rapids: Zondervan, 1995), 65.

The Jealous Christian

When is human jealousy godly? When is it ungodly? What are appropriate ways to express godly jealousy today? This final section of this study will seek to provide answers to these questions based on what we have learned thus far.

Christians should feel the jealous anger and indignation of the godly leaders we have studied. However, it is vital that one recognize the significant distinctions between the Old Testament saint, operating under the law based theocracy, and the New Testament Christian, operating under the New Covenant and the Lordship of Christ. While the depth and intensity of the jealousy that one feels for God's honor should be the same as the men we studied, this jealousy must be appropriately expressed within our context today. The roles of Priest, King, Prophet, Messiah, and Apostle gave the five jealous persons we studied unique authority and responsibility that led them to act as they did.

In addition to their roles, the theocratic context of Phinehas, David, and Elijah was based on Old Testament law and direct commands of God. This makes the bloody expression of their jealousy limited to their historical situation. Phinehas' killing of Zimri and Cozbi, David's killing of Goliath, and Elijah's slaughtering of the prophets of Baal were appropriate manifestations of their godly jealousy for their contexts, but such manifestations would no longer represent God's methods under the New Covenant.

> To infer from this act of Elijah the right to institute a bloody persecution of heretics, would not only indicate a complete oversight of the difference between heathen idolatry and Christian heretics, but the same reprehensible confounding of the evangelical standpoint of the New Testament with the legal standpoint of the Old, which Christ condemned in His own disciples in Luke 9:55-56.[23]

---

[23]Keil, *Kings*, 250 n., 1.

Care should also be taken to acknowledge the differences that may exist between one's calling today and the New Testament expressions of godly jealousy we studied. Before taking bold and violent action as Jesus did in the Temple, one must consider whether God has given that role, power and authority to us as well. As Calvin rightly says,

> In common with the Son of God we should all be zealous; but it is not for all of us to take a whip and forcibly correct vices. For the same power has not been given to us nor the same office laid upon us.[24]

The ardent desire for God's honor should be as strongly felt by the present day Christian as it was by the Old Testament believer. However, those who now live between the first and second coming of Christ defer to him the kind of swift judgment he will bring when he returns. 'Christians view idolatry as no less sinful, but see total judgment as reserved for the final Day.'[25] The Christian awaits the future judgment of Christ and does not take that judgment into his own hands. Any action taken in jealousy by the Christian should reflect the eschatological perspective of the New Testament that hopefully awaits God's intervention in human history.

Phinehas, David, Elijah, and Paul remain important examples in many ways. Each of their godly lives foreshadow or point back to Christ. However, there are significant differences between them and Christ. As we saw, Jesus experienced intense jealousy for God's honor but expressed it differently than David. In the New Testament, God's jealousy for his own honor caused him to take the lives of people (Acts 5:5-10; 12:23), but we have no example of godly men doing the same. David's imprecatory Psalms show a distinction between the expressions of godly jealousy in the Old Testament and the New. 'The very juxtaposition of David cursing his tormentors

---

[24]Calvin, *John*, 54.
[25]Wiseman, *1 and 2 Kings*, 170.

and Jesus praying for his, brings out the gulf between type and antitype and indeed between accepted attitudes among saints of the Old Testament and the New.'[26]

In the New Testament we still see God himself taking drastic, physical action on those who dishonor him (Acts 5:4-6;12:23). But when it comes to jealousy of human leaders, a shift takes place in the New Testament where jealousy for God's honor is channeled through gospel proclamation, and is, in some measure, put on hold until God unleashes his final judgment.[27] Jesus himself frowned upon violent reactions to behavior that were dishonoring to God. He rebuked Peter when he cut off Malchus' ear (Matt. 26:52). His response to James and John when they wanted to call down fire to consume the inhospitable Samaritans seems to teach the same idea:

> But He turned and rebuked them, and said, 'You do not know what kind of spirit you are of; for the Son of Man did not come to destroy men's lives, but to save them.' And they went on to another village. (Luke 9:55-56)

Another important qualification of the jealousy of a Christian is that it should always function within the other emotions that sanctification produces. Jealousy for God's honor and the true gospel should be expressed along with patience, kindness, goodness, and compassion. To determine what godly jealousy looks like in the life of the believer requires discernment, wisdom, and the leading of the Holy Spirit. It is easy to become self-righteous in the defense of truth and God's honor.

---

[26]Kidner, *Psalms 1-72*, 245.

[27]One exception to this could be Paul in 1 Corinthians 5 "delivering" an immoral man "over to Satan for the destruction of the flesh". However, I do not see this as precedent for Christians actually taking violence into their own hands, but rather precedent for excommunication and allowing for the spiritual harm that comes through that as well as the devastating physical and spiritual effects of sin. On another related issue, while the scope of this study does not allow for a treatment of the Christian's relationship to civil governments and their God-ordained role as instruments of vengeance (e.g. Rom. 13:3-4), this is certainly an area where further study is needed.

The person whose jealousy is godly is always motivated by righteousness. In his explanation of the imprecatory psalms, VanGemeren describes the necessary internal process for expressing indignant jealous anger in a godly way:

> For the Christian it is most important to uproot any selfish passions, judgmentalism, and personal vindictiveness, because those who practice these come under the judgment of God (Gal. 5:15; James 4:13-16). These psalms help us to pray through our anger, frustrations, and spite, to a submission to God's will. Only then will the godly man or woman be able to pray for the execration of evil and the full establishment of God's kingdom.[28]

It seems that this process was absent in the examples of human jealousy for God's honor that ended up as ungodly expressions of this emotion. Although Jehu had great קנא (*qna*) for the Lord (2 Kings 10:16), he obviously expressed his jealousy in an ungodly and self-serving way.

> And the LORD said to him, 'Name him Jezreel; for yet a little while, and I will punish the house of Jehu for the bloodshed of Jezreel, and I will put an end to the kingdom of the house of Israel.' (Hosea 1:4)

Along the same lines, while aspects of the Pharisee's ζῆλος (*zēlos*) for God and his law were commendable (Phil. 3:6), it was nevertheless without knowledge and consequently opposed to the gospel (Rom. 10:2).

Because jealousy is such a central characteristic of God and godly men, it should be understood as an emotion that needs to be cultivated and felt by godly Christians. If the limitations and qualifications we have discussed are heeded, this emotion should be encouraged and appreciated in the church and in marriage. True love responds with deeply felt jealousy whenever one in covenant relationship expresses infidelity.

---

[28]VanGemeren, *Psalms*, 832.

Godly jealousy primarily focuses on fidelity to God among the people of God. While godly jealousy has an interest that all men acknowledge God's glory (Exod. 14:4, 18; 1 Sam. 17:46; Isa 19:21; Jonah), it has God's covenant people as its main focus. Godly jealousy is grounded in the covenant between God and his people. This relationship that God compares to a marriage, is central to the experience of godly jealousy.

The most important characteristic for jealousy to be godly is that it must have God's honor and glory as its primary and conscious goal. It does not desire obedience to God's commands as an end in itself. It desires obedience because obedience to God is the primary way of honoring him. Godly jealousy hates idolatry because it is foolish and harmful to those who practice it, but it hates it most of all because it dishonors God.

The godly man or woman who cares deeply about God's honor will have feelings of intense jealousy whenever a rival to God receives the devotion that he alone deserves. This jealousy begins with the destruction of any rival to God within one's own heart. The godly person must be willing to turn Phinehas' jealous spear on any idolatry found within his own life. Only then is he ready to be a prophetic voice of godly jealousy into the lives of others.

As we have seen, the Old Testament examples of godly human jealousy should not be used to advocate or justify violence of any kind within the Christian perspective. They should be considered within their theocratic context and tempered with the perspective of spiritual warfare that we find in the New Testament.

> For though we walk in the flesh, we do not war according to the flesh, for the weapons of our warfare are not of the flesh, but divinely powerful for the destruction of fortresses. (2 Cor. 10:3-4)

> For our struggle is not against flesh and blood, but against the rulers, against the powers, against the world forces of this darkness, against the spiritual *forces* of wickedness in the heavenly *places*. (Eph. 6:12)

The godly Christian should hate idolatry no less than Phinehas, yet he is called to fight with different weapons now. The enemies of God should be fought with the same bold indignation David had, but righteousness, the gospel of peace, and the sword of the Spirit have replaced his stones.

The God who is the husband of his people loves his bride far too much to allow her to wander from his side for long. His jealous love will not allow her to follow her adulterous heart indefinitely. God will allow no rival to him in the lives of his people, and godly men will share in this jealousy for the faithfulness of his people and ultimately for God's eternal glory.

God's ardent interest in his own glory and honor is a part of his eternal nature. However, before creation, God's jealousy would have not had occasion for expression. The perfect expression of relationship within the triune Godhead would have left no place for God's jealousy to be provoked. After creation, God's jealousy is provoked by his finite creatures who deny him his rightful honor. From God's jealous reaction to Satan's rebellion (Isa. 14:12-15), to the final, violent reclaiming of his kingdom (Rev. 18), this jealous reaction to an abrogation of his honor is present throughout the history of redemption. God's intense desire to protect his own glory (Exod. 20:4-6; Ezek. 39:25) is not a peripheral or accidental attribute. It is a necessary aspect of his divine nature and a necessary aspect of divine love. Divine jealousy demands the best of interpersonal relationship.

The key examples of godly human jealousy occur within a broad spectrum of salvation history. The proper manner and timing of the expression of human jealousy depend upon context, discernment, and the clear leading of the Holy Spirit.

Godly human jealousy should be grounded in a theocentric perspective and the exclusive demands of the covenant. The godly person will have no tolerance for idolatry, or religious pluralism of any kind. Any rival to God will be rooted out of the jealous person's life, and he will strive to see it removed from the life of the church as well. May the God whose name is Jealous be honored through the obedience and faithfulness of his jealous bride.

Bibliography

Adamson, James B. *The Epistle of James*. Grand Rapids: Eerdmans, 1976.

Albright, W. F. *From Stone Age to Christianity*. New York: Doubleday, 1957.

Alden, Robert. *Psalms: Songs of Dedication*. Chicago: Moody, 1975.

Alexander, Ralph H. *Ezekiel*. EBC, ed. Frank E. Gaebelein., vol. 6. Grand Rapids: Eerdmans, 1986.

Allen, Leslie C. *Ezekiel: 20-48*. WBC, ed. Robert L. Hubbard, vol. 29. Waco, Tex.: Word, 1990.

Allender, Dan, and Tremper Longman. *The Cry of the Soul: How Our Emotions Reveal Our Deepest Questions About God*. Colorado Springs, Colo.: NavPress, 1994.

Anders, Peter D. 'Divine Impassibility and Our Suffering God: How an Evangelical Theology of the Cross Can and Should Affirm Both.' *Modern Reformation* July/August 1997: 24-30.

Anderson, A. A. *The Book of Psalms*. NCBC, ed. Ronald E. Clements, vol. 1. Grand Rapids: Eerdmans, 1972.

Ashbrook, James B., and Carol Rausch Albright. *The Humanizing Brain: Where Science and Religion Meet*. Cleveland, Ohio: Pilgrim Press, 1997.

Ashley, Timothy R. *The Book of Numbers*. NICOT, ed. R. K. Harrison. Grand Rapids: Eerdmans, 1993.

Baker, David W. *Nahum, Habakkuk, and Zephaniah: An Introduction and Commentary*. TOTC, ed. D. J. Wiseman, vol. 23b. Downers Grove, Ill: InterVarsity, 1988.

Baldwin, Joyce G. *1 & 2 Samuel*. TOTC, ed. D. J. Wiseman, vol. 9. Downers Grove, Ill.: InterVarsity, 1988.

Barrett, C. K. *A Commentary on the Second Epistle to the Corinthians*. Harper's New Testament Commentaries, ed. Henry Chadwick. New York: Harper & Row, 1973.

_____. *A Critical and Exegetical Commentary on the Acts of the Apostles*. ICC, ed. J. A. et al Emerton, vol. 1. Edinburgh: T & T Clark, 1994.

_____. *The First Epistle to the Corinthians*. Harper's New Testament Commentaries, ed. Henry Chadwick. New York: Harper & Row, 1968.

_____. *The Gospel According to St John*. London: S. P. C. K., 1962.

_____. *The Second Epistle to the Corinthians*. Black's New Testament Commentary, ed. Henry Chadwick, vol. 8. London: A & C Black, 1973.

Batey, R. A. *New Testament Nuptial Imagery*. Leiden: Brill, 1971.

_____. 'Paul's Bride Image: A Symbol of Realistic Eschat-ology.' *Interpretation* 17 (1963): 176-82.

Bauckham, Richard. ' "Only the Suffering God Can Help": Divine Passibility in Modern Theology.' *Themelios* 9, no. 3 (April, 1984 1985): 6-12.

Beasley-Murray, George R. *John*. WBC, ed. Ralph P. Martin, vol. 36. Waco, Tex.: Word, 1987.

Ben-Ze'ev, Aaron. 'Are Envy, Anger, and Resentment Moral Emotions?' *Philosophical Explorations* 5, no. 2 (May 2002): 148-54.

_____. 'Envy and Jealousy.' *Canadian Journal of Philosophy* December 1990: 487-516.

Block, Daniel I. *The Book of Ezekiel*. NICOT, ed. R. K. Harrison and Robert L. Hubbard, vol. 1-2. Grand Rapids: Eerdmans, 1997.

Bloesch, Donald. *God The Almighty*. Downers Grove, Ill.: InterVarsity, 1995.

Blomberg, Craig. *Matthew*. NAC, ed. David S. Dockery, vol. 8. Nashville: Broadman, 1992.

Boogaart, T. A. 'History and Drama in the Story of David and Goliath.' *Reformed Review* 38, 1985.

Borchert, Gerald, L. *John 1-11*. NAC, ed. David S. Dockery, vol. 25A. New York: Broadman & Holman, 1996.

Boyd, Gregory. *God of the Possible*. Grand Rapids: Baker, 2000.

Brown, Raymond E. *The Gospel According to John*. The Anchor Bible, ed. William F. Albright and David N. Freedman. New York: Doubleday, 1966.

Brownlee, William H. *Ezekiel 1-19*. WBC, ed. David A. Hubbard, vol. 28. Waco, Tex.: Word, 1986.

Bruce, F. F. *1 & 2 Corinthians*. NCBC, ed. Matthew Black. Grand Rapids: Eerdmans, 1971.

_____. *Hebrews*. NICNT, ed. F. F. Bruce. Grand Rapids: Eerdmans, 1990.

Budd, Philip J. *Numbers*. WBC, ed. David A. Hubbard and Glenn W. Barker, vol. 5. Waco, Tex.: Word, 1984.

Buunk, Bram P. 'Jealousy in Close Relationships: An Exchange Theoretical Perspective.' In *The Psychology of Jealousy and Envy*, ed. Peter Salovey, 148-72. New York: Guilford, 1991.

Calvin, John. *Commentaries of the Book of the Prophet Ezekiel*. Translated by Thomas Myers. Grand Rapids: Eerdmans, 1948.

_____. *Commentary of the Book of the Prophet Isaiah*. Translated by William Pringle. Grand Rapids: Eerdmans, 1957.

_____. *Commentary on the Book of Psalms*. Translated by James Anderson. Grand Rapids: Baker, 1979.

_____. *The Gospel According to St John*. 1552. Translated by T. H. L. Parker. Edited by David W. Torrance and Thomas F. Torrance. Grand Rapids: Eerdmans, 1959.

_____. *Institutes of the Christian Religion*. Translated by Henery Beveridge. Grand Rapids.: Baker, 1989.

Carlson, R. A. 'Élie a l'Horeb.' *Vetus Testamentum* 19 (1969): 416-39.

Carson, D. A. 'Matthew,' ed. Frank E. Gabelein. *Expositor's Bible Commentary*, vol. 8, 3-602. Grand Rapids: Eerdmans, 1984.

_____. *The Difficult Doctrine of the Love of God.* Wheaton Ill.: Crossway, 2000.

_____. *The Gospel According to John.* Grand Rapids: InterVarsity, 1991.

Chambers, Sarah. 'A Biblical Theology of Godly Human Anger.' Ph. D. diss., Deerfield, Ill., Trinity Evangelical Divinity School, 1996.

Childs, Brevard S. *The Book of Exodus: A Critical, Theological Commentary.* The Old Testament Library, ed. Peter Ackroyd. Philadelphia: Westminster, 1974.

Christensen, Duane L. *Deuteronomy 1-11.* WBC, ed. David A. Hubbard, vol. 6A. Waco, Tex.: Word, 1991.

Cole, Alan R. *Exodus: An Introduction and Commentary.* TOTC, ed. D. J. Wiseman, vol. 2. Downers Grove, Ill.: InterVarsity, 1973.

Conzelmann, Hans. *1 Corinthians: A Commentary on the First Epistle to the Corinthians.* Translated by James W. Litch. Hermeneia, ed. S. J. MacRae, vol. 46. Philadelphia: Fortress, 1975.

Coppes, Leonard J. 'Kana.' In *TWOT*, ed. Harris L. R., Gleason L. Archer and Bruce K. Waltke, 802-03. Chicago: Moody Press, 1980.

Cottrell, Peter. 'Linguistics, Meaning Semantics, and Discourse Analysis.' In *NIDOTTE*, ed. Willem A. VanGameren, vol. 1, 134-60. Grand Rapids: Zondervan, 1996.

Craigie, Peter C. *The Book of Deuteronomy.* NICOT, ed. R. K. Harrison, vol. 5. Grand Rapids: Eerdmans, 1976.

Curtis, Edward. 'Man as the Image of God in Genesis in Light of Ancient Near Eastern Parallels.' Ph. D. diss., University of Pennsylvania, 1984.

Darwin, Charles. *The Expression of the Emotions in Man and Animals.* Chicago: University of Chicago Press, 1965.

Davids, Peter H. *The Epistle of James: A Commentary on the Greek Text.* New International Greek Testament Commentary. Grand Rapids: Eerdmans, 1982.

Davies, Eryl W. *Numbers.* NCB, ed. Ronald E. Clements. Grand Rapids: Eerdmans, 1995.

Delitzsch, F. *Isaiah.* Translated by James Martin. Commentary on the Old Testament in Ten Volumes, ed. C. F. Keil and F. Delitzch, vol. 7. Grand Rapids: Eerdmans, reprint 1982.

DeVries, Simon J. *1 Kings.* WBC, ed. John Watts, vol. 12. Waco, Tex.: Word, 1985.

Dibelius, Martin. *A Commentary on the Epistle of James.* Translated by Williams Michael. Hermeneia, ed. Helmut Koester, vol. 59. Philadelphia: Fortress, 1975.

Dohmen, Christoph. ' "Eifersuchtiger ist Sein Name" (Ex 34,14): Ursprung und Bedeutung der Alttestamentlichen Rede von Gottes Eifersucht.' *Theologische Zeitschrift* 46, no. 4 (1990): 289.

Driver, Sammuel R. *The Book of Exodus.* The Cambridge Bible for Schools and Colleges, ed. A. F. Kirkpatrick, vol. 2. London: Cambridge University Press, 1911.

Durham, John I. *Exodus.* WBC, ed. David A. Hubbard and Glen W. Barker, vol. 3. Waco, Tex.: Word, 1987.

Eaton, J. H. *Psalms: Introduction and Commentary.* Torch Bible Commentary, ed. John Marsh and Alan Richardson. London: SCM, 1967.

Eichrodt, Walter. *Ezekiel: A Commentary.* Philadelphia: Westminster, 1970.

_____. *Theology of the Old Testament.* Translated by J. A. Baker. Philadelphia: Westminster, 1961.

Erickson, Millard J. *Christian Theology.* Grand Rapids: Eerdmans, 1985.

_____. 'God and Change.' *The Southern Baptist Journal of Theology* (1997): 38-51.

Farrell, Daniel M. 'Jealousy and Desire' in *Love Analyzed*, ed. Roger E. Lamb. Boulder: Westview Press, 1997.

_____. 'Jealousy.' *The Philosophical Review* 89, no. 4 (Oct. 1980): 527-59.

Faur, José. 'Understanding the Covenant.' *Tradition: A Journal of Orthodox Thought* 9 (1968): 33-55.

Fee, Gordon D. *The First Epistle to the Corinthians.* NICNT, ed. F. F. Bruce. Grand Rapids: Eerdmans, 1987.

Field, D. H. 'Envy.' In *NIDNTT*, ed. Colin Brown, vol. 3, 557-58. Grand Rapids, : Zondervan, 1978.

Freedman, David Noel. *The Anchor Bible Dictionary. 6 Vols.* Garden City, N. J.: Doubleday, 1992.

Fruchtenbaum, Arnold G. 'A Study of the Root Qana.' Th.M. thesis, Dallas, Dallas Theological Seminary, 1971.

Furnish, Victor P. *2 Corinthians.* AB, ed. Foxwell A. Albright and David N. Freedman, vol. 32A. Garden City: N. J.: Doubleday, 1984.

Gard, Carolyn. 'Taming Jealousy: "The Green-Eyed Monster".' *Current Health* 25, no. 7 (March 1999): 26-28.

Gerhardsson, Birgir. *The Mighty Acts of Jesus According to Matthew.* Lund: C.W.K. Gleerup, 1979.

_____. *The Testing of God's Son.* Lund: C. W. K Gleerup, 1966.

Gispen, W. H. *Exodus.* Translated by Ed van der Mass. Bible Students Commentary. Grand Rapids: Zondervan, 1982.

_____. *Het Boek Numeri.* Kampen: J. H. Kok, 1964.

Godet, F. *Commentary on the Gospel of John.* 1864. Translated by Timothy Dwight. New York: Funk & Wagnalls, 1886.

Good, E. M. 'Jealousy.' In *IDB*, vol. 2. N. Y.: Abingdon, 1962.

Goudge, H. L. *The Second Epistle to the Corinthians.* London: Methuen, 1927.

Gray, John. *1 & 2 Kings.* Edited by Peter Ackroyd. et. al. OTL. Philadelphia: Westminster, 1964.

Grogan, Geoffery W. *Isaiah.* EBC, ed. Frank E. Gabelein., vol. 6. Grand Rapids: Zondervan, 1986.

Grosheide, F. W. *Commentary on the First Epistle to the Corinthians.* NICNT, ed. F. F. Bruce. Grand Rapids: Eerdmans, 1974.

Grudem, Wayne A. *Systematic Theology: An Introduction to Biblical Doctrine.* Grand Rapids: Zondervan, 1994.

Hallman, Joseph M. 'The Emotions of God in the Theology of St. Augustine.' *Recherches de Theologie Ancienne et Medievale* 51, no. 4 (Jan-Dec 1984): 5-19.

Hals, Ronald M. *Ezekiel.* FOTL, ed. Rolf P. Knierim and Gene M. Tucker, vol. 19. Grand Rapids: Eerdmans, 1989.

Han, Hans-Christoph. 'Zalos.' In *TNIDNTT*, ed. Colin Brown, vol. 3. Grand Rapids: Zondervan, 1978.

Hanson, Richard P. *The Second Epistle to the Corinthians.* Torch Bible Commentaries, ed. John Marsh, vol. 47. London: SCM, 1954.

Harris, Laird R. 'Leviticus,' ed. Frank E. Gabelein. Expositor's Bible Commentary, vol. 2 (Genesis-Numbers), 499-654. Grand Rapids: Eerdmans, 1990.

Harris, Murray J. *2 Corinthians.* EBC, ed. Frank E. Gabelein, vol. 10. Grand Rapids: Zondervan, 1976.

Harrison, R. K. *Numbers.* The Wycliffe Exegetical Commentary, ed. Kenneth Barker, vol. 4. Chicago: Moody, 1990.

_____. *Numbers: An Exegetical Commentary.* Grand Rapids: Baker, 1992.

Hendriksen, W. *Exposition of the Gospel According to John.* Grand Rapids: Baker, 1953.

Hertzberg, Hans Wilhelm. *1 & 2 Samuel.* Translated by J. S. Bowden. OTL, ed. G. Ernst Wright, et.al. vol. 9. Philadelphia: Westminster, 1964.

Heschel, Abraham J. *The Prophets.* New York: Harper and Row, 1962.

Hick, John. *The Myth of God Incarnate.* London: SCM, 1977.

Hodge, Charles. *An Exposition of First Epistle to the Corinthians.* Grand Rapids: Eerdmans, 1976.

Horton, Michael S. 'Hellenistic or Hebrew: Open Theism and Reformed Theological Method' *JETS*, Vol. 45. No. 2. June, 2002.

House, Paul R. *1, 2 Kings.* NAC, ed. E. Ray Clendenen. Ray, vol. 8. New York: Broadman and Holman, 1995.

_____. *Old Testament Theology.* Downers Grove Ill.: InterVarsity, 1998.

Hubbard, R. L. *First and Second Kings.* EBC, ed. Frank E. Gabelein. Grand Rapids: Zondervan, 1991.

Hughes, Philip E. *Paul's Second Epistle to the Corinthians*. NICNT, ed. F. F. Bruce. Grand Rapids: Eerdmans, 1962.

Hunter, Archibald M. *The Work and Words of Jesus*. Philadelphia: Westminister, 1950.

Hupka, Ralph B. 'The Motive for the Arousal of Romantic Jealousy: Its Cultural Origin.' In *The Psychology of Jealousy and Envy*, ed. Peter Salovey, 148-72. N. Y.: Guilford, 1991.

Hyatt, J. Phillip. *Exodus*. NCBC, ed. Ronald E. Clements and Matthew Black, vol. 2. Grand Rapids: Eerdmans, 1971.

Johnson, Luke Timothy. *The Letter of James*. The Anchor Bible, ed. Foxwell A. Albright, vol. 37A. New York: Doubleday, 1995.

Jones, Gwilym H. *1 and 2 Kings*. NCBC, vol. 2. Grand Rapids: Eerdmans, 1984.

Kaiser, Walter C. *Hard Sayings of the Old Testament*. Grand Rapids: InterVarsity, 1988.

_____. *Exodus*. EBC, ed. Frank E. Gaebelein., vol. 2. Grand Rapids: Zondervan, 1990.

Kalland, Earl, S. *Deuteronomy*. EBC, ed. Frank E. Gaebelein., vol. 3. Grand Rapids: Zondervan.

Kant, Immanuel. 'Jealousy, Envy, and Spite,' translated by Louis Enfield. In *Virtue and Vice in Everyday Life*, ed. Christina Sommers and Fred Sommers, 394-92. New York: Harcourt Brace Janovich College Publishers, 1993.

Kaufman, Yehezkel. *The Religion of Israel*. Chicago: University of Chicago, 1985.

Keil, C. F. *The Books of the Kings*. Translated by James Martin. Commentary on the Old Testament in Ten Volumes, ed. C. F. Keil and F. Delitzch. Grand Rapids: Eerdmans, reprint 1982.

_____. *Ezekiel*. Translated by James Martin. Commentary on the Old Testament in Ten Volumes, ed. C. F. Keil and F. Delitzch, vol. 9. Grand Rapids: Eerdmans, reprint 1982.

_____, and F. Delitzsch. *Commentary on the Old Testament*. Vol. 2, *Biblical Commentary on the Books of Samuel*. Translated by James Martin. Grand Rapids: Eerdmans, 1956.

Kidner, Derek. *Psalms 1-72*. TOTC, ed. D. J. Wiseman, vol. 19. Downers Grove, Ill.: InterVarsity, 1973.

Kistemaker, Simon J. *Exposition of the Epistle of James and the Epistles of John*. Grand Rapids: Baker, 1986.

Klein, Ralph W. *I Samuel*. WBC, ed. John D. Watts, vol. 10. Waco, Tex.: Word, 1983.

Kline, Meredith G. *Treaty of the Great King: The Covenant Structure of Deuteronomy.* Grand Rapids: Eerdmans, 1963.

Knitter, Paul. *No Other Name? a Critical Survey of Christian Attitudes Toward the World Religions.* New York: Orbis, 1986.

Kraus, Hans-Joachim. *Psalms 60-150.* 1978. Translated by Hilton C. Oswald. Minneapolis: Augsburg, 1989.

Kristjansson, Kristjan. *Justifying Emotions: Pride and Jealousy.* NY: Routledge, 2002.

_____. 'Why Persons Need Jealousy.' *Personalist-Forum* 12, no. 2 (Fall 1996): 163-81.

Kroeger, Catherine Clark. 'Prologue.' In *Women, Abuse and the Bible: How Scripture Can Be Used to Hurt or Heal,* ed. Catherine Clark Kroeger and James R. Beck, 9-12. Grand Rapids: Baker Books, 1996.

Kruse, Colin G. *The Second Epistle of Paul to the Corinthians: An Introduction and Commentary.* TNTC, ed. Leon Morris, vol. 8. Grand Rapids: Eerdmans, 1987.

Lane, William. *Hebrews.* WBC, ed. David A. Hubbard and Glen W. Barker, vol. 47a. Waco, Tex.: Word, 1991.

Laws, Sophie. *A Commentary on the Epistle of James.* Peabody, Mass.: Hendrickson, 1980.

Lenski, R. C. H. *The Interpretation of the Epistle to the Hebrews and the Epistle of James.* Minneapolis: Augsburg, 1966.

_____. *The Interpretation of The First Epistle to the Corinthians.* Minneapolis: Augsburg, 1937.

Levine, Baruch A. *Numbers 21-36.* The Anchor Bible, ed. William F. Albright and David N. Freedman, vol. 4A. New York: Doubleday, 2000.

Luter, Boyd A., Jr. 'Jealousy, Zeal.' In *Dictionary of Paul and His Letters,* ed. Ralph P. Martin, Gerald F. Hawthorne and Daniel G. Reid, 461-63. Downers Grove, Ill.: InterVarsity, 1993.

Macleod, Donald. *Behold Your God.* revised and expanded edition. Geanies House, Fearn, Ross-shire, Scotland, Great Britain: Christian Focus, 1995.

Mare, Harold. *First Corinthians.* EBC, ed. Frank E. Gaebelein., vol. 10. Grand Rapids: Zondervan, 1986.

Martin, Ralph P. *2 Corinthians.* WBC, ed. David A. Hubbard, vol. 40. Waco: Word, 1986.

_____. *James.* WBC, ed. David A. Hubbard, vol. 48. Waco: Word, 1988.

Mayes, A. D. H. *Deuteronomy.* NCBC, vol. 5. Grand Rapids: Eerdmans, 1981.

Mayor, Joseph B. *The Epistle of St James.* Minneapolis: Klock and Klock, 1892.

McFague, Sallie. 'The Christian Paradigm.' In *Christian Theology*, ed. Peter C. Hodgson and Robert H. King, 377-90. Philadelphia: Fortress, 1985.

McGrath, Alister. 'Response to John Hick.' In *More Than One Way?: Four Views on Salvation in a Pluralistic World*, ed. Dennis Okholm and Timothy Phillips, 65-70. Grand Rapids: Zondervan, 1995.

Mcleod, J. Campbell. *The Nature of the Atonement*. Grand Rapids: Eerdmans, 1856, reprint, 1996.

Mendenhall, George E. 'The Incident at Bet Baal Peor (Nu. 25).' In *The Tenth Generation*, 105-21. Baltimore: Johns Hopkins University Free Press, 1973.

Merrill, Eugene H. *Deuteronomy*. NAC, ed. E. Ray Clendenen, vol. 4. Dallas: Broadman and Holman, 1994.

Metzger, Bruce M. *A Textual Commentary on the Greek New Testament*. London: UBS, 1975.

Milgrom, Jacob. *Numbers*. JPS Torah Commentary. Jerusalem: Jewish Publication Society, 1990.

Montgomery, James A., and Henry Snyder Gehman. *The Book of Kings*. ICC. Edinburgh: T & T Clark, 1960.

Moo, Douglas J. *The Letter of James*. PNTC, ed. D. A. Carson. Grand Rapids: Eerdmans, 2000.

Morris, Leon. *The First Epistle of Paul to the Corinthians*. TNTC, ed. R. V. G. Tasker. Grand Rapids: Eerdmans, 1958.

_____. *The Gospel According to John*. NICNT, ed. Bruce F. F. Grand Rapids: Eerdmans, 1971.

_____. *The Gospel According to John*. NICNT, ed. Ned B. Stonehouse. et al. Grand Rapids: Eerdmans, 1995.

Motyer J. Alec. *Isaiah: An Introduction and Commentary*. Downers Grove, Ill.: InterVarsity, 1993.

Nelson, Richard D. *First and Second Kings*. Interpretation, ed. Patrick D. Miller. Atlanta: John Knox, 1987.

Newbigin, Leslie. *The Gospel in a Pluralist Society*. Grand Rapids: Eerdmans, 1992.

North, Christopher R. 'The Essence of Idolatry.' In *Festschrift Otto Eissfeldt*, ed. Johannes Jempel and Leonhard Rost, 151-60. Berlin: Verlag, 1961.

_____. *Isaiah 40-55*. Edited by John Marsh, Alan Richardson and Gregor Smith. London: SCM, 1952.

Noth, Martin. *Exodus: A Commentary*. OTL, ed. G. Ernst Wright et al. Philadelphia: Westminster, 1962.

_____. *Numbers: A Commentary*. OTL, ed. James D. Martin. Philadelphia: Westminster, 1966.

Ortlund, Raymond C., Jr. *Whoredom: God's Unfaithful Wife in Biblical Theology*. Grand Rapids: Eerdmans, 1996.

Oswalt, John N. *The Book of Isaiah*. In *NICOT*, ed. R. K. Harrison and Robert L. Hummard. Grand Rapids: Eerdmans, 1988.

Packer, James I. 'The Way of Salvation, Part 4: Are Non-Christian Faiths Ways of Salvation?' *Bibliotheca Sacra* Jan-March 1973.

Peels, Hendrik G. L. 'קנא' In *NIDOTTE*, ed. Willem A. VanGemeren, vol. 3. Grand Rapids: Zondervan, 1996.

Pfeiffer, Robert. 'The Polemic Against Idolatry in the Old Testament.' *Journal of Biblical Literature* 43 (1924): 229-40.

Pinnock, Clark. *Most Moved Mover: a Theology of God's Openness*. Grand Rapids: Baker 2001.

Pinnock, Clark et al. *The Openness of God: A Biblical Challenge to the Traditional Understanding of God*. Downers Grove, Ill.: InterVarsity, 1994.

Piper, John. *Desiring God: Meditations of a Christian Hedonist*. Sisters, Oregon: Multnomah, 1996.

Plummer, Alfred. *A Critical and Exegetical Commentary on the Second Epistle of St Paul to the Corinthians*. ICC, ed. J. A. Emerton, vol. 47. Edinburgh: T & T Clark, 1915.

Pulcini, Theodore. 'Cultivating "Christian Anger": A Warning from the Fifth Century.' *Touchstone* 11, no. 1 (Jan-Feb 1988): 8-10.

Rad, Gerhard von. *Old Testament Theology: Volume I, The Theology of Israel's Historical Traditions*. Translated by D. G. M. Stalker. New York: Harper and Row, 1962.

_____. *Old Testament Theology: Volume II, The Theology of Israel's Prophetic Traditions*. Translated by D. G. M. Stalker. New York: Harper and Row, 1962.

Ramm, Bernard. *Special Revelation and the Word of God*. Grand Rapids: Eerdmans, 1961.

Reif, S. C. 'What Enraged Phinehas.' *JBL* 90 (1971): 200-06.

Reiss, Ira L. 'A Sociological Journey Into Sexuality.' *Journal of Marriage and Family* 48, no. 2 (1986): 233-42.

Renaud, Bernard. *Je Suis un Dieu Jaloux*. Paris: Les Editions du Cerf, 1963.

Rice, Gene. *A Commentary on the Book of 1 Kings*. ITC, ed. Fredrick Carlson Holmgren. Grand Rapids: Eerdmans, 1990.

Ridderbos, Herman N. *The Gospel According to John: A Theological Commentary*. 1987. Translated by John Vriend. Grand Rapids: Eerdmans, 1992.

Ringer, Gerald. 'Report from a Far Meridian: Yahweh, God of the Fireball.' In *Fireball and the Lotus: Emerging Spirituality from Ancient Roots*, ed. Ron Miller and Jim Kenney, 73-93. Santa Fe, N.M.: Bear & Co., 1987.

Robertson, Archibald. *A Critical and Exegetical Commentary on the First Epistle to the Corinthians*. ICC, ed. Samuel Driver. Edinburgh: T & T Clark, 1911.

Robinson, J. *The First Book of Kings*. CBC. London: CUP, 1972.

Robinson, Jennifer. 'Emotion, Judgment, and Desire.' *Journal of Philosophy*, 80. 1983.

Rogerson, J. W., and J. W. McKay. *Psalms 51-100*. The Cambridge Bible Commentary, ed. P. R. Ackroyd, A. R. C. Leaney and J. W. Packer. London: Cambridge University Press, 1977.

Ropes, James Hardy. *A Critical and Exegetical Commentary on the Epistle of St. James*. ICC, ed. Alfred Plummer, vol. 59. Edinburgh: T & T Clark, 1968.

Rosner, Brian S. 'Stronger Than He?: The Strength of 1 Corin-thians 10:22b.' *Tyndale Bulletin* 43, no. 1 (1992): 171-79.

_____. 'The Concept of Idolatry.' *Themelios* 23 (May 1999): 21-30.

Ross, Alexander. *The Epistles of James and John*. NICNT. Grand Rapids: Eerdmans, 1974.

Sakenfeld, Katharine D. *Journeying with God*. International Theological Commentary, ed. Fredrick C. Holmgren and George A. F. Knight. Grand Rapids: Eerdmans, 1995.

Salovey, Peter. 'Psychology of Jealousy.' In *The Psychology of Jealousy and Envy*. New York: Guilford, 1991.

Sanders, John. *The God Who Risks: A Theology of Providence*. Downers Grove, Ill.: InterVarsity, 1998.

Semdahl, D. H. 'God and the Concept of Jealousy.' Th.M. thesis, Dallas, Texas, Dallas Theological Seminary, 1983.

Snaith, Norman H. 'Jealous, Zealous.' In *A Theological Wordbook of the Bible*, ed. Alan Richardson, 879-90. London: SCM, 1957.

Stamm, Johann J., and Edward Maurice. *The Ten Commandments in Recent Research*. Naperville, Ill.: Allenson, 1967.

Stuart, Douglas. *Ezekiel*. The Communicators Commentary, ed. Loyd J. Ogilvie, vol. 18. Waco, Tex.: Word, 1989.

_____. *Hosea-Jonah*. WBC. Waco, Tex.: Word, 1987.

Stumpff, Albrecht. 'Zalos,' translated by G. W. Bromiley. In *TDNT*, ed. Gerhardt Kittel and G. Friedrich, vol. 2, 879-90. Grand Rapids: Eerdmans, 1965.

Swinburne, Richard. *The Evolution of the Soul*. Revised edition. Oxford, 1997.

Talley, D. *Three Themes about Yahweh in the Old Testament—His Person, His Presence, and His Glory: A Foundation for Spiritual Formation*.

Unpublished paper, presented at the Evangelical Theological Society in Nashville, Tenn., November 2000.

Tasker, R. V. G. *The General Epistle of James: An Introduction and Commentary*. Grand Rapids: Eerdmans, 1975.

_____. *The Gospel According to St. John*. TNTC. Tasker, R. V. G.: Eerdmans, 1960.

Tate, Marvin E. *Psalms 51-100*. WBC, ed. David A. Hubbard, vol. 20. Waco, Tex.: Word, 1990.

Tozer, Aiden W. *The Knowledge of the Holy*. New York: Harper & Row, 1961.

VanGemeren, Willem A. *The Progress of Redemption: The Story of Salvation from Creation to the New Jerusalem*. Grand Rapids: Baker, 1988.

_____. *Psalms*. EBC, ed. Frank E. Gaebelein., vol. 5. Grand Rapids: Zondervan, 1991.

Veereshwar, Anand Swami. 'Jealousy and the Abyss (Ego Defenses Against Nothingness).' *Journal of Humanistic Psychology* 23, no. 2 (Spring 1983): 70-84.

Ware, Bruce A. 'An Evangelical Reformulation of the Doctrine of the Immutability of God.' *Journal of the Evangelical Theological Society* 29, no. 4 (December 1986): 175-96.

_____. 'An Exposition and Critique of the Process Doctrines of Divine Mutability and Immutability.' *Westmnister Theological Journal* 47 (1985): 175-96.

Watson, Thomas. *The Ten Commandments*. Edinburgh: Banner of Truth, 1692, reprint 1986.

Weinfeld, Moshe. *Deuteronomy 1-11*. The Anchor Bible, ed. Foxwell A. Albright and David Noel Freedman, vol. 5. New York: Doubleday, 1971.

Wenham, Gordon J. *Genesis 1-15*. WBC. Waco, Tex.: Word, 1987.

_____. *Numbers*. TOTC, ed. D. J. Wiseman, vol. 4. Downers Grove, Ill.: InterVarsity, 1981.

Wiseman, Donald J. *1 and 2 Kings*. TOTC, ed. Donald J. Wiseman, vol. 9. Downers Grove, Ill.: InterVarsity, 1993.

Young, Edward J. *The Book of Isaiah*. Grand Rapids: Eerdmans, 1972.

Zimmerli, Walther. *A Commentary on the Book of the Prophet Ezekiel: Chapters 1-24*. Translated by Ronald E. Clements. Edited by Frank Moore Cross and Klaus Baltzer. Philadelphia: Fortress, 1969.

_____. *Ezekiel 1 and 2*. Hermeneia. Philadelphia: Fortress, 1979.

_____. 'Das Zweite Gebot.' In *Festschrift Alfred Bertholet*, ed. Walter Baumgartner, 550-63. Tübingen: J. B. C. Mohr, 1950.

Appendix 1

קנא – in the Old Testament

Passage	Subject	Object	Cause	Result	+ / -	Best Translation(s)
Gen. 26:14	Philistines	Of Isaac	Isaac's Possessions	Vandalism	-	Envied
Gen. 30:1	Rachel	Of Leah	Leah's Offspring	Fertility wars and Family Conflict	-	Resentful Jealous / envious
Gen. 37:11	Joseph's brothers	Of Joseph	Their Father's greater love	Assault and betrayal	-	Jealous/Resentful
Exod. 20:5	God	For his people	God's character	Exclusive worship demand	+	Jealous
Exod. 34:14	God	For his people	God's character	Exclusive worship demand	+	Jealous
Exod. 34:14	God	For his people	God's character	Exclusive worship demand	+	Name is Jealous
Num. 5:14	Justified husband	For his Wife	Actual infidelity	Test for infidelity	+	Spirit of Jealousy
Num. 5:14	Justified husband	For his Wife	Actual infidelity	Test for infidelity	+	Jealous
Num. 5:14	Unjustified husband	For his Wife	Inaccurate Suspicion	Test for infidelity	-	Spirit of Jealousy
Num. 5:14	Unjustified husband	For his Wife	Inaccurate Suspicion	Test for infidelity	-	Jealous
Num. 5:15	A husband	For his Wife	Unspecified Suspicion	Test for infidelity	?	Offering for Jealousy
Num. 5:18	A husband	For his Wife	Unspecified Suspicion	Test for infidelity	?	Offering for Jealousy
Num. 5:25	A husband	For his Wife	Unspecified Suspicion	Test for infidelity	?	Offering for Jealousy
Num. 5:29	A husband	For his Wife	Unspecified Suspicion	Test for infidelity	?	Law of Jealousy
Num. 5:30	A husband	For his Wife	Unspecified Suspicion	Test for infidelity	?	Feelings of Jealousy
Num. 5:30	A husband	For his Wife	Unspecified Suspicion	Test for infidelity	?	Jealous
Num. 11:29	Joshua	For Moses	Threat to authority	Attempt to protect Moses	+	Jealous
Num. 25:11	Phinehas	For God's honor	Sexual immorality	Killing and atonement	+	Jealous
Num. 25:11	God	For his people	Sexual immorality	Wrath and judgment	+	Jealous
Num. 25:11	God	For his people	Sexual immorality	Wrath and judgment	+	Jealousy
Num. 25:13	Phinehas	For God's honor	Sexual immorality	Killing and atonement	+	Jealous
Deut. 4:24	God	For his people	God's charater	Condemnation of idolatry	+	Jealous
Deut. 5:9	God	For his people	God's charater	Condemnation of idolatry	+	Jealous
Deut. 6:15	God	For his people	God's charater	Condemnation of other god's	+	Jealous
Deut. 29:20	God	For his people	Idolatry	Wrath and disaster	+	Jealousy
Deut. 32:16	God	For his people	Strange gods	Anger and rejection	+	Jealous
Deut. 32:21	God	For his people	That which is no God	Acceptance of gentiles	+	Envious / Jealous
Deut. 32:21	Israel	For God's favor	God's favor toward gentiles	Captivity	+	Jealousy
Josh. 24:19	God	For his people	Their rebellion and sin	Israel's inability to serve him	+	Jealous
2 Sam. 21:2	Saul	For Israel's loyalty	Israel's favor toward David	Broken covenant to Gibeonites	-	Envy / Jealousy
1 Kings 14:22	God	For Israel	Idolatry and immorality	Anger	+	Jealousy
1 Kings 19:10	Eiljah	For God's honor	High places, idolatry	Public challenge and killing	+	Jealous
1 Kings 19:10	Eiljah	For God's honor	High places, idolatry	Public challenge and killing	+	Very jealous (for emphasis)
1 Kings 19:14	Eiljah	For God's honor	High places, idolatry	Public challenge and killing	+	Jealous
1 Kings 19:14	Eiljah	For God's honor	High places, idolatry	Public challenge and killing	+	Very jealous (for emphasis)
2 Kings 10:16	Jehu	For God	Idolatry (Baal worship)	Killing	+/-	Jealous / Zeal
2 Kings 19:31	God	On behalf of his people	Blasphemy by Assyrians	Preservation of a remnant	+	Zealous
Job 5:2	A simple person		Desire for restitution	Death	-	Envy
Ps. 37:1	A person	Of evil-doers	"Unfair" prosperity	Failure to trust God	-	Envious
Ps. 69:9	David	For God's house	David's devotion	David endures persecution	+	Jealousy
Ps. 73:3	Asaph	Of the arrogant	"Unfair" prosperity	Despair	-	Envied

Passage	Subject	Object	Cause	Result	+ / -	Best Translation(s)
Ps. 78:58	God	For his people	Graven images, idolatry	Anger and rejection	+	Jealousy
Ps. 79:5	God	For his people	Their disobedience	Wrath and Israel's captivity	+	Jealousy
Ps. 106:16	Korah and his followers	Of Moses	Moses' unique authority	Rebellion	-	Envious / resentful
Ps. 119:139	The psalmist	For God's honor	Ignoring God's words	He is consumed	+	Jealousy
Prov. 3:31	A young man	Of a violent man	Lack of wisdom		-	Envy
Prov. 6:34	A husband	For his wife	Infidelity	Fury and revenge	+	Jealousy
Prov. 14:30	A person		Lack of wisdom	Rotten bones	-	Envy
Prov. 23:17	A young man	For fear of the Lord		A future hope	+	Jealous / zealous
Prov. 24:1	A young man	Of wicked men		Violence and trouble	-	Envy
Prov. 24:19	A young man	Of the wicked		You will be snuffed out	-	Envious
Prov. 27:4				No one can stand before it	-	Envy / jealous
Eccl. 4:4	Man	Of one's neighbor		Labor and achievement	?	Emulation / envy
Eccl. 9:6	The dead			It's absence is a sign of death	?	Zeal / jealous / envy
Song 8:6	The wife	For her husband	Love	Request for exclusivity	+	Jealousy
Isa. 9:7	God	On behalf of his people	Oppression of his people	Salvation in the messiah	+	Jealousy / zeal
Isa. 11:13	Ephraim	Of Judah	Family conflict	Unified conquest	-	Jealousy / zeal
Isa. 11:13	Ephraim	Of Judah	Family conflict	Unified conquest	-	Jealousy / zeal
Isa. 26:11	God	On behalf of his people	The wicked	The wicked are put to shame	+	Zealously
Isa. 37:32	God	On behalf of his people	Assyria	The restoration of the remnant	+	Zealously
Isa. 42:13	God	For his own glory	The enemies of God / Israel	Triumph of enemies	+	Jealousy
Isa. 59:17	God	On behalf of his people	Enemies and foes of God	Retribution and salvation	+	Zealously
Isa. 63:15	God	On behalf of his people	Enemies of God	Restoration of God's people	+	Zeal / jealousy
Ezek. 5:13	God	For his people	Idolatry	Anger and punishment	+	Jealousy
Ezek. 8:3	God	For his people	An idol	Anger and judgment	+	Idol of jealousy
Ezek. 8:3	God	For his people	An idol	Anger and judgment	+	Jealous
Ezek. 8:3	God	For his people	An idol	Anger and judgment	+	Idol of jealousy
Ezek. 16:38	God	For his people	Idolatry	Anger and Vengeance	+	Jealous anger
Ezek. 16:42	God	For his people	Idolatry	Anger and Vengeance	+	Jealous anger
Ezek. 23:25	God	For his people	Idolatry	Destruction	+	Jealous anger
Ezek. 31:9	Other nations	Of Assyria	Her power and prosperity	Destructive pride	?	Envy / emulation
Ezek. 35:11	Edom	Of Israel and Judah	Israel's prosperity	Oppression of Israel	-	Envy
Ezek. 36:5	God	On Israel's behalf	Other nations and Edom	Judgment and vengeance	+	Burning zealousy
Ezek. 36:6	God	On Israel's behalf	Other nations	Judgment and vengeance	+	Zealous wrath
Ezek. 38:19	God	On Israel's behalf	Gog	Judgment and vengeance	+	Zealous and fiery wrath
Ezek. 39:25	God	For his holy name	Israel's captivity	Restoration and salvation	+	Jealous
Joel 2:18	God	For his land	The nations	Restoration and salvation	+	Jealous
Nahum 1:2	God	On behalf of his people	Nineveh	Wrath wengeance and punishament	+	Jealous
Zeph. 1:18	God	For his creation	Human sin	Wrath and the final judgment	+	Jealousy
Zeph. 3:8	God	For his creation	Human sin	Wrath and the final judgment	+	Jealous anger
Zech. 1:14	God	For Zion and Jerusalem	The nations	Restoration of Israel	+	Jealous
Zech. 1:14	God	For Zion and Jerusalem	The nations	Restoration of Israel	+	Very jealous (for emphasis)
Zech. 8:2	God	For Zion	The nations	Restoration of Jerusalem	+	Jealous
Zech. 8:2	God	For Zion	The nations	Restoration of Jerusalem	+	Very jealous (for emphasis)
Zech. 8:2	God	For Zion	The nations	Restoration of Jerusalem	+	Burning wih Jealousy

Appendix 2
ζηλ– in the New Testament

Passage	Subject	Object	Cause	Result	+/-	Best Translation(s)
Luke 6:15	Simon					The Zealot
John 2:17	Jesus	For God's house	Materialism / irreverence	Temple cleansing	+	Jealousy
Acts 1:13	Simon					The Zealot
Acts 5:17	Sadducees	Of The apostles	The apostle's healing ministry	Persecution	-	Envy / Jealousy
Acts 7:9	Joseph's brothers	Of Joseph	Their father's greater love	Betrayal and persecution	-	Envious / Jealous
Acts 13:45	The Jews	Of Paul and Barnabas	The crowd's attention	Abusive speaking	-	Envious / Jealous
Acts 17:5	the Jews	Of Paul and Silas	Large numbers of conversions	Persecution and a riot	-	Envious / Jealous
Acts 21:20	Believing Jews	For the law	Their religious backgrounds	Legalism	+/-	Zealous / Jealous
Acts 22:3	Paul	For God	His religious training	Persecution of the Church	+/-	Spirit of Jealousy
Rom. 10:2	The Israelites	For God	Legalism	Self-righteousness	-	Zeal
Rom. 10:19	The Jews	For God's Exclusive favor	Gentile Salvation	Isreal's return to God	+	Provoke to Jealousy
Rom. 11:11	The Jews	For God's Exclusive favor	Gentile Salvation	Isreal's return to God	+	Provoke to Jealousy
Rom. 11:14	The Jews	For God's Exclusive favor	Gentile Salvation	Isreal's return to God	+	Provoke to Jealousy
Rom. 13:13	The Romans				-	Envy
1 Cor. 3:3	The Corinthians		Worldliness		-	Envy
1 Cor. 10:22	God	For his people	Participation with demons		+	Jealousy
1 Cor. 12:31	The Corinthians	For the greater gifts	Desiring to fulfill one's role	Edification of the body	+	Be zealous for
1 Cor. 13:4	Love				-	Does not envy
1 Cor. 14:1	The Corinthians	For the greater gifts	Following the way of love	Edification of the church	+	Be zealous for
1 Cor. 14:12	The Corinthians	For spiritual gifts			+	Are zealous
1 Cor .14:39	The Corinthians	For the gift of prophecy			+	Be zealous for
2 Cor. 7:7	The Corinthians	For Paul	Love for Paul	Paul is comforted	+	Zeal
2 Cor. 7:11	The Corinthians	For Vindication	Godly Sorrow	They are proved innocent	+	Zeal
2 Cor. 9:2	The Corinthians	For acts of service	Eagerness to help	Others were stirred to action	+	Zeal
2 Cor. 11:2	Paul	For the Corinthians	False Teaching	Paul corrects them	+	Jealous
2 Cor. 11:2	God	For the Corinthians	False teaching		+	Jealousy of God
2 Cor. 12:20	The Corinthians			Paul will be grieved	+	Envy
Gal. 1:14	Paul	For Jewish traditions			+/-	Zealous
Gal. 4:17	The Judaizers	For the Galatians	To alienate them from Paul		-	Jealous
Gal. 4:17	The Galatians	For the Judaizers	The zeal of the Judaizers	No good	-	Jealous
Gal. 4:18	The Galatians				+/-	Zealous
Gal. 5:20	The Galatians		The sinful nature	Failure to inherit the Kingdom	-	Jealousy
Phil. 3:6	Paul	For Judaism	The church	Confidence in the flesh	-	Jealousy / zeal
Titus 2:14	Christians	For good deeds	Christ gave himself	These things should be taught	+	Zealous / jealous
Heb. 10:27	Fire of judgment	For judgment	The enemies of God	The enemies are consumed	+	Zeal
James 3:14	Scattered 12 tribes		The devil	Disorder and evil	-	Envy
James 3:16	Scattered 12 tribes		The devil	Disorder and evil	-	Envy
James 4:2	Scattered 12 tribes	Of things not attainable	The battle within	Quarrals and conflicts	-	Envious / covetous
1 Pet. 3:13	God's elect	For what is good	Their calling		+	Zealous / eager
Rev. 3:19	The Church at Laodicea		God's rebuke and discipline	Repentance	+	Zealous

Appendix 3
Godly Human Jealousy in the History of Redemption

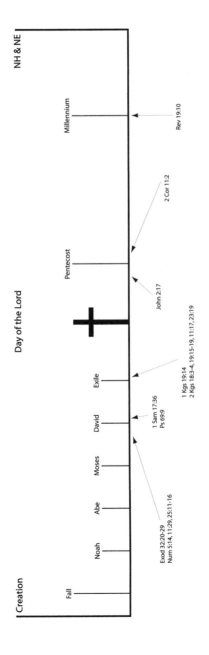

Scripture Index

Author Index

Where authors are quoted their names may only appear
in the footnotes of the relevant pages.

Subject Index

Christian Focus Publications

publishes books for all ages

Our mission statement –

STAYING FAITHFUL

In dependence upon God we seek to help make His infallible Word, the Bible, relevant. Our aim is to ensure that the Lord Jesus Christ is presented as the only hope to obtain forgiveness of sin, live a useful life and look forward to heaven with Him.

REACHING OUT

Christ's last command requires us to reach out to our world with His gospel. We seek to help fulfill that by publishing books that point people towards Jesus and help them develop a Christ-like maturity. We aim to equip all levels of readers for life, work, ministry and mission.

Books in our adult range are published in three imprints.

Christian Focus contains popular works including biographies, commentaries, basic doctrine and Christian living. Our children's books are also published in this imprint.

Mentor focuses on books written at a level suitable for Bible College and seminary students, pastors, and other serious readers. The imprint includes commentaries, doctrinal studies, examination of current issues and church history.

Christian Heritage contains classic writings from the past.

Christian Focus Publications,
Geanies House, Fearn, Ross-shire,
IV20 1TW, Scotland, United Kingdom
info@christianfocus.com
www.christianfocus.com